John Hoskins, possibly Serjeant Hoskyns, from the
Miniature in the Collection of His Grace the
Duke of Buccleuch

The

Life, Letters, and Writings

of

JOHN HOSKYNS

1566-1638

By

LOUISE BROWN OSBORN

ARCHON BOOKS

1973

Library of Congress Cataloging in Publication Data

Osborn, Louise Brown.
 The life, letters, and writings of John Hoskyns,
1566—1638.

 Original ed. issued as v. 87 of Yale studies in English.
 A revision of the author's thesis, Yale, 1930.
 Includes bibliographical references.
 1. Hoskins, John, 1566—1638. I. Series: Yale studies
in English, v. 87.
PR2294.H5808   1973   828'.3'07   72—8893
ISBN 0-208-01132-3

[Yale Studies in English, vol. 87]

Printed in the United States of America

CONTENTS

ILLUSTRATIONS

PREFACE

THIS study makes available the collected writings of John Hoskyns and brings together biographical facts about this versatile, distinguished wit, lawyer, parliamentarian, and stylist.

Much of the material of this book was presented, in somewhat different form, to the Faculty of the Graduate School of Yale University in partial fulfilment of the requirement for the degree of Doctor of Philosophy.

My debts to Canon Sir Edwyn Clement Hoskyns, Bart.; Miss W. B. de La Chere; and Mr. Henry Hornyold-Strickland for permission to use manuscripts in their possession are indeed great. Especially am I indebted to Mr. Hornyold-Strickland for transcribing the extraordinary collection of Hoskyns' letters which he possesses and for giving me access to the originals. To the American Council of Learned Societies I am obligated for a grant which enabled me to go to England to see the letters.

To the authorities and staffs of the following libraries I am grateful for the privilege of using their resources: the Yale Library; the British Museum; the Bodleian; University Library, Cambridge; the Library of Trinity College, Cambridge; the Library of the Society of Antiquaries in Edinburgh; the Chetham Library; the Library of Lambeth Palace; the Guildhall Library, London; the Public Record Office; the Library of the Marquis of Salisbury at Hatfield House; and that of the Grolier Club in New York. For gracious replies to various queries and sometimes for rotographs or other copies I have to thank the authorities of Winchester College; the National Library of Wales; the Harvard Library; the Henry E. Huntington Library; and Mr. Francis Needham, librarian of Welbeck Abbey.

Sir Herbert Grierson graciously sent me most useful suggestions. Through the generosity of Mr. Percy Dobell I was able to see a commonplace book in his possession, and Dr. A. S. W. Rosenbach gave me access to several in his collec-

tion. Mr. R. E. Bennett and Miss Marcella Hartman have
helped me; and Professor C. Bowie Millican has given me
the benefit of his critical reading of a part of the manuscript.
In Chapter IX and the notes I have indicated items for which
I am indebted to Professor Hoyt H. Hudson's edition,
Directions for Speech and Style by John Hoskins (1935).

His Grace the late seventh Duke of Buccleuch permitted me
to examine the miniature reproduced as the frontispiece, and
his Grace the present Duke has permitted its use in this
volume. To Dr. George C. Williamson I am grateful for
several items on the history of the miniature.

I owe much to members of the faculty of Yale University.
Professor Wallace Notestein lent me helpful material on
political aspects of Hoskyns' career. From Professor Karl
Young I have received good counsel. Professor John M.
Berdan gave wise suggestions about investigation, and his
careful and stimulating criticism during the period in which
most of the book was written and his continued interest have
been of utmost value. To the erudition, judgment, and
generous helpfulness of Professor Tucker Brooke I cannot
measure my indebtedness.

LOUISE B. OSBORN

EVANSVILLE, INDIANA
NOVEMBER, 1936

CHAPTER I

INTRODUCTORY

IN late Elizabethan and early Jacobean days John Hoskyns[1] was wont to bring his own spark of gaiety and his own weight of erudition into circles of some of London's bravest wits. The obscurity[2] that has since cloaked the name of this scholar, lawyer, parliamentarian, occasional poet, wit, stylist, and critic affords but another example of the fickleness of reputation.[3] A man in touch with some of his greatest contemporaries passed almost completely out of the ken of succeeding generations, and his work lay virtually unobserved for three centuries. A survey of his claims to recognition in his own time emphasises the loss arising from neglect of so versatile a representative of the period which may be said to have begun in the heyday of Elizabethan energy and buoyancy and to have closed just before open rebellion followed the dissension of the first third of the seventeenth century.

One of Hoskyns' claims to literary recognition is the fact that within a decade of the publication of the *Arcadia* he analysed Sidney's prose with careful regard for contemporary and permanent standards of excellence and commented illuminatingly upon Sidney himself and upon numerous other great figures of the age. From this manuscript treatise[4] Ben Jonson transcribed a lengthy extract[5] into his commonplace book posthumously published as *Discoveries* in the folio of 1640-41. Embedded in Jonson's book, Hoskyns' precepts, sensible, unaffected, sound as they are, have helped to mould English prose style. Their influence was strengthened, in purely academic circles at least, by the further borrowings of two lesser men, Thomas Blount[6] and John Smith,[7] who, without acknowledgement, adopted much of Hoskyns' treatise for their rhetorics. His verse in Latin and in English circulated in the commonplace books of the time alongside the poetry of Donne, Carew, Ben Jonson, Ralegh, and the rest. His thirty domestic letters which have been preserved[8] provide a charming, intimate account of their author and are themselves examples frequently of distinguished prose. Moreover, Hoskyns is reputed to have compiled a Greek lexicon as far as the letter *Mu*;[9] to have written an article on memory,[10] some legal studies, and an autobiography; and to have revised Sir Walter Ralegh's *History of the World*.[11]

In his profession Hoskyns rose to two of the very high dignities the law could offer: in 1621[12] he was appointed a judge in Wales, and two years later was named one of his Majesty's Serjeants-at-Law. His entrance into the law, moreover, furnished him his easiest way into the House of Commons. There, on one occasion in 1606, his arguments were answered in debate by no less distinguished a man than Sir Francis Bacon.[13] At intervals these two were serving together on committees, of which Hoskyns had a share of more than forty in a single Parliament. Some of his concerns therein were the problems of free trade, the searching out of grievances, the proposed union with Scotland, and methods for curtailing subsidies to the Crown.

Professor Wallace Notestein has developed a theory that the lawyers in Parliament in the first twenty years of the reign of James I were responsible for the shift of power into the hands of the Lower House. 'The lawyers,' he says, 'crowded into the Commons and brought with them not only legal skill but initiative.' Their influence, he continues,

upon the new developments in the Commons can hardly be over-estimated . . . . No doubt . . . the late Elizabethan and early Stuart period saw in England a wider dissemination than ever before of legal knowledge and a more general interest in the nature of legal principles . . . . If the life of the time was infused with law, certainly its politics was infused with lawyers. By virtue of their manner of education and discipline, they had become almost a class held without bloodshed, Hoskyns' part in the struggle was waged in the early and intellectual stages and carried on by debates in Parliament or during conferences with the Lords in the Painted Chamber or through the search for precedents among the ancient documents stored away in the Tower.

If in political activity Hoskyns stands at the period of transition from Elizabethan practices and patterns of thought to those of the era of the Commonwealth, he occupies a similarly interesting position in literary history, for his extant writings reflect the transition from Elizabethan fashions of literary expression to those current in the early seventeenth century. A fellow of New College when Sir Philip Sidney died, Hoskyns outlived John Donne by seven years. By the fortune of his span of life he can hardly fail to mirror for us something of the changing standards. Other circumstances, however, operated to make him now an interesting study in the development of English literary style. Hoskyns had the advantage of the best classical background that England could provide: he was a thorough product of the Revival of Learning as it flourished in Wykeham's two 'famous Nurseries,'[17] Winchester and New College. That he was a student of Aristotle, Demosthenes, Cicero, Isocrates, and Ovid he tells us himself.[18] His mastery of the principles of style he doubtless had derived from these writers, together with Quintilian and later but 'honest men,' as he calls them, like Sturmius, Talaeus, Ascham, and Lipsius. Hoskyns' soundness in this field we may believe was recognized in the English universities in his own time.[19] Yet he was by no means enchained by the academic fetters of the erudition of the sixteenth century, for his active life in London kept him in touch with changing ideas and brought him into competition with the sharp-tongued wits of the early seventeenth century. His *Direccōns For Speech and Style* is weighted and charged with devotion to the principles that developed the conceited, involved, copious, and often majestic prose of the sixteenth century. Nevertheless, the same treatise, lightened at intervals by a sensible distrust of some of the old principles governing literary expression, reveals its author's quickened interest in the less elaborate, the more direct utterance which was to supersede the Arcadian prose of Sidney. Hoskyns could not only compose a thorough-going and technical treatise on Elizabethan prose, which even Ben Jonson found worthy of study, but he could also write the charmingly direct lyric 'Absence, hear my protestation' so savouring of the 'metaphysical' vein of the school of Donne that from 1721 for more than one hundred and fifty years it easily lodged in the Donne canon.[20]

Just as Hoskyns is interesting for his achievements and significance in the fields of law, politics, and literature, he is also interesting, if elusive, for his social and intellectual connections. From his early youth he found himself in the company of wits. At Winchester College John Owen,[21] who for a time was to be extraordinarily popular as an epigrammatist, became Hoskyns' friend when the latter was only thirteen. Winchester, just at this period, fostered a veritable school of aspiring young epigrammatists. Thomas Bastard,[22] who published *Chrestoleros. Seven Bookes of Epigrams* in 1598, was one of these, and the more famous John Davies[23] was another. Of a somewhat different turn was the gentle, studious Henry Wotton, who, though not registered among the scholars, passed some time there,[24] doubtless as a commoner,[25] during Hoskyns' period. It is interesting to observe that young Wotton, at the age of sixteen, proceeded to New College, where he matriculated on 5 June 1584.[26] The next October John Donne, a precocious boy of about twelve, entered Hart Hall for a two years' residence in Oxford.[27] Walton tells us that Wotton and Donne began their life-long friendship during this period. Hoskyns was admitted a probationer[28] of New College just four months after Donne's arrival in Oxford and nine months after Wotton's. It is natural to suppose that Hoskyns, although nineteen at the time, may soon have formed an acquaintanceship with Donne, through Wotton, their mutual friend. Owen[29] and Bastard,[30] like Hoskyns, also proceeded to New College, where as Old Boys from Winton the three may well have been close associates. That

Owen, at least, continued his friendship begun at Winchester is recorded in these Latin verses:

Ad D. Jo. Hoskins.

Ambiguos tecum peragens socialiter annos,
    Oxonia[e] juvenis, VVintoniaeque puer,
Saepe tuum in dubiis sine fuco expertus amorem,
    Rebus & indubiam sum sine fraude fidem.
Hoc tibi mnemosynon me mittere jussit amoris
    Qui mihi te junxit, me tibi vinxit, Amor.[31]

In London, outside the cloistering influence of college and university, Hoskyns was to find the law, which also provided his way into politics, a ready means of keeping him in touch with friends of his academic days and of introducing him to the society of equally interesting and often more influential men. For a period of more than thirty years Hoskyns was to maintain chambers in his Inn of Court, the Middle Temple.

To realize the importance for him of residence in one of the Inns of Court one must recall their function and position in the life of London before and during his time. From the days of Edward I young men had been coming up from the provinces to lodge near Westminster during term-time that they might observe practice in the courts and receive advice and instruction from skilful jurists and thus, in time, be prepared to plead. The hostels in which they naturally drew together evolved into the societies known as the Inns of Court, four in number: Lincoln's Inn, Gray's Inn, the Inner Temple, and the Middle Temple. The two latter societies took over the properties of the militant, monastic order of the Knights Templar, and used jointly the ancient church of that abolished order. Lincoln's Inn and Gray's Inn, each with its own chapel, were not far distant. The young men lodged in their Inns, ate there in commons, attended services in their own chapels, and, besides the advantages of conversation with men of similar interests and more experience, received no mean instruction in the law. Though the routine was perhaps somewhat informal, the instruction offered and required in Hoskyns' day for those who expected to be admitted to the bar was thorough and extensive.[32]

The Inns of Court, however, must not be regarded as mere hostels and training schools for lawyers. To sense their full significance one has to recall, first of all, the fact that the English of the sixteenth century seem to have been happiest and healthiest in the country. As a rule, those who could returned there as soon as their business or pleasure had been consummated in London. Secondly, the periods for transacting business were definitely fixed and corresponded with the four terms of court: Hilary, Easter, Trinity, and Michaelmas.[33] Furthermore, men of affairs who found it desirable or necessary to come up for a term seldom transplanted their families to London for various obvious reasons, among which may be mentioned the difficulties of travel and the constant fear of an outbreak of the plague. If elder men found term-time the logical period for residence in London, young noblemen, knights, gentlemen, and university wits, perhaps uninterested in the profession of law, also came up at these seasons, looking for preferment at court or for a post with some powerful lord or for a place on the staff of an embassy. The ingress of these groups of men created the necessity for lodgings that were at once congenial and exclusive and capable of long lease. The lawyers, with their instinct for organization and the perpetuating of forms and traditions, had evolved just such a satisfactory mode of living in their Inns of Court. Moreover, finding advantages attendant upon their influential connections, the lawyers were not loath, at least until 1614, to offer accommodation in their Inns to the two groups of gentlemen already mentioned, even when the latter had no interest whatever in the study or practice of law.[34] The latter, in turn, were eager to avail themselves of the reciprocal advantages of participation in the life of the Inns. To recall but a few of the men who lodged there at various periods is to summon up a list of England's distinguished names. Roger Ascham[35] was a member of the Middle

Temple in 1554. Frobisher and Sir John Hawkins were admitted there,[36] and Ralegh procured his admission[37] not to become a barrister[38] but to enjoy suitable quarters among men who counted and to gain thereby convenient access to rumours of Court and Parliament. Nor is it hard to imagine the excitement in commons when on 4 August 1586 'Francis Drake, knt., one of the Society . . . after his voyage came into the Middle Temple Hall at dinner time and acknowledged to John Savile, esq., then Reader, . . . and . . . Masters of the Bench, and others present, his old friendship with the Society, those present congratulating him on his happy return with great joy.'[39] Shortly after Hoskyns' own admission there Wotton[40] became a member by special favour of the Reader, but there is no record of his having been called to the bar, nor is there reason to suppose that he aimed at a legal career. Donne lodged for a while in Lincoln's Inn with no very resolute purpose of studying law. Thomas Carew, the poet, was admitted to the Middle Temple in 1612, 'by consent of the Reader and other Masters of the Bench.'[41] It was undoubtedly in the Inns of Court that young wits fresh from the universities and young gentlemen, even noblemen, up from the country to look for preferment oriented themselves in London's ways more pleasurably and profitably than they could have done elsewhere. In their later years, they were not likely to surrender the advantages they had thus obtained but were well pleased to retain as long as possible the connections that had been, often, well-nigh requisite to their subsequent advancement. The Inns of Court by Hoskyns' time had reached the full flower of their development which was at once curious and natural. Partaking somewhat of the qualities of university and cloister, furnished with chambers, commons, and chapel, they had also the essential qualities of the exclusive club. They were the logical and unique resort of knights and noblemen, scholars and *literati*, as well as of Benchers and Ancients, some of whom were to become grave Judges and learned Serjeants-at-Law. Under these circumstances, Hoskyns could not have failed to find himself, in the Temple, amidst the society of some of London's most influential, gifted, and ambitious men.

During his period there, the revels were being kept up with splendour, and the feasts were sometimes lavish entertainments. Perhaps the most famous affair of the sort was the presentation of *Twelfth Night* at the Reader's Feast on 2 February 1602, an event which John Manningham records in his diary.[42] On another occasion, 15 February 1613, the lawyers of the Middle Temple and those of Lincoln's Inn defrayed the heavy charge of £1,086.8s.11d, a sum apparently assessed each house, for presenting George Chapman's masque at Whitehall upon the occasion of the marriage of James's daughter, the Princess Elizabeth, with the Prince Palatine.[43] The masque was an elaborate affair, performed chiefly by members of the two Inns. They all met at the house of Sir Edward Philips and set forth with fifty

Gentlemen, richly attirde, and as gallantly mounted. . . . Next (a fit distance obseru'd betweene them) marcht a mock-Maske of Baboons, attir'd like fantasticall Trauailers, in Neapolitane sutes, and great ruffes, all horst with Asses; and dwarf Palfries, . . . and casting Cockle-demois about, in courtesie, by way of lardges; Torches boarn on either hand of them; lighting their state as ridiculously, as the rest Nobly. After them sorted two Carrs Triumphall, . . . and in them aduanc't, the choice Musitions of our Kingdome, sixe in each; attir'd like Virginean Priests . . . . Then rode the chiefe Maskers, in Indian habits, all of a resemblance . . . imitating Indian worke . . . . Altogether estrangfull . . . . The Torch-bearers habits were likewise of the *Indian* garb, but more strauagant . . . all showfully garnisht with seueral-hewd fethers.[44]

The great procession winding up to Whitehall was kept in order by 'two Marshals (being choice Gentlemen, of either house) Commaunder-like attir'd.' The King, the bride, the bridegroom, and the Lords of the Privy Council and the chief nobility 'stood in the Gallery before the Tilt-yeard, to behold their arriuall.' The whole procession 'for the more ful satisfaction of his Maiesties view,' and perhaps their own lusty enjoyment, 'made one turn about the yeard, and dismounted: being then honorably attended . . . to a Chamber appointed, where they were to make ready for their performance in the Hall.'

In the course of the masque, a great rock was rent asunder by the skilful devices of Inigo Jones, a member of the Middle Temple;[45] and the spectators gazed upon the wealth of Indian mines, beheld a grotesque dance of the baboons, and heard charming hymns to the sun rendered to the accompaniment of six lutes. Ingeniously enough, through the mazes of this medley, the performers arrived at suitable songs of compliment to the bride and bridegroom and concluded with the maskers dancing with the ladies of Court. Thereupon there was feasting, and the King complimented the performers and assured them that he had never seen so many proper gentlemen, and Winwood, praising the elegance of the masque, told the Venetian ambassador that 'it left nothing to be desired.'[46]   Although evidence that Hoskyns took part in the performance is lacking,[47] it is hardly likely that any members shirked their duties in its presentation.[48] Affairs of this sort furnished the members of the Inns of Court contacts with men in the dramatic profession and often brought their societies no small measure of recognition in Court circles.[49]

On an earlier occasion, 8 February 1602, some negotiations were under way between Sir John Popham and Sir Robert Cecil for an entertainment for Queen Elizabeth. Popham states that he has brought it about that the Middle Temple will 'be willing to bear 200 marks toward the charge of what is wished to be done, to her Majesty's good liking, and if the young gentlemen will be drawn in to perform what is of their part,' he hopes it may be effected.[50]   He is rather fearful, however, of the outcome, since 'some of the young men have their humors.'   There is no record that this projected entertainment was ever given.

A still earlier affair, the revel of *Le Prince d'Amour*, acted perhaps in the Christmas festivities of 1597-8, has interesting connections with Hoskyns. There are reasons for supposing that he had a hand in its preparation and performance, since one of its speeches is assigned to him in a manuscript in the British Museum and in another in the Huntington Library,[53] and since in his *Direccōns* Hoskyns quotes from it in a tone of modest pride. In the manuscript in the British Museum and in one in the Bodleian Library[54] the speech is headed thus: 'Refused to answer at extempore being importuned by yᵉ Prince & Sʳ Walter Rawlegh began.' The *Prince d'Amour* was Richard Martin,[55] reigning for the brief season of Christmas. The reference to Ralegh indicates that Hoskyns knew him by 1597 and that together they were making merry in a holiday revel in Middle Temple Hall.

Outside the Temple, as well as within its confines, Hoskyns moved in interesting society.[56] His continued friendship with Wotton is recorded in their joint poem written while they were 'riding on the way.'[57] Another poem[58] furnishes the only record available of a supper party at the Mitre in London on 2 September sometime between 1608 and 1612. Hoskyns appears to have met on that occasion with a group of twelve, all men of unusual interest. One was Lionel Cranfield,[59] the parliamentarian and a man of 'exact information about the finances of the realm,' whom, Professor Notestein remarks, James I might have made his Thomas Cromwell.[60] Another guest was Inigo Jones, the 'Kingdomes most Artfull and Ingenious Architect.'[61] Still another member of the group was Richard Martin,[62] the *prince* of the Templars' revel already mentioned and later Recorder of London. The most distinguished guest of the evening, however, was the poet John Donne.

Basing conjecture upon the publications of Thomas Coryate, one may conclude that Hoskyns, about this period, was seeing a good deal of Donne and also of Ben Jonson as well as of the lesser wits just mentioned. It is a well-known fact that Thomas Coryate,[63] after making a hasty tour of the continent in 1608, was extraordinarly eager to publish for the avid readers of travel literature the account of his rather stupendous five months' travels on foot to Venice and back. This he contrived to do in 1611, after he had obtained from some sixty wits an amazing collection of pseudo-panegyric, prefatory verses. Hoskyns, Donne, Jonson, Inigo Jones, Richard Martin, and Michael Drayton were among the contributors, the last writing in a really affectionate and respectful vein. In 1612 Coryate set out again on his travels; and, writing from the court of the great Mogul in Asmere, in India, he sent back to London a series of letters to certain gentlemen there. In these letters he styles himself 'the Traueller for the English VVits.'[64] Hoskyns belonged to this group of wits. In the first letter, addressed to Sir Edward Philips,[65] Master of the Rolls 'at his house in Chancery-Lane, or VVanstead,' Coryate, after an account of his travels, commends himself to Sir Edward and his 'vertuous Lady'; their son, Sir Robert; Richard Martin; Christopher Brooke; William Hackwell; John Hoskyns;[66] and the rest of the worthy gentlemen frequenting Sir Edward's table, all gentlemen 'that sauour vertue, and the sacred Muses.' Of these friends of Hoskyns' Hackwell[67] was his fellow parliamentarian; Christopher Brooke was a minor poet and a friend of Donne's and his former 'Chamber-fellow in Lincolns-Inn.'[68] If Brooke was a frequent guest at Sir Edward's, it is probable that Donne was also.

The second letter in Coryate's volume, addressed to his 'Most deare and beloued Friend, Maister L. W.,'[69] concludes with his 'humble seruice' to Sir Edward, Sir Robert, and their ladies; to Martin; Hugh Holland; and Inigo Jones. In a postscript he asks to be commended to 'M. Protoplast[70] and all the Sireniacall gentlemen' and suggests that 'L. W.' read the enclosed facetious verses to his friends 'and especially to the Sireniacall gentlemen; for they are elegant and delectable.' He asks that his commendations be remembered also 'with all respect to . . . Beniamin Iohnson.'

The third letter is addressed 'To the High Seneschall of the right *Worshipfull Fraternitie of Sireniacal* Gentlemen, that meet the first *Fridaie of euery Moneth, at the signe of the Mere*-Maide in Breadstreete in London.' After his salutation to the 'Right Generous, Iouiall, and Mercuriall Sirenaicks,' Coryate recalls a meeting with them before his departure, a meeting presided over by 'the quondam Seneschall of the noblest society, M L. VV.' This remark suggests that the party held in September, at which Coryate had been present, was not the only gathering of the sort, since Lawrence Whitaker, it seems, was not present on that occasion.[71] The letter concludes with Coryate's commendations listed under twenty-three heads. Among the recipients of his greetings are Sir Robert Cotton; 'M. John Donne,[72] the author of two most elegant Latine Bookes, *Pseudo-martyr*, and *I*gnatÿ Conclaue'; Richard Martin; Christopher Brooke; and 'M. *Iohn Hoskins*, alias *Aequinoctial Pasticrust*, of the citie of Hereford, Counsellor, at his chamber in the middle Temple.' Hackwell, Inigo Jones, Hugh Holland, and Samuel Purchas[73] are others remembered. Still another commendation is addressed 'to Maister Beniamin Iohnson[74] the poet at his chamber at the Blacke Friars.'

These letters indicate that Hoskyns was recognized as an associate of Jonson and Donne and the other wits mentioned. They also suggest that these wits maintained some sort of organization. Lawrence Whitaker had been *quondam* seneschal. Coryate anticipated a different one who would be reigning over the group upon the arrival of his letter. Though the 'seneschall' was probably no more than the master of ceremonies at a given meeting, Coryate's phrase suggests a series of these presiding officers. There seems also to have been some regularity as well as frequency in the 'Sireniacal' meetings,[75] if reliance can be placed upon Coryate's statement that they met the first Friday of every month at the Mermaid in Bread Street. With all his love of extravagant and absurd expression, Coryate is probably to be relied on for these conclusions. It is therefore apparent that Hoskyns was on terms of intimacy with Donne and Jonson as well as with the lesser wits.

Aubrey indicates that Hoskyns knew also William Herbert, third Earl of Pembroke; for, commenting on Hoskyns' strong and vigorous body, he remarks that Hoskyns 'did the pomado in the saddle of the third horse in his armour . . . before William, earle of Pembroke.'[76] Pembroke,[77] a patron

of the greatest literary men of his time, was also compara-
tively intimate with Hoskyns' fellow-Templar and friend,
Benjamin Rudyerd.[78]   If Rudyerd knew Pembroke, it is
probable that Hoskyns also enjoyed the society of that
nobleman.

The life of a versatile man allied by various ties with
several of the great personages of his time invites investigation.   His critical views are of unusual interest.   His verse
warrants as faithful a collection as can now be made.   The
obscurity of a man so representative of his age is in part
due to the fact that Hoskyns' son lost the manuscript collection of his verse, which he is reputed to have had transcribed by one of his clerks.   Further explanation, however,
is to be found in the ephemeral nature of wit itself and in
his own thoroughly unprofessional attitude toward his literary productions.   Everything he wrote was occasional, usually
a mere *jeu d'esprit*, intended for no wider circle of readers
than that which his friends afforded.   With the Elizabethans
it was the fashion for a gentleman to write verse but not to
publish.   Puttenham[79] complains of the difficulty he experienced in 1589 in laying hands on the acknowledged work of
Dyer, Ralegh, and other courtly poets who chose to conceal
their identity.   This conventional reticence continued to be
the fashion in Jacobean days.   In 1613 Michael Drayton,
in his address to the 'General Reader' of *Poly-Olbion*,
remarks: 'In Publishing this Essay of my Poeme, there is
this great disadvantage against me; that it commeth out at
this time, when Verses are wholly deduc't to Chambers, and
nothing esteem'd in this lunatique Age, but what is kept in
Cabinets, and must only passe by Transcription. . . .'[80]   In
1627, in his epistle to Reynolds, Drayton, again speaks of
'poems, be they nere so rare, In private chambers, that
incloistered are, And by transcription daintyly must goe.'[81]
In 1614, Donne deplores the fact that he seems brought to
the necessity of printing his poems.   'This,' he writes, 'I
mean to do . . . not for much public view, but at mine own
cost, a few copies, I apprehend some incongruities in the
resolution; and I shall have to suffer from many interpreta-

tions . . . yet in this particular, I am under an unescapable necessity . . . .'[82] Of course, there was by no means the same degree of justification for the publication of Hoskyns' verse as is patent in the cases of Donne and Drayton, but there can be little doubt that Hoskyns held the conventional view regarding all his writings. His treatise on style was, for example, but a gift to a young Templar, dedicated to the latter's 'future discretion.'[83]

The contemplation of publication would have enforced pruning and modification with attendant enhancement of the intrinsic merit of his work. On the other hand, a certain gain has accrued from his complete indifference to a general body of readers. Recompensing spontaneity, lack of reserve, and informality now pervade his writings. These qualities enable his work to reveal the author and his times with veracity and colour to a generation remote in time and manners but responsive to the charm of a singular personality and eager for additional glimpses of the age which was fascinated with Sidney's studied grace but was also, in time, to sense the clear splendour of Jonson and to acknowledge the insinuating spell of Donne. Through the medium of Hoskyns' life and writings one may obtain a fresh and intimate view of the activity, the thought, and the literary taste of his England.

CHAPTER II

EARLY LIFE
1566-1593

JOHN HOSKYNS was born on 1 March 1566[1] in the village of Mouncton, now Monnington-upon-Wye, in the parish of Llanwarne and the county and diocese of Hereford. He was the second[2] of the seven sons of John and Margery, and the grandson of John and Elizabeth, Hoskyns, also of Mouncton.[3] The paternal grandfather died in 1558, leaving, besides his wife Elizabeth and their daughters, four sons: John, the eldest; John, Junior; William; and Thomas. It is not clear which John was the father of Serjeant Hoskyns; but if the Middle Temple records are accurate in designating him as the second son, he was likely the son of John, Junior, since Hoskyns' paternal grandmother, in her will drawn up in 1558, mentions the two children of John, her eldest son.[4] Like the Paston[5] family in the fifteenth century that of Hoskyns in the sixteenth seems to have been resolved to maintain a double hold upon the name *John* in each generation; for, like his father, Serjeant Hoskyns had a brother John, with whom he has occasionally been confused.[6]

Not much is known of his family before the year 1558, but the name indicates their Welsh extraction. In the middle of the fifteenth century they were owners of property in the parish of Llanwarne, and in 1510 a John Hoskyns was a lessee of Abbey property, which the family later purchased upon the dissolution of the religious houses.[7] Aubrey records that Hoskyns' ancestors held the office of cupbearer to the prior of Llanthony.[8] It has sometimes been supposed erroneously[9] that Hoskyns' father was a member of Parliament from 1604 to 1611, but a reading of the *Journals of the House of Commons* makes obvious the fact that it was John Hoskyns (1566-1638), the son, who was a member of that Parliament. However, Thomas Jones, probably Hoskyns' maternal grandfather, was returned for the city of Hereford on 27 September 1586 and on 6 October 1601.[10] The foregoing meagre facts constitute what is now known of Hoskyns' forebears.

In Herefordshire in the village of Mouncton upon the river Wye Hoskyns passed the first twelve years of his life. Aubrey says that he was then sent to the Latin grammar school at Westminster,[11] but, 'not speeding there,' was transferred to Winchester College, where, as already observed, he was entered as a scholar on 15 December 1579. It has sometimes been stated[12] that he was admitted as Founder's Kin, a privilege which would have given him a number of advantages such as that of being placed in the charge of one of the advanced pupils who would have made him 'perfect in grammar'[13] at a charge of six shillings, eight pence, borne by the college. Moreover, by the provisions of William of Wykeham he would have received at Christmas, besides the usual cloth to make him a long gown, his linen and woolen clothes, shoes, and other necessities. A final advantage would have been the privilege of proceeding to New College as a fellow instead of undergoing a probation there of two years. Since, however, he passed the usual time as probationer at Oxford[14] and since the records of Winchester do not designate him as Founder's Kin,[15] we must assume that he entered as a regular scholar. Without the special consignments at Christmas and the watchful tuition of a 'discreeter sort' of scholar, he, no doubt, necessarily profited from all the usual advantages of this 'place of strict Discipline and Order,' where one 'might in his youth be moulded into a living by Rule.'[16] During each meal he heard some scholar 'read aloud from the Lives of the Fathers, The *Dicta Doctorum*, or Holy Writ.'[17] Nor could his attention to these sound principles have been distracted by delicacy or variety of fare, for the diet at Winchester in the sixteenth century was still characterized by the simplicity which the Bishop of Winchester had thought seemly for boys preparing for New College immediately and for holy orders event-

ually. The cost of each scholar's food for a week was esti-
mated to be one shilling, nine pence, and a farthing. This
sum provided a slight variation of these simple items: beef
broth; roast mutton and beef; boiled beef, 'cold or sodden
in water'; cheese and butter; and 'baked pudding made up
with water.' In addition, about one-half pound of 'good
wheaten bread' was alloted each scholar at every meal and
'something more than a pint of beer . . . at dinner and
supper and . . . less than a pint at breakfast.'[18] However,
each week there were three meals, breakfast on Friday and
Saturday and supper on Friday, for which the accounts call
for nothing besides the customary beer and bread. It was
only in the sixteenth century that the floors of the school
had been boarded and that bedsteads had replaced the heaps
of straw on the floor. During Hoskyns' period the boys
swept the floors and made their own beds. Notwithstanding
the simplicity, rigour, and discipline of life in a Latin school
like Winchester in the sixteenth century, he probably led a
normal schoolboy's existence.[19] Certainly he has been privileged in retaining for himself at Winton a place in the affections of the Old Boys, for it was he who made the Latin
verses[20] painted beside his emblematic figure of the Trusty
Servant on the wall near the kitchen, 'at the cocks where the
boyes wash their hands,'[21]—a relic so highly esteemed that in
the college accounts there are, at intervals since 1612, entries
for the sum of twenty shillings or so for renewing the
Trusty Servant.[22]

At the age of nineteen, Hoskyns proceeded to New College,
where he matriculated as a scholar on 5 March 1585,[23]
being described in the register as *plebii filius*, or the son of
a yeoman, or commoner. On 21 April the term began,[24]
with John Donne, Henry Wotton, John Owen, and Hoskyns
among those matriculated. On 22 June that year Hoskyns
was actually admitted probationer,[25] and two years later a
fellow.[26] On 6 May 1588 he was admitted to the degree
Bachelor of Arts;[27] in 1589 he 'determined';[28] and on 26
February 1592 was licensed Master of Arts, and in the same
year completed[29] that degree.[30]

At this particular time he was selected to perform the part
of University buffoon,[31] or *terrae filius*, the 'orator privileged
to make humorous and satirical strictures in a speech at the
public "act," '[32] or ceremonies accompanying the conferring
of degrees. Blount, writing in 1656, describes such a person
as 'the *bon drol* . . . who must be a Master of Arts, to qualifie
him for this Office, and is commonly chosen out of the best
Wits of the University.'[33] The public 'acts,' including
apparently the speech delivered by the *terrae filius*, were, in
Hoskyns' time, 'kept' in the Church of St. Mary Le Virgin.[34]
According to Evelyn, writing in 1669, the proper function of
any *terrae filius* was the 'old facetious way of raillying upon
the questions.'[35] However, it had, apparently, always been
much easier to fall into personal satire and abuse, a 'sar-
castical rhapsodie, most unbecoming the gravity of the
Universitie.'[36] Into this obvious danger Hoskyns was the
very person to plunge headlong, and '*propter dicteria
maledica sub persona Terrae filii*,'[37] he was forced to resign
his fellowship and leave the university.

Though Hoskyns had perhaps expected to remain, for a
time at least, as a fellow, he had now to look about for a
livelihood. He appears to have procured at once a teaching
position at Ilchester in Somersetshire.[38] Here in 1592 one
might have seen 'in part the Carkesse of an auncient Citty
that flourished in ye Brittaines Saxons Romans Danes and
Normans times,' but by 1592 '(such is the fate of places as
well as families) almost wholly decayed.'[39] No record
remains of Hoskyns' experiences during the year in
Ilchester, but probably he was reading very carefully and
annotating systematically a vast amount of Greek, for it was
at this period that he compiled a Greek lexicon as far as the
letter *Mu*.[40] That he should have done so indicates his
marked scholarly tastes. Winchester and New College had
left upon him the stamp of their humanism.

CHAPTER III

A YOUNG MIDDLE TEMPLAR
1593-1601

THE isolation of Ilchester, this village 'content with a Common gaol, the County Courts, and one of the Quarter Sessions,' though it did 'enjoy a weekly market on yᵉ Wednesday,'[1] Hoskyns was to exchange at the end of one year for the busy life of Fleet Street and of Westminster, for on 13 March 1593 he procured his admission to the Middle Temple[2] and, with the studious lawyers, took chambers in one of 'those bricky towres, The which on Themmes brode aged backe doe ryde.'[3] From the first, according to Aubrey, Hoskyns wore good clothes, kept good company, got himself acquainted with under-secretaries at Court, and often wrote their Latin letters for them.[4]

Upon his entrance into the Temple he was bound, generally, at a fine of three pounds, with John Davies[5] and James Kirton.[6] Two years later, Hoskyns had bound with himself and Davies his own first young master of the Temple.[7] From that time onward until 1619 he was to receive fourteen young students of the law,[8] one of whom was Robert Harley[9] of Brampton Castle in Herefordshire, later the eminent Puritan parliamentarian in the Long Parliament. Another was John Manningham,[10] the diarist. It is interesting to note that, of the fourteen, six were from Hoskyns' native Herefordshire, and two were from neighbouring Welsh counties. Though there seems to be no definite record of the circumstances governing the placing of young Templars, the fact that nearly half of the number who received their first supervision from Hoskyns came from Herefordshire may suggest that they were regularly bound with acquaintances or relatives.[11] If such was the case, we may conjecture that Hoskyns early had some repute in his own shire. That he soon gained recognition in the Temple for his wit and cleverness has already been suggested by his part in the preparation and performance of *Le Prince d'Amour*.[12] The Middle Temple Records tell little about Hoskyns at this period, aside from a few notices of his removal to different quarters[13] in the Temple lodgings. In the usual time, however, he fulfilled the requirements of study and residence, and on 2 May 1600 his call to the bar, during the preceding reading, was confirmed by the Parliament of the Society.[14]

The readings, such as the one during which he was called to the bar, constituted an important part of the formal legal training which the Temple offered. They were held twice a year: the summer reading at the beginning of August, between the Trinity and Michaelmas terms, and the Lent reading between Hilary and Easter. For each of these periods a Master of the Bench[15] was chosen by the society as Reader, whose duty it was to expound a statute of his own choosing, to lecture on its possible interpretations, and to point out previous decisions rendered thereon.[16] Four senior barristers who had not yet served in the office of Reader 'were stationed at the Cupboard during the Reader's discourses, ready to argue points of law'[17] that might arise. These discourses were attended with a good deal of formality. The Reader, moreover, dispensed lavish hospitality[18] during this period, the cost of which sometimes reached about six hundred pounds in twelve days' time.[19] Those young men preparing to be called to the Bar and those who were already Utter Barristers[20] were expected to be in commons and to attend these lectures. The records show, however, that from fourteen to nineteen Utter Barristers[21] were regularly fined twenty shillings each for absence at a given reading.

It is interesting to observe that Hoskyns was among those so fined for absence from the first five readings after his own admission to the bar.[22] He was never similarly fined thereafter. No very plausible reason presents itself for his absence from commons during four of these readings, but doubtless the explanation for his absence in early August

1601 is the fact that on 1 August that year 'M[r] John Hoskins & Bennet Borne' were married in the Abbey Church of SS. Peter and Paul, in Bath.[23]   Benedicta Bourne, or Bennet, as she was frequently called, was the daughter of John Moyle of Buckwell, Kent, by Mary, daughter of Robert Honywood of Charing, Kent,[24] and was the widow of Hoskyns' fellow-Templar, Francis Bourne.[25]   Francis Bourne had been buried on the preceding 24 February in the same Abbey Church of SS. Peter and Paul.[26]   In his will[27] he had left his wife 'the manor of Sutton Saint cleere' conveyed to them by his father upon their marriage. To his son Walter he left his 'landes in Bristowe for 80 yeares if he live so long, the lease to begin after the decease of his mother.' But this son, Walter, was buried beside his father in Bath Abbey on 17 April the same year.[28]   Benedicta Bourne survived with a son,[29] a daughter,[30] and Francis Bourne's posthumous child, christened Elizabeth in the same abbey on 15 March 1601.[31]

From his entrance into the Temple Hoskyns had probably known Francis Bourne. Since Bourne's manor near Long Sutton was not far distant from Ilchester, the two men may even have met during Hoskyns' year in that village. Just when he was introduced to Benedicta Moyle Bourne is not known; but, at any rate, less than six months after the death of Bourne, Hoskyns, at the age of thirty-five, was married to Bourne's widow, a woman of twenty-six,[32] possessed of a considerable fortune[33] and doubtless of wisdom and charm.[34]

From this time onward, Hoskyns' career in the Middle Temple is characterized by his steady advancement toward the dignities of standing at the Cupboard and serving as Reader to his House. The eight years just considered together with the ensuing twelve mark the period of Hoskyns' most interesting social and literary connections.

CHAPTER IV

IN THE FIRST JACOBEAN PARLIAMENT
1604-1611

JOHN HOSKYNS took his seat in Parliament for the city of Hereford on 19 March 1604.[1] He found himself in a Parliament that had not forgotten the fervour of unified national feeling with which England had welcomed Drake home after his voyage or which she had felt when she knew herself mistress of the seas and longed for adventures westward in successful competition with Spain. But, at the same time, Hoskyns found himself in a Parliament[2] made up of men whose ambitious hopes for building a world empire on trade were being thwarted by powerful monopolies and by the heavy duties imposed upon imported commodities.[3] In the very language of their debates lies something of the Elizabethan romance of adventure as well as a record of the growing discontent of the ambitious middle class. They were protesting that the impositions 'upon Marchandise after their long Voyages, and great adventures, be grievous to the Marchants, and to the other Subiects, by inhancing the prices of such things which are of good use, and hath bene, and will be the decay of great Shipps, to the Damage of the Realme.'[4] It was a time when the problem of free trade, though couched in phrases redolent of romance and adventure on the high seas, was nevertheless an extraordinarily poignant concern of the knights and burgesses of England. With Hoskyns, they believed that since an Englishman is an islander born, 'it is proper unto him to traffique.'[5] The position of the Established Church was scarcely a less immediate concern. The projected union with Scotland presented insurmountable difficulties. Moreover, throughout the first Jacobean Parliament the Lower House was intent upon remedying accumulated grievances and upon holding within limits the kingly prerogative.

In these endeavours Hoskyns, from the beginning, was an advocate of the popular cause. He was bold and outspoken but not radical; cautious regarding the surrender of any portion of the power which he conceived to be vested in the Commons; and judicial in his point of view. His caution to safeguard popular rights is suggested by his insistence upon a limitation and definition of the power of the Speaker of the Commons to deliver messages from the King or to the King from the House.[6] On one occasion he opposed the reading of the Bill of Attainder of 'some Offenders in the late most barbarous, detestable, monstrous, and damnable Treason,' the Gunpowder Plot.[7] It appears that Sir Robert Wingfield and others wanted a petition sent to the King that the persons involved in the plot might be tried in Parliament 'that some more greavous death might be by the parliament appointed to the said traitors then the lawe inflicteth.'[8] That Hoskyns opposed any effort to bring their punishment within the jurisdiction of the House indicates his judicial poise maintained even when his position, however unfairly, might have cast a shadow of suspicion upon his loyalty.

In the matter of religion, he was anti-Papist but conservative. When a grievance was read in the House to the effect that the Papists were 'collecting all the *Lives* of Ministers in England,' Hoskyns exclaimed, 'He hath a dull Spirit, that hath no feeling in this Cause —We ought to be Intercessors for such as are Intercessors for us to God,'[9] meaning apparently that Parliament should protect the livings or benefices of the clergy from the encroachments of Roman priests. In 1604 he served on the committee for the bill for disabling recusants[10] and in 1607 was on the committee for the bill to assure the execution of justice in the ecclesiastical courts.[11] On 5 July 1610 he was added to the committee for religion.[12] His conservatism is shown by his speaking for the bill to prohibit the residence of married men with their wives and families in colleges, cathedral churches, and the Universities of Oxford and Cambridge, on the grounds that virginity is a virtue, that marriage is not a necessity, and that the founders' will that the heads of their houses should be unmarried ought to be observed.[13] An opponent of Hoskyns thereupon exclaimed, 'And yet this ientleman saieth he is not popish!'[14] In cooler appraisal, however, his point of view marks him not necessarily as a Papist but merely as a conservative Churchman.

To realize how able a man of affairs Hoskyns was, one has but to follow his activities in Parliament on some of the minor issues. That he was a person of unusual energy and one to be charged with details is evident from the scope of his activities. Recognition of his ability to carry on business in an approved parliamentary fashion is suggested by his appointment during the first five weeks of the Parliament to serve on the committee for a bill restraining 'frivolous actions,'[15] that is, unnecessary or ill-drawn bills.

On 20 June 1604 he and Sir Charles Cornwallis, Thomas Fuller, Sir Thomas Hoby, and others were at work in the 'Chequer Chamber' on a bill 'to encourage Seamen of England to take Fish,' whereby these seamen might 'increase, to furnish the Navy of England.'[16] The same month Hoskyns was added to the committee for the bill 'concerning Tanners and Curriers, Shoemakers, and others' occupied in the cutting of leather.[17] He investigated deceits in dyeing[18] and disputed the bill for the 'true making of woolen clothes.'[19] He served on a committee dealing with the transportation of beer over seas[20] and concerned himself with the problems of butter and cheese at home.[21] He considered the relief of 'such as lawfully use the Trade and Handicraft of Skinners'[22] and served on the committee for a bill for the preservation of game,[23] and on another for a bill 'against Aliens and Strangers retailing' hawks within the realm.[24] He helped prepare a bill against turning coppices and underwoods into pasture or tillage[25] and another for the 'better provision of Meadow and Pastures' in Herefordshire.[26] The 'new Making and Keeping in Reparation of Chepstowe Bridge';[27] the problems of the Minehead, Yarmouth, and Lowestoft harbours;[28] and the confirmation of the charter of Southampton,[29] all came under his notice. The establishment of a free grammar school in Cumberland[30] and the conversion of a Devonshire manor into another[31] were his concerns. Bills regarding jointures, the confirming of titles, the sale of lands, and the settlement of estates were affairs in which he frequently had a hand.[32] Bills for the naturalization of foreigners, chiefly the Scots, he often helped to draw up.[33] He advocated important reforms in the jurisdiction of the courts in the Marches of Wales.[34] It would be impossible to think of Hoskyns as lethargic in the first Jacobean Parliament when he was thus engrossed with problems of parliamentary procedure, the encouragement of industries at home and on the seas, the conservation of resources,[35] the building and improvement of bridges and harbours, the establishment of free schools, the settling of estates, the drawing up of papers for naturalization, and the reform of the courts in the Welsh Marches. These multifarious duties represent the routine tasks of the period, but there is every suggestion that Hoskyns dealt with them promptly and with zest.[36] The dependence which the Commons felt upon its lawyers is evident from the numerous provisions made to assure their continued presence.[37] Certainly Hoskyns was one of the most energetic members of this group.

One of the major issues of the first Jacobean Parliament was the proposed union with Scotland. The difficulties of union were so numerous that although James eagerly and persistently urged it, his efforts were futile in his lifetime; and indeed the union was not achieved until 1707. In Hoskyns' time Scotland was still something of a traditional foe of England. When James became king, the two nations were not drawn together in any sort of amity. Though James admitted to the Commons that Scotland was, for the most part, a bleak and not too fertile country, he reminded them that sturdy men were also part of the wealth of a nation.[38] England, reaping the fruits of peace at the moment, felt no particular need for the hordes of sturdy Scots who followed their monarch into England. Neither was she willing to share her wealth with her northern neighbours. The English merchant traders were unwilling to open their monopolies to Scottish trade, nor had Scotland many commodities that England wanted. The rift between the established churches of the two nations was wide enough to preclude the most friendly and sympathetic feelings. Each country had its own laws. The coinage was distinct in each nation. Finally, the late sympathies between France and Scotland were looked upon with distrust in England. When all things were considered, there were, from the English point of view, many arguments against union. There was but one reason for tearing down old barriers: both nations found themselves under the rule of a single king. Since, however, union was one of the dearest concerns of the King, on 13 April 1604 he urged the Commons to consider that question.

Five days after the King's announcement of his wishes, Hoskyns delivered in the House a speech outlined under three points: '1. What God hath done: 2. What we are to do: 3. What we cannot do.' The briefly recorded notes indicate that he spoke as follows:

God hath made an Union. Without God's Supportance nothing can stand. *Tigris* and *Euphrates* are run together, and the Noise is gone throughout the World. The King may name it at his pleasure. —

2. We Subjects, since wee see it done by God, are to join to give Obedience to the King; neither for Reason of Policy, nor Reason of . . . [*sic*] but for Christianity, in imitating God. —

Princes affect Length of Titles. One took up his Breath, in reciting the Titles of the Emperor of *Russia*: Ill taken; and he not entertained, except he could go through. —

3. What can we not do? We cannot make it perpetual. —*Unus Rex, una Britannia unum imperium: Unus Deus, una fides, unum baptisma.*[39]

Hoskyns' speech indicates that he may have been willing to accept a limited form of union but that he opposed the complete and perfect union for which James so ardently wished. To Hoskyns the difficulties seemed too great to warrant making the union perpetual and complete. That he should have stated these views boldly five days after the

King's proposal marks him as a daring opponent of the royal policy.

In June of the same year Hoskyns was one of a committee from the House to confer with forty lords in the Painted Chamber on the proposed union with Scotland.[40] As the discussion went on, Sir Edwyn Sandys hesitated lest England's bounty might be her bane.[41] Another questioned 'whither it be safe to entertaine into our Bosomes them whom he shewed to be so fast annexed to an other Kingdome and People.'[42] By 1607 Hoskyns was advising further deliberation before any decision might be arrived at.[43] Thus he steadfastly held himself in opposition to this measure urged upon the Commons by the King.

Recurrent as the question of union was, the Parliament spent its greatest energy in the gathering together of grievances. In 1606 a committee of which Hoskyns was a member framed the collected grievances into a petition to present to the King.[44] Later we find Hoskyns limiting grievances by pointing out those which are 'unproper.'[45] Excellently equipped by his legal training, he was systematic in the work of assembling grievances,[46] and on 6 June 1610 he moved 'that Bowyer[47] and other clerks give attendance at the Tower in place where his Majesty's Records are kept,' to aid in this work.

The first grievance dealt with came up in sudden fashion. At the opening of Parliament the King proposed to have all doubtful elections turned over to the jurisdiction of the Court of Chancery, a situation which would have lessened materially the power of the Commons. Naturally they promptly protested that their privileges were being challenged and proceeded to maintain their own power to disable a man from a seat in Parliament by drawing up a bill to that effect. Hoskyns was a member of the committee for this bill.[48] Throughout the Parliament he was watchful to preserve the privileges[49] of the House and quick to argue for a definition of those privileges. We find him exclaiming: 'No privilege in Matter of Peace. Walking late— No Privilege.'[50] On 12 March 1606, Hoskyns, sitting with one of the committees,

declared: 'Greavances weare aunciently sent upp to the King:
but to treate of them att Conference or Committees doth butt
disclose our harts and make our selves to be singled out.'[51]
Though Hoskyns thus valued circumspection, he nevertheless
was willing upon necessity to present a grievance to the
House with a boldness scarcely paralleled in this session.
Respecting the sanctity of records, he became thoroughly
aroused over one Tipper's abuse of the right of access to
records of titles. According to Hoskyns' accusations this
Tipper had been unscrupulous in his activities as a commis-
sioner empowered to accept composition for rectifying
defects in titles of estates derived out of the Crown.[52] No
other than Sir Edward Dyer was the 'partaker' with Tipper
in this business,[53] and Hoskyns' attack upon Tipper is indirectly an attack upon Sir Edward Dyer as well. It was on
7 April 1606, in the Parliament Chamber, that Hoskyns
spoke

of a Grievance by a Commission, by rolle, whereof one now is easily
perspicuous, for that he rideth on horseback, doth prevent the Kings
Subiects of the Benefitt of his Majesty Grace, whereby they may
establish, and have their Estates amended upon Composition with Certaine Commissionors. And his Course is, First he sendeth for the
Party by a Letter from the Commissionors, when such Partie cometh
to him, he telleth him to this Effect, You hold such Lands, That Tytle
is defective, This is the Case, and then he delivereth him such Cases
he thinketh good, and with all he requireth to see the Parties Evidence
and upon Sight thereof, and notes taken out of it, or having such
Evidence left with him, he then seeketh how a Quirke may be found
in the Tytle, and for this Purpose he hath obtayned Warrants for
Sight of the Kings Records in diverse Offices, as namely in the Aug-
mentation Records which he hath soe handled, That a man may
tracke him easily where he hath bene (and note here, Mr. Hoskyns
used plaine words signifying that this Fellowe hath blotted and falsi-
fied many Records there) yea said he, he hath gotten a lease of 40.
or 41. Mannors and when the Tenants or Owners of them come up
to compound, they come too late: And all this he doth upon Promise
to bring one hundred thousand Pounds to the King in fyve yeares;
And for reward, he and an other[54] have the fourth Part of all they
shall soe bring in: But hitherto he hath not brought to the King, I
thinck one thousand Pounds. In Conclusion his name is Tipper.[55]

Nine days after this speech Hoskyns delivered to Fuller, the chairman of the committee on grievances, a grievance in writing against Tipper:

Many Cathedrall Churches, Colledges, Hospitalls, Corporations and Foundations erected to charitable uses, infinite Numbers of the Kings Tenants are grieved with the uniust vexation and subtill Practices of Tipper, he pretendeth himselfe to be an Officer authorized to deale with all such as have defective Tytles and Estates derived out of the Crowne, and by Color thereof carrieth a great Port and Countenance Keepeth an Office without Warrant, and he and his Clerk takes unlawfull Fees, and Extorts of the Kings Subiects great Summes of Money; He hath accesse to the Kings Records, perswadeth the Clerks of the Court of Augmentations and the Exchequer that they suffer not the Subiect to have sight of the Records for strengthning their Tytles; And since his Accesse, the Records are misplaced, unperfect, and imbezelled: He hath procured to himself Grants of the whole Estates of Cathedrall Churches, and other Corporations, and of particular Persons, and vexed them without Cause: He hath now a Grant of 41. Mannors, with diverse other Granges and Fermes to his use, for the Consideration of 20£ — only paid by Clerck and Clerck: And when the Kings Tenants and others called up to compound for defective Tytles by his Majesty honorable Commissioners authorized to make them good Estates, doe offer Composition, after such tyme as the said Tipper hath by long Molestation discovered their Tytles, then he interposeth his said lease betwixt them, and his Majesty favour intended by the said Commission, in fraud of his Majestyes Grace, and dishonour of the Commission, he first giveth false Coppies to such as come to Compound, then searcheth their Evidences, and either taketh bribes, or multiplieth Endlesse Suites. He and his Partaker hath covenanted to bring into his Majesty 100000£ — in few yeares by discovery of Tytles, and is to have together with his Partaker either a fourth part of the same 100000£ — and what ever else he shall bring in in money, or a fourth part of the Lands so evicted in lease for 90 yeares at his Election. And hath undertaken debts due to the King, but little or nothing is brought in by this Course to the King, infinite Number of Subiects troubled, and Scandall raysed by this Course, which in Common Persons is Barretry[56] and Maintenance.[57] It is humbly desired that his Majesty Service be supplied by a man of honnor, Reputation, and by the direction of his Majesty Judges or learned Counsell, and that they be not referred over to such a person to worke upon them by undirect Sleights to their great Charge and Grievance.[58]

Hoskyns' suggestion that the lawyers be granted some authority in the selection of one of his Majesty's agents emphasises the growing power of the lawyers. Moreover, the tenor of his speech indicates that he did not lack boldness and courage in exposing a grievance which might disparage the King's methods of increasing his funds.

A grievance of longer standing, however, than that of the commission of the rolls was the abuse of purveyance, or the system by which appointees of the Crown, known as purveyors, were authorized to take supplies for the King's household and to command carts and equipment for his progresses. By Hoskyns' time the supplies were taken at appraised rates; yet when the purveyors were unscrupulous men, abuses arose from this method of providing for the King's household and for the expenses of his travel. The Commons maintained, for the most part, that since these abuses were illegal, the King could not seek compensation for abandoning them. The Lords, on the other hand, were willing to make the King an annual grant of fifty thousand pounds in lieu of the right of purveyance. It is on this point of 'composition' for a grievance that Hoskyns' views clashed with those of Sir Francis Bacon. On 5 March 1606 the Commons disputed the question of granting composition for purveyance. Hoskyns was against proceeding that day to the question. He spoke

Inter alia to prove the King had no such valuable right in purveiance as might be woorth much he disproved that which the Lord Archbishop did speake att the last conference, uppon this text. *Hoc est ius regis*: for quoth he in the booke of Samuell from whence this text is drawen, God spake of an evell King whom he would sett over the people who should oppresse them as there appeareth, but quoth he in the 17 of Deutronomy wheare a good King is described there is not such power saied to be in the King as that he could take the goods of the subiects: He concluded merily, viz. that if wee proceeded in a composicion he feared wee should do like unthrifts who begin with a Rent charge, then proceede to a Mortgage, and in conclusion departe with the land itselfe.[59]

Two days later, Sir Francis Bacon, persuading composition, in the course of his argument answered some objections:

1. It is objected that hereby we shall bring a perpetuall taxe on the Realme. To which it is aunswered, that it is not desiered it should be perpetuall nor other then a probation for a tyme so as Doomes day (herin he glaunced at Mr. Hoskyns who two days before had used that woorde) is not to be expected before the Inconvenience hereof be founde, except the next parliament be saied to be the day of doome, if for anie inconvenience it take away and censure this composicion.[60]

After answering other objections Bacon concluded thus regarding the matter of composition for the right of purveyance:

I say it is not a buyeing of Justice but agreeing or buying if you will of Interest of ease of quiet for say the King have nothing but as some call it preemption, and power to buy and take carrages for the veary valew against the owners will (wherof is no doubt) yet may this be doon at such tymes and in such place as may be exceeding inconvenient.[61]

It is interesting to observe that Bacon was expedient and willing to make concessions in abstract theory in order to meet the needs of the moment, whereas Hoskyns was unwilling to recognize any valuable legal right in royal purveyance and was cautious lest the Commons 'should doe like unthrifts' and thus finally surrender their right to the land itself.

Subsidies and impositions furnished another fertile ground for search and dispute in the first Jacobean Parliament. The extant records of Hoskyns' part in this battle for funds, which James was to carry on throughout his reign, suggest that he was one of the frugal burgesses resolved to keep at a minimum the taxes of their shires, let happen what might regarding the increased cost of the monarch's household, the standing debts of the late queen, the charge of ten thousand pounds for James's coming to England, the twenty thousand pounds for the burial of Elizabeth, and an equal sum for James's coronation.[62]

In February 1606, Hoskyns was serving on a committee with Sir Francis Bacon, Lord Howard, and others to discuss

the drawing of a bill for subsidies.[63]   On 12 March of that
year, in the same committee, Hoskyns remarked: 'I must
say that betweene theis proposicions: 1: A Kinge may not
waunt: 2. Subiects ought not to examine how it is spent:
A supply may easily be spent so may a resupply, and so the
Fortunes of the crowne may runne a circle and whatsoever
wee give, wee cannot give that [which] may suffice.'[64]   In
the same month Hoskyns, opposing a suggestion that the first
payment be hastened, said: 'The King in Possession of the
Subsidy.—He would not have the Sheep to say, the Bramble
was more merciful than the Shepherd.'[65]   On another occasion when the Parliament was discussing how it might
express its love to the King through the granting of a subsidy, Hoskyns remarked: 'We have no Sheep that yields
Two Fleeces in the Year.'[66]   The substance of one of his
speeches in February 1610 is recorded as follows:

Neither was it thought tyme to enter into consideracion of subsidies,
for that the former were not yet payd, and to grante subsidies in
reversion was not usuall, nor warranted by any president, especially
considering that His Majestie did declare in his proclamacion for the
parliament, that he did not call that parliament for any private bene-
fite to hymselfe, but for the good of the Comonwealth. And that also
it was sayd in the last grante of subsidy, that that grante was without
president, and should not be drawne into example in after tymes.[67]

On 6 November of that year Hoskyns declared that it
was 'not fitt to conferre with the Lords, for the mene matter
of supplie ought to proceed' from the House. 'No danger,'
he said, 'to proceede to the question, for it may please His
Majesty to recommend it unto us agayne in the same state
it was.' Thereupon the matter was put to the question, the
House following Hoskyns' suggestion, '*unâ voce.*'[68]   Here
one observes Hoskyns' care to keep the initiative regarding
subsidies firmly fixed in the Commons.
    The fullest report of his views on subsidies is found in
the following notes on his speech delivered in the last session
of the Parliament:

The question whither wee will give, *rebus sic stantibus,* is like to be
with childe with another. *Quomodo possunt res mutari in melius?*

Henry the 7th and Tiberius both rich, but not taking all from the people. Tacitus.

Cato had a double revenue: frugality is one. Well governing of revenue hathe bene a meanes used by princes to supplie his revenue.

The falt of those that so presse upon the Prince as to hold his Parliament to sitt 7 yeares together to fynde meanes how to supplie the King.

1. Theise not English. They were wont to spend theyre owne revenue in the King's service.

2. Not Irish; they will be costermongers rather than want.

Not Dutch; for they are ingenious and industrious.

They be such as hold a consultacion how to draw out of this cesterne as fast as wee fill it.[69]

In regard to subsidies, then, Hoskyns consistently strove to delay the grants, to keep them moderate, and to keep their control in the hands of the Lower House.

In 1610 Hoskyns, with Bacon, Sandys, Fuller, Hackwell, and others, served on a committee to search and dispute the grievance arising from heavy impositions.[70] Hoskyns' views are recorded in the following fragmentary notes:

'Expectation,' he said [is] a great adversary; and I will free myself of it as soone as I can.' He then denied that 'Custome is the Kinge's inheritance' and continued thus:

Jeffrey's case proves an imposition may be made where the Comon lawe gives authority . . . . Generall and comon customes are but the Comon lawe of England. So, if it be proved by the Comon lawe the King may impose, then that argument is of weight: *aliter non* . . . . The King accepts not that as a guift which is due unto hym by prerogative . . . . The King may inhibite, *igitur* he may impose . . . . The Kinge may restrayne me from suing in one Courte; therefore he may take money to release me.

So the Lord Chancellor may injoyne me from suing: therefore he may take money to sett me at liberty.

Judges may judge the excesse, if the imposition be unreasonable.

Neither the Judge nor the Jury can judge what gaynes is reasonable for a merchant his aventure.

If it be excessive then voyd, say they. But it is voyd for want of power or knowledge. I should be loth to say the King's power is above his knowledge, or that he should borrowe knowledge of his subjects when he hath power of his owne.[71]

In Hoskyns' opinion custom was a toll but not a good toll
if the subject received no benefit from it. He continued thus:

> The regal power from God, but the actuating thearof is from the
> people.
> To have this power illimitated is contrary to reason. . . .
> So an unlimited power is contrary to reason. . . . Customes due to
> the King by Comon law . . . .
> If toll be due whense comes the lymitation? Thoe he have custome
> *de jure,* yet the lymitation is *de pacto* by Parliament . . . .[72]

These shreds of his speech indicate that he did not chal-
lenge kingly prerogative but that he did maintain by virtue
of common law, the right of Parliament to limit that
prerogative.

The outcome of the matter was that on 23 November 1610
James 'sent a writ in his own hand' to the effect that, provided certain other levies were made, 'he would be content to
give way that there should be an act of parliament made
that no impositions hereafter should be laid out but by act.'[73]
The King, pressed for funds, offered to relinquish the position he had been holding on royal prerogative for the sake
of an immediate grant. Doubtless he had begun to find
annoying, among others, this man Hoskyns, who argued
freely that though the regal power be from God, the actuat-
ing thereof is from the people; although the King 'have
custome *de jure,* yet the lymitation is *de pacto* by Parliament.'

CHAPTER V

IN THE ADDLED PARLIAMENT AND THE ENSUING YEAR IN THE TOWER 1614-1615

ON 5 April 1614, about 'Twelve of the Clock, my Lord Admiral, Lord High Steward for this Time came into the Roome, commonly called the *Whyte-hall*, or Court of Requests,' and administered the oaths of allegiance and supremacy to about one hundred and sixty knights and burgesses elected to sit in James's second Parliament.[1] Hoskyns was one of the number, and again represented the city of Hereford.[2] After waiting about an hour these gentlemen received their summons to the banqueting room in the House of Lords to hear the King's opening address. The crowd was already so great, however, that many of them, somewhat disgruntled, returned to the Parliament Chamber without hearing James's long speech in which he entreated for relief of his wants. He compared himself to a mirror in which they might see the integrity of his purpose, but pointed out that some of the Lower House in the preceding Parliament had looked upon him with polluted eyes, and, as he might say, defiled his mirror.[3] He reminded those who had crowded into the banqueting hall that there had been many great occasions of expense: 'by enterteynem^t: of forraine Princes, and Ambassadors, the great and long Christmas' he had kept at his coming to England ten years before, but had not yet paid for, 'the feare of Ireland,' and the general 'consideration that the Nerues both of peace and warr, are many.' For these reasons he hoped that the Parliament might begin 'wth alacrytie and loue, and conclude soe,' when suitable provisions had been made for his needs. It concluded with alacrity, but scarcely with love, in early June of that year without granting any subsidies. Nor is there reason to suppose that on 5 April Hoskyns and the other burgesses and the knights gathered for the Parliament felt much assurance that the King's hopes were warranted.[4]

Within a fortnight of this none too auspicious opening of
Parliament Hoskyns was again energetically engaged in the
concerns of the Commons.   Before the House should consider subsidies, he was insisting[5] that the issue of the matter
might be known.[6]   A few days later he moved that a warrant be issued from the House for search in the Tower and
Exchequer, and that the very material records and precedents
found there be copied and examined 'at the Charge of the
House.'[7]   Not long afterwards, Hoskyns grumbled: 'This a
Parliament of Love.—All the arguments now used, [are]
Arguments of Feare.'[8]   At the same time, he continued his
reasoning of 1610 by asserting: 'To be, *potestas emendi et
vendendi in terra aliena*, this is liberty . . . . Greater peace,
greater securitie, when the K. is limited by Parlament and
the rates allowed . . . not withstanding the Judgment of y[e]
Exchequer, we should desire we might enjoy our auncient
liberties, and that the Custome should be rated and allowed
by Parlament.'[9]   Though the substance of his arguments was
virtually unchanged, the manner of delivering them was
more feverish than it had been in 1610.   At the same time
others were somewhat frantically declaring that 'Sampson
must be bound wth Cords, not Cobwebbs' and that 'Custome
like Juice . . . will moderate it self to preserue it selfe.'[10]

Bishop Neile of Lincoln, resenting the boldness of leaders
in the Lower House, declared that the impositions were a
'noli me tangere, the questioning whereof struck . . . at the
root of the prerogative, nay would tumble down the imperial
crown itself.'[11]   Regarding a projected conference with
members of the House, he declared that 'he could not enter-
tain the dispute,' lest in the heat of argument 'it might be
seditious words might fall from some of the Commons'
House.'[12]

His fears appear in a measure to have been justified.[13]
Moreover, Bacon's implication in 1606[14] that this Parliament
might prove to be the Day of Doom was almost prophetic
so far as Hoskyns was concerned.   In the forenoon of
7 June 1614, in a speech before the House, he applied 'the

Sicilianae Vesperae[15] to the Scots who consumed both king
and kingdom in insolency and all kind of riot.'[16]   On the
same afternoon, the Privy Council dispatched a messenger
'to bring John Hoskins, esquier, before their lordships,'
assembled in Whitehall, 'to answer such matters as should
be objected agaynst him.'[17]   The next morning the Council,
with the Lord Archbishop of Canterbury, the Duke of
Lennox, the Earl of Pembroke, the Earl of Somerset, and
others present, dispatched this letter to Sir Gervase Helwys,
Knight, Lieutenant of the Tower:

> Wheras we finde cause to restrayne the person of John Hoskins,
> esquire, for offences committed against his Majestye and the State,
> these are therefore to will and require you to receave into your custody
> and safe keeping in the Tower and sayd John Hoskins, and to keep
> him close prisoner, untill yow shall receave further directyon from
> us concerning him.[18]

On the same day Thomas Wentworth,[19] Christopher
Neville,[20] and Sir Walter Chute[21] were similarly dispatched
to the Tower for their own speeches in Parliament on
7 June.[22]   Five days later Dr. Lionel Sharpe[23] and Sir
Charles Cornwallis[24] were also committed to the Tower on
the charge of having furnished Hoskyns with the speech he
had delivered.[25]

A short time after this the following rimes were being
circulated about town:

> 'The Counsell by committing 4
> Haue sent 8 humors to y[e] Tower
> Hoskins the poet is merrily sad,
> Sharpe y[e] devine is soberly mad.
> Cornwallis y[e] states-man is popishly p[re]cise
> And Chute y[e] Caruer is foolishly wise.'[26]

Cornwallis on 22 June sent the King a lengthy and 'pre-
cise' explanation of his conduct:
'Accept I humblie beseech you (most gracious Soueraigne)
the true and plaine discouery of a soule afflicted & greiued
in all extremitie for yo[r] Ma:[ties] displeasure, occasioned by
some conferrences concerning yo[r] late Parliament.'[27]   After

beginning thus, Cornwallis thereupon protested that he had
been indeed zealous and ardent that his Majesty's 'desires
might haue been effected,' and his 'deere countrie cared for &
contented.' For a reason not very plausibly explained he
had found it impossible to be in the Parliament himself, but
had 'conceiued & projected' what he would wish to say were
his presence there possible, the whole purpose of his speech
being to draw from the Parliament 'matter of so great consequence' as the payment of the King's debts; the providing
of his 'Treasure'; and the establishing of the state of his
revenue fit to support him 'in y^t Royall Lustre, y^t hitherto'
he had enjoyed.   To arrive at this worthy end, he had
planned to remind the House that they ought not 'to seeke
to depriue' the king 'of any of the Gemes, or fflowers of
his crowne, nor make him so deare an earner' of their money.
'My humble motion,' he continued, 'should be, y^t we might
all vnitely wth one hart & voice cast ourselues at his Ma:^{ties}
feete, offeringe vnto him whatsoeuer this kingedome can possiblie yeild for ye releife of his necessities.'   Yet he humbly
desired that the King might take into consideration the
'thinges of great consequence vnto him: & of most contentm:^{t}
to his subjects.'   In the first place, he hoped James would
not insist upon the marriage of Prince Charles with a
Princess of the 'Romish' religion, particularly not with a
Princess of France, for 'such is the neereness of ffrance vnto
us,' he reminded the King, 'as should a daughter of y^t
kingdome, be brought hither: such and so many would be
the visitts, as wee should euery month be enforced to entertaine a new Mounsieur: wch to a Prince of so magnificent &
liberall a disposition, as his Ma:^{tie} would breed no little
trouble, and a great deale of expence & charge.'   In the
second place, he would request his Majesty to be 'pleased,
to stopp the current of future comers, of the Scottish nation
to reside' in England.   This, he declared, was the substance
of the speech he would have delivered in Parliament.
Unable to be there himself, he communicated the matter to
Dr. Lionel Sharpe, who got 'by some meanes correspondencie
wth Mr Hoskins, who made . . . a speach in Parliam:^{t} con-

cerning the Scotts but such as neither agreed with' Cornwallis' 'in forme, or matter.'[28]

Just what Hoskyns said and what forces influenced him
to do so remain conjectural. Gardiner[29] believed that Northhampton was his abettor, since the latter may have believed
that his plans for a Spanish alliance and a measure of toler-
ation to the English Catholics could be furthered by maintaining unfriendly relations between the King and the
Commons. Gardiner seems to have supposed that Hoskyns
was hired to make his rash speech under assurance of protection from Sir Charles Cornwallis and even from the Earl
of Northhampton.[30] It is true that Chamberlain wrote
Carleton that Hoskyns and others had been 'hired to forward
the plot.'[31] But since Chamberlain was gossipy rather than
very well-informed,[32] full credence may not be placed in his
remark. It seems likely enough that Hoskyns may have been
offered some protection for the risk he took in voicing
general opinions in unvarnished terms, but there is no evidence that he was bribed to perform his part. Moreover,
the views he expressed appear to be exactly the ones he had
voiced throughout the first Jacobean Parliament. In speaking out plainly against the Scots he was only somewhat
bolder than he had been on earlier occasions and more
straightforward than Cornwallis and many others dared to
be. This time he acted, in the opinion of the circumspect
Sir Henry Wotton, as though he were a member of the
'Senate of *Venice*, where the Treaters are perpetual Princes,
then where those that speak so irreverently, are so soon to
return (which they should remember) to the natural capacity
of Subjects.'[33]

Though in 1610 Hoskyns had reminded the House that a
statute in the time of Henry VII declared that no man should
be impeached for speaking in Parliament freely,[34] he was,
nevertheless, on 8 June 1614 to find himself a close prisoner
in the Tower for the offense of voicing in unglossed language the widespread dissatisfaction of his countrymen.

Sir Henry Wotton on Midsummer Morning 1614 wrote
to his nephew: '*Chute*,[35] *Hoskyns, Sharp,* and Sir *Charles*

Cornwallis are still in the Tower, and I like not the com-plexion of the place.'[36]   But on Midsummer Morning Hoskyns' full year of imprisonment had barely begun, dur-ing which, as Aubrey records, the sight once of a crow and at another time of a kite afforded him great pleasure.   The most intimate view of his own and his family's distress is furnished by the following four letters[37] from Benedicta Hoskyns to her husband, dated at intervals during the period of 18 July to 15 August 1614:

I

Good sir.   I with my family doe continue our prayers to God for the kings ma^tie and his most honourable counsayle, I am persw^aded that if I were there I would so petitio^n to his maiestie[38] that I should sure obtayn your liberty which I doe more desire than any treasure this world can afforde concerni^nge your priuate affaires they are all in good order as for setlinge of tytley[39] I will referre that vntill your cominge home which I hope will be shortly; your little sonne is a great scholler and remembers his humble duty vnto you: Julie this xviii^th

your Ben
Hoskynes

To Mr John Hoskins
at the Tower
give these

II

To the worthy Mr John Hoskyns in
the Tower give
these.

I pray you good Ma^r hoskynes come home: and commaund to do w^hat you plase: and I will obaye: I rely one none in this world: it tis a bad husband that a wife and child [MS. torn] not miss: if I shall bee harte by none but such as [MS. torn] flater mee: the dangear is not nere: for I am not com [MS. torn] fayer wordes and kinde vsages where I haue deserued [MS. torn] and as for that Judgment and beauty w^hich you out of your Loue thought I had had: is now with age and siecnes decaed and gone: I thinke the bering of children the breding them vp: the extreame griue I haue sufferred for your miserye dese^rues Loue: and this I will swere: if I dye befoare I see you agane: I loue you truly and no other in the worled: so well: and as for your London papor that is so sawcy toe abues. a poore woman.[40]   Is worthy to bee bornt I receued to toknes ffrom you for w^hich I thanke you. and I haue sent you my wedding ring by M^r

gyellem: for a token: and whold bee ruled by you in all thinges If
that whold please you trie mee in any on thinge. if I doe it not. then
ves me ase you do. and that is punieshment enoght: I know ther are
worse husbands then yoe: and better wyffes then I: yet[41] I se no
cause but wee to may liue contentedly to gether: if wee pray to god
to bless our Loues: without the which blessinge: all our loue is
nothing and so I end: showing you by this letter as litle wit as your
plesuer is I sholld.

your Ben Hoskynes.

III

deare hart I beg for gods sake: let peticion bee made vnto his maiesty
and the priuy counsayle for your deliuerance, that euen as god of his
mercy hath miraculously delyuered the king out of the traiterous hand
of gowry and his bloudy confederates, and from the damnable powder
treson: so hee in imitation of this diuine quality of mercy would be
so princely compassionate as to grant your liberty to mee being in
this case hauing no way deserued to be barred of that comfort which
I might haue enioied by your company. therefore good sweet hart if
you loue mee use all possible meanes to procure your enlargement: if
you meane to see mee aliue, for I growe weake and heauy and therefore vnfit to trauell, or els all the perswasions which you or any other
could vse should not keepe me from you so long. thus trusting to god
that my patience and hope shall not be in vaine but that our gratious
and mercifull king (whom I beseech god long to preserue) will grant
you your liberty I end. viii agust

your
Ben Hoskyn^s

IV

Good Sir
I pray god move his maiesties hart y^t he may have compassion in y^u
vppon vs all and your enlargement. set our sorrowefull harts at
liberty. surely there is great mercy in ye kinge and we are now
subiect to great misery and therefore we are fitt matter for mercy
to worke vppon; when please ye Lord and him: we must expect still
y^{ur} deliverance and pray for more patience for we have spent a greate
dele I beseech god give y^u comfort and all ye meanes y^u shall vse
to com vnto vs good successe.

Aug 15 1614
Your Ben
Hoskynes

To the wor^{ipp} M^r
  John Hoskyns
    Esquire in
      the Tower
        give these.

In spite of the distress which Hoskyns and his family suffered, it is gratifying to find no letters or petitions from Hoskyns himself to the King during the first five months of his imprisonment. Unlike Cornwallis he presented, apparently, no excuses nor did he veil bitter dissatisfaction with the Government under vaguely flattering references to his majesty's 'Royal and pious heart.' By no circumlocutions did he seek to minimize his violent protest against the Scottish favourites. Neither did he, like Cornwallis, maintain that by some indirect and circuitous route his speech had aimed at drawing from the House 'matter of so great consequence, as the payment' of the King's debts, the providing of his treasury, and the establishing of the state of his revenue fit to support him 'in y^t Royall Lustre' to which he was accustomed. Hoskyns had never stood on equivocal ground. He had openly attacked James's unfair and lavish parcelling out of English lands, monopolies, and honours to the Scots.

The strictness with which Hoskyns' isolation in the Tower was observed during the first three months of his confinement there is indicated by the following letter[42] to the Lieutenant of the Tower, from the Privy Council, dated 8 September 1614:

> Wheras humble suite is made unto us by John Hoskins and Oswald Hoskins,[43] brothers unto John Hoskins, now prisoner in the Tower, that for the better settling and managing of the estate of the sayd prisoner, and also to treate with him of such busynes as may concerne his wife, children and familye, accesse might be gyven them unto the sayd prisoner: we have therfore thought fytt and doe hereby require you to gyve leave unto the sayd John and Oswald Hoskins to repaire unto him and to have conference with him at fytt and convenyent tymes, so that it be in your presence or hearing of such as you shall appoint.

We need not suppose, however, that a genuine scholar in the days of Ralegh was less idle than his distinguished fellow prisoner. Hoskyns passed part of his time turning his reflections into verse, sometimes in Latin, sometimes in English. As a New Year's gift to the King he prepared a plea for his liberty, couched in Latin verses.[44]   They failed, however, to win any response from James. On 10 February 1615 the Privy Council sent another letter to the Lieutenant of the Tower, this time 'to gyve leave unto the wife of John Hoskins, close prisoner there, and some of his counsell in lawe, to have accesse unto him, for the setling of his estate, and to conferre with him at such convenyent tymes as the Leiuetenant should think fytting, so as it be in his presence or such as he should appoint.'[45]

By early March the clouds of disfavour had sufficiently dispersed to enable Hoskyns to draw again upon his irrepressible wit in a letter to his wife. His release he expected as soon as 'som new rumor & opinion' could be 'fashioned fitt for the wearinge of vulgar fancy' or when it was assured that some obligation would bind his wit. 'I was never unkynd in earnest or bitter in jest,' he protests.

So then why should I be sorry? . . . no man ever suffered for mere witt: but yf he lived not to requitt it hymselfe, yet the witt of all posterity took penaunce on his name that oppressed hym . . . and for my part I had rather dy with witt then live without it. for the other part of beinge assured of me to be bound for ever therin I am courted for he that feares least he shall not be suer of me, would fayne have me fast bound to him: & so he shall . . . but the knott is to long in knittinge. Now Ben yf I shalbe delivered when I am a thanckfull man & will not abuse my friends, I shall tarry very little. For speake thou nurse of my love, mother of the experience of all my thanckfulnes, thou mistresse of my wit, when did I abuse thee? . . . . you must com Ben & refute them, ... God forgive me for this idle letter & yf whereas I have somtymes wept & prayd, I somtymes laugh & pray hereafter.[46]

At length, three months later, at 'Whitehall, on Thursday in the afternoone, the 8th day of June, 1615,' the Privy Council recorded that

This day Sir Charles Cornewallis, knight, Leonell Sharpe, Doctor of Divinity and John Hoskins, Councellor at Law, prisoners in the Tower, were by his Majesty's comaundment called to the Board, and the severall peticions and submissions which each of them had formerly made in acknowledgment of their grevious offence, were particularly reade unto them: which, as each of them respectively did avowe to be subscribed by their hands, soe they did acknowledge the same to proceede from the true sense and meaninge of their harte. And thereupon it was signified unto them that his Majestie, in his singuler mercy and clemency, was graciously pleased to accept of their submissions, and the acknowledgement made by them of their offences, and to give order for their enlargment out of the Tower of London: which their lordships thought fitt, and soe ordered should be done in this manner. First, that their peticions now reade and acknowledged by them should be entered in the Register of Councell Causes, and that each of them should subscribe his name respectively to his peticion soe entered . . . .

And lastly, that John Hoskins, Councellor at Law, may . . . . (haveing his wife and famylie here) remayne in London this next Tearme, to be confined to some such house as he shall make choice of, without repareinge either to his chamber in the Temple or to Westmynster Hall, or to any other publique place; and the Tearme beinge done, to goe downe into the country, to remayne confined at his house there, and within five miles compasse thereof, untill his Majesty's pleasure be further knowne.[47]

All three were required, moreover, to give notice to the Clerk of the Council of their lodgings both in London during the term and in the country afterwards.

Hoskyns' petition 'To the Right Honourable the Lords and others of his Majesty's most honourable Privy Councell,' read at this meeting, is recorded as follows:

Out of the bitterness of an afflicted soule and from the bottom of a most penitent harte, not for his libertie's sake, but for his conscience sake, he acknowledgeth his imprisonment to be just, his offence to be heaynous, in his too inconsiderate speeches in the last Parliament, in medling with matters that became him not, in alledginge impertinent histories and that one of damned memory and detestable consequence, which, as God knows, he conceived not when he spoke, nor intended to mencion when he first stood up to speak.

He hath suffered five monethes close imprisonment, sustayned greate losses in his estate by accidentes which his only liberty might have prevented, and acknowledgeth the same to be the just and woefull effectes of a most dreadfull cause, the displeasure of God, and the King's sacred Majestie.

Most humbly beseecheth your Honours to mediate for him to his most gratious Soveraigne for his mercy, whereunto he wholey and most humbly submittes himself, and whereon only he reposeth himself, and most instantly desireth it next to the mercy of God in another world.[48]

Cornwallis upon his release from the Tower was confined within five miles of his house in Norfolk until 8 October 1615;[49] and Sharpe, to his benefice in Devon for an even longer period.[50]   Hoskyns, in this respect, however, was more fortunate than either, for, on 21 July 1615, the Council drew up this decision:

Whereas John Hoskins, esquire, Councellor at Lawe, late prisoner in the Tower of London, and since confined to his dwelling howse in the countye of Hereford, and within 5 myles compasse there-aboutes, is become an humble peticioner to this honourable Boorde for his enlargement, and to be restored to his former libertie, in respect of the greate losse which he hath susteined, and still doth susteine in his fortune, being kept from the place of his conference and studie, and hindered from his practise, besides many other detrimentes happening to his private estate upon this occasion; their lordships, having taken the same into their favorable consideracion, and not doubting but that his future demeanor wilbe suche as shall merritt the good opinion of his Majestie and this Boorde, do order and agree that from hence-forthe hee shalbe released of his sayd confinement, and that it shalbe free for him to repayre to London and Westminster Hall for his practise in the lawe, or otherwise to dispose of himselfe wheresoever and as hee shall think fitt, as before his imprisonment it was lawefull for him to do.[51]

In this manner a situation that had proved grave indeed for Hoskyns terminated, after a year of personal losses and deprivations, which he had borne with some dignity.   But it may be noted that he had not wholly retracted his protests against James's policy toward the Scots.   In his petition for liberty and his confession of the justness of his imprisonment, he acknowledged that his speeches had been 'too inconsiderate'; that he had meddled 'with matters that became him not'; and that 'when he first stood up to speak,' he had not intended to mention the Sicilian Vespers.   He avoided saying that the parallel had not occurred to him; he stated that he had not intended to speak of it.   Nor did he minimize the seriousness and soundness of the grievance he had been expressing.   With skill he evaded retraction of the substance of his speech.

In his parliamentary career under James, Hoskyns was a

supporter of the principles which in less than twenty years were to be fought for in the Civil War. With straightforward facing of facts he, with others, laid before the Government genuine grievances which might have been remedied in sufficient measure to avert the impending catastrophe of war. Instead of meeting the opposition in a rational way the King and Privy Council clapped Hoskyns and two others into the Tower for a year. The King dissolved Parliament and strove to live extravagantly without subsidies for the next seven years and, in doing so, only plunged the country into still greater confusion.

CHAPTER VI

A SERJEANT-AT-LAW

HOSKYNS had been at liberty only a month or so when, if John Chamberlain can be trusted, he composed a riming libel for which as late as February 1617 he was standing in danger of the Star Chamber itself. Chamberlain, writing on that date to Dudley Carleton about numerous rimes on Buckingham which were circulating in London, went on to say that

> now for matter of rimes Hoskins the lawier is in a laberinth being brought into question for a rime or libel (as it is termed) made some yeare and halfe agon, yᵗ he find not the bett. friends yt is feared he shalbe brought into the star-chamber and then he is vndon. yt is saide they had him in a dilemma either to confesse or to denie yt upon his oath, and then they haue sufficient witnes to conuince hm the best hope they haue is that my L. Chauncellor is his frend, but he hath greater adversaries.[1]

By the death of Sir Thomas Egerton, the Lord Chancellor, in March 1617 Hoskyns lost the powerful friend counted upon to help him in his dilemma, and yet the matter seems never to have got into the Star Chamber.[2] Chamberlain's relation of the incident in connection with his references to Buckingham suggests that possibly Hoskyns had been protesting once more against James's policy towards his favourites of whom Buckingham was one of the most grasping, and who perhaps was one of Hoskyns' greater adversaries.

Aside from this single caprice, Hoskyns' movements and words seem to have been tempered with caution and a desire to avoid further royal displeasure. In October 1615 he had been able to report to Benedicta that he had derived some comfort from the 'honorable words' spoken in his behalf publicly and privately by the Lord Chancellor, Sir Thomas Egerton, and by the Master of the Rolls, Sir Julius Caesar.

He had also felt some assurance of forgiveness for his indiscretion of 1614, for the King, speaking of Sir Thomas Overbury, had said that the Earl of Somerset dealt falsely with him as he did with Hoskyns, since he had promised to speak for Overbury's deliverance but failed to do so and had promised to speak for Hoskyns but spoke against him.[3] In 1621 he was repressing members of the Lower House when they wished to question his commitment to the Tower and to provide, as they said, against the possibility of another such occurrence. Not wishing to revive the King's displeasure towards himself, Hoskyns obtained their assurance that they would do nothing that would bring him again into unfavourable notice.[4] With other parliamentary matters he had nothing to do until 1628, except to collect from the city of Hereford the remuneration due him for his services in the first and second Jacobean Parliaments, the whole sum amounting to ninety-two pounds.[5]

Although Hoskyns was not 'burning his fingers'[6] with much parliamentary business during the ensuing decade, he was by no means idle. To further his late brother Oswald's business in woolen drapery he wrote on 15 March 1619 to his 'Sireniacal' friend, Sir Lionel Cranfield, Master of the Wards and Liveries, to say that the servants of his brother's shop wished to furnish part of the 'blacks' for Queen Anne's funeral, shockingly delayed so many weeks before arrangements could be made to conduct it in proper splendour. In the same letter in gossipy vein regarding the proposed marriage of Prince Charles with the Infanta of Spain Hoskyns adds:

When they receive the money, we shall tell you how well it spends in better meat than the proclamation allows us at this time, when the air is so infected with the smell of red herring, that it is thought it will turn back the Spanish fleet. Our lieutenants are all fethers, our clowns all iron, our beacons themselves are ready to spit fire; whereby you may see how well the Spaniard's coming is taken.[7]

Hoskyns' own affairs in the Temple were bringing increasing responsibilities and honours. On 5 February 1619 he was appointed to stand at the Cupboard during the Lent reading,[8]

and he served in the same capacity the following August.[9]
In October he was appointed to the distinguished if costly
post of Reader for the ensuing Lenten vacation.[10]   The
nature of his entertainment and the extent of the hospitality
he dispensed are hinted at in the following letter from his
brother Dr. John Hoskyns to Benedicta in the country,
giving her a first-hand account of how things were going in
Middle Temple Hall and also in the pantry:

> I can acquaint y[u] with nothinge amisse, ye readinge is half gon
> over in good fashiõ, all (except myself) very rich & brave for y[e]
> tyme, and nobly disposed for the honor of Mr Reader, a reasonable
> portiõ of Lords have ben at his table already, and the greate
> marquesses meane to be heere to-morrowe being sunday, others on
> tuesday & on thursday, friday we break our fast and away. I heare
> not yeat of any strãgers y[t] come downe. I beleeve it will be tuesday
> following y[e] next weeke ere y[u] see any of y[e] company—som escapes
> and slipps you shall not knowe. It hath gon well with abundance
> yea sup[er]fluity rather then want; beyond Readers of other houses &
> former tymes they say. my brother Boorne hath donn his exercise
> well, and M[r] Reader going to the hall at 7 of y[e] clocke cannot con-
> clude his matter untill allmost 2. they say preachers are longe, but
> sure the law is very tedious. Y[e] things y[u] sent up were well handled,
> I sawe thẽ takẽ out of ye hãper & they will serve on Sũday &
> tomorrow I pray you send noe more for M[r] pyes chãber is full of his
> kindread . . . . God send us a good end.[11]

Though in his entertainment as Reader Hoskyns was
extravagant,[12] he was at the same time thrifty enough to
have his young son, Benedict, a boy of eleven,[13] admitted to
the Middle Temple; for the records show that on 11 February 1620 'Mr. Benedict, only son of John Hoskines, esq.,'
was admitted specially, with 'no fine, his father being
Reader.'[14]   In June of the same year Hoskyns was appointed
to serve as assistant Reader for the next autumn,[15] and in
1621 was again appointed to that post.[16]   Thus he served
almost continuously as a lecturer in law from the spring of
1619, when he first 'stood at the Cupboard,' until the Lent
Reading of 1621.   From the length of his service one may
suppose that he proved an able, willing, acceptable lecturer
to his fellows in the Temple.

Twelve days later the busy Mr. Hoskyns found time himself to write hastily, warning her that he expected to trouble
her patience soon with a Welsh judge.[29]   In this appointment
Hoskyns had obtained a post much sought after, since the
work took little time and the circuits were often arranged so
as not to interfere with practice in London.[30]   The sessions
of the courts usually convened in the Guild Hall of the towns
mentioned.[31]   Hoskyns held the judgeship 'during pleasure,'
which so continued that he was still actively engaged in the
legal business of his Welsh circuit at the time of his death.

Though it appears to have been customary to appoint
judges from the ranks of the serjeants,[32] Hoskyns' preferment came in the reverse order.   He was not to wait long,
however, to be appointed to the latter dignity by virtue of a
writ from King James, for in the twenty-first year of the
reign of that sovereign, on 26 June, Hoskyns was raised to
the state and rank of Serjeant-at-Law.[33]   Although James
had probably not entirely forgiven the man who openly
opposed him in important issues in his first and second
Parliaments, a Parliament being not far off, the Lord Keeper
John Williams 'was provident; that the Worthies of the Law
should be well entreated.   Their Learning being most com-
prehensive of Civil Causes and Affairs, they had ever a great
Stroke in that Honorable Council.   Therefore he wrought
with his Majesty, to sign a Writ for the Advancement of
some of the Gravest and Greatest Pleaders who were ripe
for Dignity,'[34] of which number Hoskyns was one.   Perhaps
James thought to placate him and to center his whole attention upon his profession rather than upon another trial at a
parliamentary career.   At any rate when 'a Call for Serjeants
was splendidly solemnized, for Number Thirteen, for Quality
of the best Reputation,'[35] Hoskyns was one of the lawyers
singled out for the distinction.   The rank of Serjeant-at-Law
was an ancient and unique honour, so great that in the days
before the twenty-sixth year of the reign of Henry VIII no
serjeants were ever knights, the dignity of serjeant seeming
to transcend that of knighthood.[36]   The history and nature
of this degree the Lord Keeper Williams dealt with quaintly

in the oration with which he congratulated the newly-appointed serjeants at Westminster, but with which he detained them so long that their feast, 'though otherwise plentiful and magnificent,' had to be served in confusion so that they could reach St. Paul's to hear Dr. Donne's sermon for the occasion.[37] Unmindful of later exactions upon his hearers' time, the Lord Keeper spoke, in part, as follows:

Remember the Title of your Degree . . . . You are call'd *Servientes ad Legem*, Sergeants at the law; . . . Words very malleable and extensive . . . .

The word Serjeant, no doubt, is Originally a Stranger born, though now for many Years denizen'd among us. It came over at the first from *France*, ... But *Sergiens* in the old French is so much as *Serviens* . . . a Servant, or an *Attendant:* As *Sergens de Dieu* . . . And *Sergens d'Amour*, Servants of Love in the Romance of the Rose, A Book well known in our Country, because of the Translator thereof *Geoffry Chaucer* . . . . Great Titles have grown up from small Originals, as *Dux, Comes, Baro,* and others, and so hath this, which is Enobled by the affix unto it, a *Sergeant at the Law* . . . .

It is your Pre-eminence that you are the chief Servants at the Bar: . . . you are the Principal of all that practise in the Courts of Law; Servants, that is, Officers preferr'd above all Ranks of Pleaders . . . . You are next in the Train of my Lords the Judges: And some of your file not seldom employ'd to be Judges Itinerant . . . . Secondly . . . You are, by reason of your Degrees, our Letters of Recommendation unto the Kings Majesty, for his Choice and Election for the Judges of the Kingdom . . . . Thirdly and lastly, This Degree of Honour is . . . a kind of Spur and Incentive to all the Students of the Law, that they might more easily concoct those otherwise, insupportable Difficulties, and Harshness of their Studies, in hope one Day to attein unto those Honours, wherewith all of you by his Majesties Favour, and your own Merits, are now to be Invested. Those outward *Decorums* of Magnificence which set forth your Exaltation this Day, are very specious, and sparkle so much in the Eyes of the young Fry, that swim up after you, that they cannot but . . . follow your Industry . . . . That Gold which you give away[38] . . . implies that by your faithful Labour and Gods Providence, you have attein'd to the Wealth of a fair Estate . . . . Then your great and sumptuous Feast[39] is like that at a Kings Coronation . . . . I should be too long if I should speak of the Ornament of your Head, your pure Linen Coif, which evidences that you are Candidates of higher Honour. So likewise your *Librata Magna,*[40] your abundance of Cloth and Liveries, your Purple Habits,

belonging antiently to great Senators, yea to Emperors; all these
. . . are but so many Flags, and Ensigns to call up those young
Students, that fight in the Valleys, to those Hills and Mountains of
Honour, which you by your Merits have now atchieved . . . .

To be elected the prime Servants of our most wise, and most equal
Laws, supposeth in you great Reading, great Reason, great Experience; which deservedly calls Honour upon your Persons . . . .

Now, I have told you as a Judge, that you are Servants, but
Honourable Servants of the Law; before I conclude, let me admonish
you as a Bishop, that you are in your highest Title the Servants of
God. Therefore keep a good Conscience in all things. Serve that
holy Law, which bids you *Not to pervert the Right and Cause of the
Innocent* . . . . Serve God; Serve the King; Serve the Law. *Ite
alacres, tantaeque precor confidite Causae.* I have ended. The Fear
of God go with you; and his Blessing be upon you.[41]

The Serjeants had sat through the oration rather wet and
uncomfortable, for that forenoon they had gone 'dabbling
on foot and bareheaded, save their beavers, to Westminster,
in all the rain,' it being a 'sad season, by reason of the continual wet.'[42] Yet in their 'long Priestlike' parti-coloured
robes, with their capes lined with white lamb, thrown about
their shoulders 'and thereupon a Hood,'[43] they must have
made, even in the rain, a rather picturesque procession as
they 'dabbled' on foot to and from Westminster.

Because Hoskyns had risen to the rank of Serjeant it did
not follow that all his cases thenceforth would be extraordinarily imposing ones, for it was a Serjeant's obligation
to undertake any cause for which he was solicited to secure
justice.[44] A sample of the litigation which a distinguished
barrister might be called upon to direct is found in the
record of a long suit in Chancery in which Hoskyns appears
to have represented his brother Thomas against one William
Pyrry of Shobden in Herefordshire. The suit, with almost
interminable litigation, grew out of the simple act of Thomas'
'cutting downe a small tree growing upon' his own land
and 'not worth aboue six pence.' The tree, however, was
one of the peculiarly troublesome variety which are wont
to spring up on boundary lines. It occasioned 'severall
supposed assaultes and affrayes . . . in the daytyme and

at the place aforesaid,' at its 'falinge and cutting downe,'
for it fell the wrong way just into Mr. Pyrry's 'backside,
and the same tree being in the defts said backside, this
deft did wish the plt. and his company not to carry away
the same tree, but . . . wth force & against' Mr. Pyrry's
will they 'did take & carry away the said tree.' The ensuing
quarrel, though not very serious, occasioned Serjeant Hoskyns no end of pains, as a great bundle of parchment leaves
still attests.[45]

With his preferment to the rank of Serjeant, Hoskyns'
residence in the Middle Temple was technically at an end,
for it was customary for the Serjeants to be 'translated[46]
to one of the . . . two Innes, called Serjeants Innes, where
none but the Serjeants and Judges' conversed.[47]   However,
on 2 May 1623 he had arranged for his son Benedict to
share with him his chambers in Essex Court. Because a
great part of the establishment had been built at Hoskyns'
own charge, the Society agreed to permit Benedict to enter
his father's study without payments to the Middle Temple,
until he should 'come into commons.'[48]   Perhaps because he
had made this arrangement, Serjeant Hoskyns was in no
haste to be 'translated' to Serjeants' Inn in Fleet Street. At
any rate, in 1627 he and Benedict were still occupying these
chambers.[49]   John Bourne, Hoskyns' step-son, who had also
lodged there in the latter years, died shortly before this date,
and we find that one John Cockes was admitted by the Treasurer of the Society 'to the part of a chamber late of Mr. John
Bourne, deceased, with Mr. Benedick Hoskines, now in the
possession of Mr. Serjeant Hoskines, father of the said
Benedick.'[50]   Apparently Mr. Cockes was not given a hearty
welcome to this chamber, for the Parliament of the Society
found it necessary to decree he should have 'a place in the
said chamber to set a bed in, and a convenient study.' 'After
Mr. Serjeant's departure a competent partition of the
chamber' was to be made between Benedict and Cockes. A
decision was recorded at the same time to the effect that the
'Serjeants-at-Law now lodging in any chambers of this
House shall have warning to depart before Hilary term

next,' that is, by early January 1628. In November of 1627 it was decided that 'Mr. Treasurer and Mr. Wotton' should 'view Mr. Hoskines' chamber . . . to a part whereof Mr. John Cockes' had been admitted 'and do right therein in accordance with a former order.'[51]   Since this is the last reference to the Serjeant in Middle Temple records, we may assume that he soon left to establish himself at Serjeants' Inn in Fleet Street,[52] loath, perhaps, to take his leave of the Honourable Society of the Middle Temple of which he had been a resident for so many years.

At about this time, doubtless, Hoskyns was improving his newly acquired country seat of Morehampton, where, Aubrey records, under 'severall venerable and shady oakes in the parke, he had seats made' and where he curbed the 'fine purling stream' with stone.   In the chapel was an organ that had belonged to Queen Elizabeth.   In the gallery were pictures of Dr. John Hoskyns, of the Serjeant in his robes, and of the house and park, with Latin verses[53] of the Serjeant's composition on the walls.   In what seems to have been something of a continental custom of the time, Hoskyns drew at the gatehouse a picture of the old man who made the fires and on the wall in the garden a sketch of Adam the gardener with his rake, spade, and waterpot in his hand, and wrote beside them Latin distichs.   The Welsh judge and Serjeant still possessed his boyish propensity for drawing and versifying, of which a record remains in the Trusty Servant at Winchester.

Benedicta Hoskyns did not long enjoy with her husband and their children[54] the estate of Morehampton,[55] for her death occurred on 6 October 1625.[56]   She was buried in Vow Church, a few miles away, in the Golden Valley, and Hoskyns prepared a simple epitaph[57] for her tomb.

In 1627 he drew up a will,[58] which, however, did not prove to be his last one.   By December of the same year, he was engaged in plans for a second marriage.   After some anxiety briefly hinted at in his letters, a marriage was solemnized at the church in the parish of Great Rissington, Gloucestershire, on 10 December 1627, between 'John Hoskins Servyante at

Law and Mrs Isabel Barrett.'[59]   The license had been issued
on 7 December.[60]   It was to Elizabeth Bourne, Hoskyns'
step-daughter, who was acting as mistress of his household
after the death of her mother, that Hoskyns sent two letters[61]
which furnish an interesting commentary on social conditions
in 1627, and afford, besides, a view of Hoskyns as an
agitated if not a very young or altogether enthusiastic
bridegroom.

The day before the ceremony the Serjeant had much on
his mind: his son and his nephew at Oxford would, within
a few days, be expecting transportation home for Christmas;
the claret and the sack were still to be ordered from Monmouth or Hereford.   But he was harried by the further and
desperate contemplation of the awkwardness of arriving with
his bride and her attendants at Ross and of finding no means
of conveyance for the remaining thirteen miles or so to
Morehampton over the muddy roads and sodden fields of
December, when the hedges often had to be broken through
for safe passage.   Naturally, then, it was a feverish note
that he sent to Elizabeth Bourne, praying that she go presently about the matter day and night until assured that a
good coach and four horses would be on hand for the bridal
party at Ross.   'Mistake me not,' he adds, 'no man resisteth
me we want nothing but coach & horses.'

A second letter, though still emphasizing that dire necessity, conveys a tone of greater composure.   He thinks every-
one at Morehampton will be as happy as himself in the
match, for the lady will prove a 'godly worthy mother-in-law
kynde and quiet.'   'Let us all pray, to God with thanks-
gevinge,' he adds, 'for the least of his benefitts.'

Whether or not the Serjeant was able to pray with thanks-
giving for the blessing he had received in the person of his
second wife is not known.   No further mention of her has
come to light.[62]

The next year Hoskyns turned once more to parliamentary
affairs and sat for the city of Hereford in the third Parliament of King Charles, which began on 16 March 1628 and
continued into the next year.[63]   Here again he served on

various committees,[64] but was apparently not so active in these affairs as he had been twenty-four years earlier. By this time the Commons were in an agitated state, fearful on the one hand of the spread of Arminianism and on the other of the growing influence of the Roman Church. One parliamentarian in January 1629 declared: 'It is apparent to every man that new opinions are brought in by some of our Churchmen to disturb the peace that our Church was formerly in; the meaning of it can be no other but to bring in the Romish Religion amongst us; for it hath ever been a Jesuited policy, first to work a disturbance, and after that a change.'[65]

Sir Robert Philips[66] expressed it as his opinion that two sects had 'dangerously crept in to undermine King and Kingdom . . . the one ancient Popery, the other new Arminianism.'[67]

The knights and burgesses were alarmed to see five hundred at a time leave the Queen's[68] mass at Somerset House. They were annoyed to hear 'the outfacing Jesuits' casually inquiring, 'Will you go to Mass, or have you been at Mass at Somerset-house?'[69]

To realize the feeling of the time one must recall that the penalty for conviction on the charge of being a Roman priest was execution. Ten persons so suspected were imprisoned in Newgate about this time.[70] There was adequate proof that they were Jesuits,[71] but insufficient evidence that they were priests. The indictments, by chance or design, charged three of them with being priests. The proof being inadequate, they were not convicted. In reviewing the matter in the Committee of Religion, Serjeant Hoskyns insisted that they ask 'the Atturney why he gave direction to indicte these as priests: the only way to have them escape.'[72] In his irritation at this procedure, he exclaimed that there was 'never the like to lett a whole Colledge of Jesuits to Bayle. There have bene wolves in Wales, and foxes in the Isle of Wight: if they were there now; the people wold not lett them to Bayle.'[73]

His animosity towards the Papists seems, however, somewhat tempered with justice in a later speech. The Committee of Religion, with Mr. Pym in the chair, had been attempting to define the public acts of the Church.[74] Selden asserted that they were the catechism, the book of homilies, the book of ordination of ministers, the book of common prayer, and the articles of 1571, but not the Articles of Lambeth nor the proceedings of the Synod at Dort, the former because they were drawn up without parliamentary sanction, the latter because other nations sent representatives, who were outside the control of England. Selden's interpretation was one to curb the authority of the King and the Bishops and to safeguard parliamentary power in the government of the Church. Hoskyns, like Selden, was also cautious to limit by careful definition the public acts of the Church, and to prevent any future group from making in Convocation articles that might be construed as 'public acts,' but which might not meet with the sanction of Parliament. On this point he maintained 'that by the Church is to be understood all the beleevers of the Church, and the Convocacion house is not to be termed the church nor hath power to doe a publique act; for that is only said to be a publique act which is considered of, debated, disputed and resolved on by the King and all the State.'[75]

'The papists, and we,' he continued, 'agree all in the Scripture and differ only in the interpretacion, and for that wee offer to be tryed by the 3 generall Creedes, the 4 first generall Councells, and all the antient fathers that wrote in the first 400 yeares.'

Though Hoskyns consistently allied himself with the cause of democratized government, the foregoing speech indicates that he had not gone so far as to link himself with the Puritan cause in religious tenets. He was a conservative supporter of the Church as it had been understood in the days of Elizabeth.[76]

On Hoskyns' position regarding the other great issues of this Parliament, those of impositions and tonnage and poundage, the records are strangely silent. This is partially due to the fact that Hoskyns was not present on 2 March 1629 when the House drew up its forbidding protestations: first, 'Whoesoever shall counsel or advise taking and levying of Subsidies of Tonnage and Poundage, not being granted by Parliament . . . shall be . . . reputed . . . an innovator in the government, and a capital enemy to this Kingdom and Commonwealth';[77] and, secondly, 'If any merchant or person whatsoever shall voluntarily yield or pay the said subsidies of Tonnage and Poundage, not being granted by Parliament, he shall . . . be reputed a betrayer of the liberties of England and an enemy to the same.'[78]

Hoskyns was not present when these protestations were drawn up because on 21 February 1629 he had been granted a leave of absence[79] to go down to the country, 'being a Judge of a Circuit,' and a mayor[80] as well. Though he was to return 'with all convenient Speed,' it is not likely that he could have been present on 2 March. Thus he was not called upon to commit himself to a position regarding those protestations, nor was he a witness of the disorder that held sway in the House that day when the King sent orders to adjourn Parliament and the House forbade the Speaker to do so. On that occasion the House rose just in time to save bloodshed that must certainly have followed the arrival of the Pensioners and the Guard, sent by the King to force the door.[81] Not long after, Parliament was dissolved, and there is every reason to suppose that Hoskyns took his permanent leave of that body in February 1629. In what measure he shared the later unrelenting determination of his Puritanical contemporaries is uncertain. There is no doubt, however, that he was a leader of the early and intellectual insurrection against King and Bishops waged in Parliament Hall during the years of 1604-1611, 1614, and 1628-1629. The intellectual revolt had met with such stubborn opposition that it is hardly likely that Hoskyns, had he lived until the Long Parliament, could have followed any course but that taken by Selden and Pym.

But two years before the Long Parliament began, Hoskyns had already exceeded the traditional limits of human life. In August 1638 it happened that a country fellow, at the assizes in Hereford, unwittingly stepped on his foot.[82]   A surgeon from Gloucester was unable to check a subsequent infection, and on 27 August Hoskyns died at his house at Morehampton.   He was buried in the south choir of the ancient Cistercian Abbey Dore, on the Dore River in the Golden Vale, in his own shire of Hereford which he had served with energy and enthusiasm during a long period of years.[83]

A biographer of one of Hoskyns' contemporaries wrote as follows in the late seventeenth century:

> This Century of our Account . . . now wasting beyond the middle, hath been happy in this, That it hath brought forth in our Kingdom of England many of great Renown, Wise and Eloquent, deep in Learning, and sage in Counsels, in a word, to be praised as much as the best of their Forefathers; yet granting to all, both former and latter, an Allowance for some Grains of Frailties. It were pity their Memorial should perish with them.[84]

Though John Hoskyns took no heed lest his 'Memorial should perish' with him, though a fragment of his work has long masked as merely one evidence of the judgement and humour and learning of a great contemporary, and though his keen insight into government taught his Scottish monarch little indeed, his name has nevertheless faintly persisted in history and tradition.

The records of his activity suggest that he may still claim attention as a true servant of the law, as a clear-sighted statesman, and as a Jacobean wit worthy of the privilege he enjoyed of conversing with Ralegh and Ben Jonson and Donne while they drained their bowls of the best Spanish, French, and Rhenish wine that the Mermaid could yield. When due allowance has been made for the 'grains of frailties' in the body of his informal and casual literary work, it is still apparent that it were pity indeed that his memorial should perish with him.

CHAPTER VII

HIS FAMILIAR LETTERS

THE letters printed here for the first time present with arresting vividness a picture of life in the early seventeenth century. Covering a period of twenty-eight years from 1601 to 1629, they tell, moreover, with an almost dramatic quality the story of Hoskyns' domestic life during that time. The first letter shows him, with attention to his own precepts on letter-writing, recording his devotion to Benedicta, the young woman he had married a few weeks earlier. From the charm and passion and glancing wit of this letter we pass by degrees to other moods, even to the smouldering infelicities of their later years. Admitted to a view of varied situations in the life of the writer, we glimpse by the way something of conditions in London lodgings; we hear prayerful messages from a prisoner in the Tower to his wife ill in the country; we look in upon his family there and gain a clear notion of household duties and of the way children were reared in the family of a gentleman and scholar. We hear a warm and penitent apology for a fit of ill temper. We learn how distraught a man can be when, after acting upon sudden resolution, he must borrow coach and horses for escorting his second bride halfway across two counties in mid-December.

These are letters written with such candour and ingenuousness and charged so often with deep personal feeling that now more than three hundred years after they were written one has almost a sense of indelicacy in perusing them. But they clearly etch the portrait of their writer, John Hoskyns, a warm, ambitious, spirited, persuasive, volatile man, one who possessed, moreover, a genuine command of language.

A history of the manuscripts and various explanatory items will be found in the notes for this chapter.

I

To m^rs Hoskyns at her
house in Widmarshe streete
in Heref giue these
wth speed

midle temple
13 Nov: 1601

 My very good M^rs /.
I would intreate y^u to thincke a lyttle vpon the solytary passions of y^r servaunt./ Yf I fynd not my patience, to be
from y^u six weeks, to grow to greater strength hereafter I
must geue over my profession. For I sweare might I
dissemble my habit I had rather be in your skullion boys
place then where I am: for soe should I be a creature,
whereas now I am but a shadow devided from myne own
lyfe & essence. I am lyke an owld pryest that commes to
church to reade a chapter and hath lefte his spectacles at
home so am I [a second *I* crossed out] come to behold the
pracktise of the Law and have lefte myne eys [*in* crossed
out] of my mynd in your bosom. O send me those eys that
they may tell me how little y^u remember me, how much
gladder y^u are to be kyndely intreated by som other then by
myselfe, and how sorry y^u are that my returne shall soe
soe [*sic*] soone interrupt y^r libertye, Let them make relation
of y^r slight regarde of my earnest affeccon, of y^r secret
smyles at my folly, y^r setled resolution to feede me w^th
shows, & make a fidlers bridge of my hart, over wch the
musique passeth to others eares, but it self hath neyther
sence nor share in it.
 Let those eys of my mynd wch I left wth y^u come and make
report to me of som thinge true or false that may be a
psuasion to me that it is in vayn for me to loue you, for till
then I shall neuer leue louinge over much, wch wilbe but
lothsom to y^u and thancklesse, troblesom to me and endlesse.
 But o sweete troble that hast w^thin these [MS. torn]
weekes assured me that the only [MS. torn] absence is
gryef w^thout intermission [MS. torn] proceedes from my

imperfecͨon, for yʳ [MS. torn] hath taken order to the
contrary: [MS. torn] hath neyther sent letter, nor message,
[MS. torn] geuen any demonstration of longinge f[or]
me, wᶜʰ had ben the only fuell to mayntain the passions
of loue, the only wynd that would fild the sayles of those
thoughts wᶜʰ might loose themselues in an Ocean of sighs,
teares, throbs, and tempests, that poore louers endure./
but yʳ discretion hath forborn all such occasions, and yʳ
silence hath pleaded agaynst my vanity: whoe yf I be asked,
why doe yᵘ loue her soe much I cañot say so much for
myselfe as She would haue me doe soe./ No No fayr, witty
and worthy mistresse I haue to longe deceaued myself bycause
when I was wᵗʰ yᵘ my hart was soe fixed vpon you that I
could not looke into myselfe, Now I coͫe to pvse my dis-
ordred study from that survey I came to behold my dis-
tempered selfe; I fynd neyther noblenes nor richesse, nor
government, nor knowledge, nor eloquence, nor coͫelynesse
nor any thinge loue worthy in me, for my welth yᵘ may
disdayn me for my behaviour yᵘ may shuñe me, for my witt
yᵘ may laughe at me, for my speech yᵘ may reprehende me,
for my letters yᵘ may be weary of me, and for my face yᵘ
may most iustely hate me, and therefore I am I must be

yʳ most vnworthy outcast

J : H

II

To my lovinge Mrs. Ben. Hoskyns.

Ben: I could easily condemne myselfe for an unkynd husband yf I knew one hower wherein I thought not vpon yᵘ.
My fellow Mr. Pembrug steales away: both cañot possiblie;
and I worse than he; such is the reward of a mans service
as is among carters for horses and oxen; he that draws well
shall never out of the plow or teeme: Good sweete hart yf
I knew that it touched yʳ hart wᵗʰ such impatiĕce as it doth
almost teare myne to be thus asunder: had I an horse heere
I would leve all & coͫ to thee but then must I be discredited

for ever: for there are divers bills of the parliament cõmitted unto me wch are to be sate upon, som to morrow som on munday.

O deere Ben the longer I love thee the more impotently & infinitely I love. Now my little Mr. Pembrug angers me that he lets me know his parting but on the instant. I have receaved no rent or debt. I have payed five pound that the taylor tooke up at the mercers in searge &c. and rãne away wth it: I have bought a filthy blacke suiet & worn it out. I have payed my cõmons I know y^u may want I have sent you 8^l in gold, I have a little left, I have yet lived by my labours: though now out of terme publi*que* paynes make me weary without fees. Tell by brother John on this suddain I could not speake with Doctor Lake. Much wranglinge I have with my brother about a cloake, but shall have it & I will sett it on makinge presently. I will send by the next messeng^r what D. Lake hath done. Thus in hast I could wish I might carry Mr. Pembrug cloakebagge so that I might but cõm by the doore and see you. I have spoken to Sr Henry Williams for Morgan, but he is gone on a suddain. I have spoken to Wotton but he coms not down I feare: tell Mr. Wallwyn I relye on him to goe to the Judge y^t neede be. Let Thom Gwillim return my recognisances & examinations taken before me to the Judge carefully. God blesse thee, sweet, lovinge excellent Ben, & John, franke, Bess & Ben, & god be m^rcyfull to us all & ever.

Y^r J. H.

My hũble duty to my Lord
& most harty & thanckfull remembr̃ce
to Mr. D. Bradshaw & his wife.

III

A Note to instruct the servants what they ought to doe and how they ought to behave themselves towards their Mistress.

Imprimis. Wait on your Mistress abroad civilly & reverently, not to bee out of call or absent at the hower of her returne.

To study and forcast to help to searchen out such meat as your Mistress loves yong rabbetts hens partridg or fowle, & to bee carfull at all times to please her & her children.

At 9 at night. To see all the doores shut say praiers and go to bed. to see that John Bourne drink not after supper that hee lodg cleane. and to lay up your things in your lodging handsumly.

Never to leave your study doore open, or the middle hatch unshut after 9 nor the doore open at night. Never to go abroad without leave, or with leave to tarry long or in bad companie drinking or quarrelling In no case to speake any lewd word before my children.

Take not tobacco too much. Serve god every morning and at all times. To rise every morning at 5 of clock before John Bourne to look to his clothes hose & shoes that they be cleane & repaired. To goe with him to morning praier. to returne from my Brothers chamber to write. to know what things your Mistress will have Brushed.

To step sometimes to the stable to see the horses & furniture cleane kept when you are weary of writing to read and study Litleton West presedents and the booke of entries.

On Court Days. To goe to the Maiors Court, but first to ask leave of your Mistress—there to observe the practise & look upon the declarations and answeres and mark the evidence but not to prate or drink going or coming.

At eleven. To fetch home John Bourne, to cover the table, & serve it reverently.

In the afternoone to bring John Bourne to my Brother, to return to write reade & study as before.

For exchange of businesse. To see the hall and too parlors decent not filled with trash. to brush my gownes, to go over the other roomes wherto you may have accesse, to see nothing sluttishly spoiled or mislaid, to cutt wood, to teach ffrank to write, Bes to read, both to know the figures in Arithmeticke, to see the garden drest up, & John to mend the walls. Cover the table & attend. At five to fetch John

Bourne home, at night to learn latin of him and law with him.

Yf any stranger com, to attend your mistress in a reverent posture of body and readiness to serve.

Read this over every day and observe it and I shall find you fitter to be forgiven what is past and gladder of your company hereafter.

God grant you grace.

Finis.

IV

To my most lovinge wyfe Mrs. Ben: Hoskins.

Good sweet hart—I was not very well upon my travayll. Mrs. Richard came one Jorney to this house under color to fetch fier & saw me not, then when I came furth again into the fold to see my horse she came wth the letter enclosed from my lord president. I told her before she spake anything I knew her arrant bid her wellcom & desired her to deliv^r me the letter. I receyved it as from a lord that I had just cause to honor & when I had done with my horse I would goe in & read it & repair to my lord or otherwise accomplish what he should expect of me: she would had the matt^r put to frends: I told I knew her husband's disposition, the matt^r betwixt hym & me was known in the best courts in England, and when I had satisfied my lord president thē let her husband use his discrecion. she would had me reade the letter in her presence. I told her my lord had other matt^rs heretofore wch he comunicated with me it may be som such are in the letter also wch concern her not nor her husband, so she departed & I turnd my backe & reade the lett^r. I had a should^r & umbles the umbles I send y^u none here can dress them, the sholder I keepe for Mr. Delehays supp^r yf he coms.

I have som pills from filly who was heere yesterday when I was at Goodrich. I am promised halfe a bucke agaynst sunday wch I will keepe in steed of our marriage day for

wch I am to thancke God above all his worldly blessings, &
therefore doe more rejoyce in this title thē any mortall
dignity.

Y^r true lovinge husband

1611.   J. Hoskyns.

    1 August our marriage day
full ten yeares since
   God be blessed.

V

To Mrs. Ben: Hoskyns at Hereford.

Sweethart: I have agreed to sell the parsonage for 830^l
and 10 angells for you I could get no more possibly for
parsonages are at xij yeres purchase & this price comes to
above 13 yeares purchase. Sr James Freere calls for his
money, & Seymores wydow being married to a needy fellow
her husband haunts me by hymselfe & others every day for
80^l so doth one kinge likewise for 50^l that I ow for morse
pt of the money for Dydley. And the Taylor to whom I
ow 72^l for Rawlinges and some 10^l more for myself yf he
forbeare req̃res use. Bacon calls for 10^l that I undertooke
8 yeres since for Colipep part of the price of my chamber.
I must be out of debt heere or else I may give over my
pracktise wch I hope wilbe in London better then 200^l a yeare
and I would be loth it should goe to pay use & the principall
undischarged. this day my gaignes this term com̃es to 23^l
I hope the terme will make it above xxx^l. I have receyved
of kattle three pound for Rent of Churchehill & Bemwell
lands. I have sent ȳ a letter or warrant inclosed to receyve
it of Mr. Clarke to whose soñe James I lent it as Mr. Clarke
usually desires me & hee had occasion therefor. J. assures
me he will not fayle ȳ or allow it Mr. John Clarke. I
receyved no other rent of Som̃setshire nor the 10^l yet of
Mr. Whitson though he evry day he sayth he will send it.
my rent to Tomchester this yeare came to 25^l wch was all
the rent of Dover Court my lease of Titley expires at

Michaelmas next therefore I must sue to renue it as I have written. So that now I have payd the seven pound 10ˢ to the Kinge for Dover Court out of my poore gaignes. I accoumpt I must pay in debts above 300ˡ heere besides I must lay out above 20ˡ for John Delehay to gett the cause heard the next terme wᶜʰ he promiseth to allow or pay me by his lettei written wᵗʰ Morgan Delehays hand. If I could so compasse it that I owed nothinge but to Thomas Webb & John Delehay I would thincke myselfe happy for Clement expects his money & yf Doctor Bradshaw or his wyfe will have any money payd heere send me word. I thincke I must send down one of my men to take a fine of yᵘ for it must be sent up & the money receyved before I cã cõm down. the comission shalbe directed to my lord Byshop to whom I will undertake to make ȳ what estate ȳ will in Dydley & Bernithen. I have receyved all this terme but xxˡ in gold wᶜʰ I send ȳ by this messenger my Cosen Bevan of Garway. So having many grievous conflicts evening & morninge betwixt me & my debts I am in hope to conquer the mayn battle of them this term & skatter the rest as I can single them within a yeare or 2 and then I hope to live merrylie with my 2 Bens & provide for yʳ 2 girles. I will bringe down every penny that remaynes above the forsaid debts discharged that must of necessity be discharged heere in London. my deare lovinge kynd earnest resolute weake mighty desperat tender harted brave miserable dayntie boun-tyfull carefull cruell godly sweet honest Ben: god keepe yᵘ & your daughters & yʳ little boy whom I pray ȳ doe not breed a clown. Send word whether I shall bring John Boorne down wᵗʰ me. pray god I may finish this bargain for yet it is but a spech write to me where ȳ will keepe yʳ Christmas & what small provision I shall heere make for it & as ȳ will it shall be. God keepe ȳ sweet deere hart.

Yʳ J. H.

Mid. Temp.
4 of clocke in the morning
vi Novēb:
1611.

VI

To my lovinge wyfe
  Mrs. Ben Hoskyns at her house in Heref[d].

Good Ben: by my accoumpt y[u] are not yet in straw. I neuer
prayde soe earnestly for any thinge, not for health, ease,
or lyfe it selfe, in extremyty of sicknesse as I doe that I
might see y[u] before y[u] lye in. notw[th]standinge yf that may
not be, yet I pray w[th] assurance of fayth to obtayne, & fynd
comfort when I pray, that y[u] & y[r] chyld both may live &
haue health, & ioy in the companie of this poore prisoner
that now wrytes to y[u]. I haue intelligence (god graũt it
be true) that there is a purpose to deliver vs vpon som
vnexpected day neere the end of the terme. Whatever
becom of me it shall nothinge greeue me yf y[u] retayn a
comfortable spirit, & vndiscouraged hart in Christ Jesus.
I haue endured a triall I am out of feare of my offences, I
feare nothinge now, but only pray that god & his maiesty
would testyfy theyr recõciliatiõ to me by my deliverãce: and
I patiently attende it: I pray y[u] thancke Mr James Clarke
very hartily he came twise very lovingely & kyndely to the
Tower. Vpõ the notice of his suddayn departure I intreate
ỹ to accept this short letter. God strengthen & preserue ỹ
& blesse all your children.
                              Y[r] true Joh: Hoskyns.

I thancke god, I never was in better health in all my lyfe
        Then now I am,
                      J H
Tower
23 Nov 1614.

VII

To my only comfort & only earthly joy
  my Ben: the mother of my Bens:

My best deservinge Ben. I only write that y[u] may under-
stand I am in health since he is returned without me who
can tell y[u] no reason for it, but that w[ch] I ever conceyved:

Good Ser: In my accounte y'are not y' in strait . I neuer
brayde soe earnestly for any thinge, not for health
ease or life it selfe in extremity of sicknesse
as y' doe that I might see y' before I dye, in
notwithstandinge if that may not be yet I pray
with assurance of fayth to obtayne, & fynd comfort
when I pray that y' & y' chyld both may have
& haue health, & may in the companie of this
poore prisoner that now wrytes to y' I haue
intelligence, god graunt it be true that there
is a purpose to deliuer vpon som vnexpected
day neere the end of the terme . what euer
becom of me it shall nothinge greeue me
yf y' retayn a comfortable spirit, & true couraig
hart in Christ Jesus . I haue endured a triall
I am out of feare of my offences, I feare nothinge
now, but only pray that god & his maiesty
would testify theyr reciocitatio to me by my
deliueraice: and I patiently attende it. I pray
y' thancke mr James Clarke very hartily he
came twise very honestly & kyndely to the
Tower vpon the notice of his suddayn departur
I intreate y' to accept this short letter
God strengthen & preserue y' & blesse all
your children .   y' true ffr: Hoskyns

A Letter by John Hoskyns to Benedicta, from the Tower,
November, 1614

that other things must be determined of before my deliverance. that som new rumor & opinion must be first fashioned fitt for the wearinge of vulgar fancy, before this vayne cloake be cast of that poore I was the impedimēt of those great matters expected. All my honest brothers hopes, to prosecucōn whereof I submitted myselfe, are proved no other then Courtly delusñs of the tyme, & appropriatinge the successe of my suiet to som certayn meanes yf it had falne right: & in that it is deferd imputinge the delayes to some feares as that I will not be a thankefull mā: that no obligacion will bynd my witt &c. I am well contented and now leve pityinge myselfe & fall to pytie those greate ones that are so abused as to be misledde by colours that my conscience knows to be false. for no greate person by whom I benefitted ever found me ungratefull or presumtuous to taxe hym but rather embraced me for the contrary. Witnesse no less then the greatest Judges of law and equity in this kingdom, y'selfe & the family of wch I com: & all that ever I gaygned or receyved in this world proceeded from no other meanes. And towards these my conscience cries aloud: that I was never unkynd in earnest or bitter in jest. So then why should I be sorry? but yet alass the poor honest gentlemā informer of greate ones, hymselfe no doubt of no greater degree then myselfe or lesse, as it should seeme by the smallness of his hart that he so much feares a jest & desires to imprison witt. It is like a mā that cañot endure cheese & psuades others to sound at the sight of it as he doth: he sayth it hath odious ingrediences in it, as ryñett, & calves maw wth wch his maw holdeth an antipathy. and suer he hath reade little history: for no man ever suffered for mere witt: but yf he lived not to requitt it hymselfe, yet the witt of all posterity took penaunce on his name that oppressed hym. Be cheerefull noble Ben I cañot be psuaded that any mā that hath witt of his own is afrayd of anothers witt as no good soldier that hath a sword feares another mans sword. and for my part I had rather dy with witt then live without it. for the other part of beinge assured of me to be bound for ever therin I am courted for he that

feares least he shall not be suer of me, would fayne have me
fast bound to him: & so he shall & y^u shalbe my suertie,
when he hath tyed me: but the knott is to longe in knittinge.
Now Ben yf I shalbe delivered when I am a thanckfull man
& will not abuse my friends, I shall tarry very little. For
speake thou nurse of my love, mother of the experiencȩ of
all my thanckfullnes, thou mistresse of my witt, when did I
abuse thee? when did I deal ungratefully wth thee? you
must com Ben & refute them. In meane while take home
y^r Doctor the late rare example of suictors now made a
greate kinge of beggars, a Mr. of an hospitall, & take my
first servaunt Mr. Pateshall, delivered frõ Wilsheere assises,
restored to his office see that he be not ungratefull nor ruñe
not over us wth his witt. Forgive me Ben, & God forgive
me for this idle letter & yf whereas I have somtymes wept &
prayd, I somtymes laugh & pray hereafter. howsoever I
will ever pray will remayn malitiouse to none infinitely &
eternally loving to y^u. God ever preserve y^u John, Francke,
Besse, Ben, dic & all yr family
     thyne only thyne all thyne ever

                                        J. Hoskyns.
2: March 1614.

                         VIII

To my most deere & lovinge
   Ben Hoskyns at Heref.

Sweet hart   I am alive & in health, desirous yf it be gods
will to take further paynes for the supportation of a poore
estate, wherein gods favour to our prayers may effect more
then the strength of our labours. Your sonne John Boorne
is well, & hath a special affeccõn to musiq*ue* & sayth he will
goe to the dauncinge schoole, but keepes his study & good
order wherein I beseech the Lord that I may continue hym.
I have ben with my lord Chaũcelour & found hym most
lovinge & honourable in his favours to me.   My lord Chyefe
Justice came home yesternight from the Kinge wth whom
as the generall report is (& I thincke it was so) he was to
relate the state of the cause of the poysoninge or attempting

to poyson Sr Thomas Overbery in the Tower, what Mr. Page
shall relate to you therin is that wch I receyved from them to
whom the Lieuetenāt hymselfe spake it. I pray God I may
get my money of the Lieuetenāt before any danger fall to
hym, for concealing what he now hath revealed whatever it
be. And let us draw home our eys eares & senses from
others cases to ourselves & gods greate mercy in our preservation. I heare Mrs Kempe came on friday wth her soñes
Smith & Jeffreys & that yesterday her mā sayd to my
mā she would speake with me. I will goe to her & doe
whatever I can for y^r sake. but to go abroad is not our
order it is the office of a sollicitor. I wish she had a skilful
one for her ease & mine. yf Page be as willinge to requitt
kyndnesse as he is to receave kyndnesse that wch I have done
for hym is well don: otherwise I will recon hym in the
nūber of them that I ow nothinge to, & to whom god owes
a reproofe. I speake for nothing that I expect but the
triall of his neighbourly affeccōn hereafter to you & yours.
We have sent down my brothers nagge by hym that brings
down Mistresse Kempes horses. I pray you pray for us
& we doe & will pray for you. God keepe you deare good
sweet hart god blesse francke Besse Ben & little Dic that I
am sorry I saw not at partinge.

Your true lovinge
J. Hoskyns.

14 October 1615.

IX

To Mris Benedicta Hoskyns
   at her house in Heref^d these.

Sweet hart
   We are in helth the lord be thancked & preserve us in his
feare & obedience to his worde. I have lighted on a bargayn
of a new barre gown that cost me v^l so that I may keepe one
heere & another at Hereford.
   On Wednesday last Weston was executed for poysoninge
Sr Thomas Overbery, yesterday the Lieuetenāt of the Tower,
Sr Gervase Hellwisse was coñitted to Sr John Swyñerton &

Sr John Keys was sworne Lieuetenãt. Sr John Wentworth & Sr John Lidcot & Mr. Sarcevile were committed for askinge questions of Weston at his execucõn. Sr John Hollis & Sr Tho Vavasor were sent for for the same cause but appeered not. On thursday last the Earle of Som'sett was convented before the lords Commissioners but I heare of nothinge confest by hym. Mrs Turnor was examined on thursday she shalbe shortely tried, but the generall report is that the lievetenãt shalbe tried on tuesday next. Soe it will goe hard with me for my 50^l yf it goe ill wth hym. I pray you therefore returne some money by Mr Philips to pay Winchester rent, for part of the 14^l is gone for a gown, & part for other things.

I have ben favourably heard but I had but few clientes. I dyned on Sunday wth the Countesse. Y^u must needs send her som Turneps seed. Mrs Kempe I thincke proceeds not in her bargayn. Sr Humfry hath many ways disabled hyselfe to pforme what he should, but Mrs Kempe is contented. This bearer desired to carry this letter for he would be y^r tenãt at Burtons poole his security he offers is every halfe yeares rent before hand. I tell hym he may have BernIthen the house, orchard grasse for 2 kine and 2 horses, & certayn acres to halves, for a rent agreeinge wth me to dyet a servaũt that shall keepe my sheep, Inne my teythes, & wynter my cattle that shall eat up my straw, & plantinge yearely some trees & agreeinge to make som certayn perch of the ringe hedge yearely. You may conferre wth hym & conclude on whether bargayn you please levinge the upshott to me. I lyke his security well & his pson indifferently.

For your steele I would gladly heare how much is delivered, and I would but heare that it is once delivered for Oswald lookes for it & every man else for every peñy that I ow nay I tooke but two fees before my coñitment for wch I moved not & I thancke my clients both, they came & made me move for the both w^thout further fee or thancks. So I hope I shall grow pfectly out of debt & ow nothinge but a care of our children & myselfe, for as my Lord Chauncelour and my lord Cooke told me I hope I shall be the better whilst I live I am so well disciplined. I am much comforted wth the honorable words both of the Lord Chaūcelour and the M^r of the Rolls both privately & publiq*uely* but discomforted by the present state of the Chaūcery the mill grynds slowly. It pleased the kinge in discourse of Sr Thomas Overbery to say that the Earl of somerset dealt falsely with hym as he did wth me. for he promised to speake for his deliverauce & spake not & promised to speake for me but spake agaynst me. Sturgeon is at 23^s a kegge. Yf it please y^u to have any y^u shall, but the longer it stays the more I shall fynde when I come. I wonder I heare not from Thomas nor Harry Waythen. Thomas promised to rayse the ponde head. I would have him cut the outlett straighter through the end of the stanke though the ditch fall to ruñe a furrow lower yet it will ruñe more easily & cõtinually. I pray y^u in any case let Thomas presently bargayn with workmen to quicksett all my ringe hedge by the perch to make a ditch halfe a foot broader & deeper then the best is usually & to sett two rows of quicksett, this wynter must not be lost. I would have som body bwy me som pere trees at Dymocke & set them at Bernithen I told Thomas where. I troble y^u wth to much husbandry. I love y^u only & infinitly. god keepe you all & blesse our children.

I heeve nothinge fro y^u by this carrier.

J. H.

17 Octr 1615.

X

To my Mrs. Ben. Hoskyns.

Sweet hart. I only write to the intent y^t y^u should have it under my hand that I love y^u better thē myselfe & all the world besides. how we doe Taylor can tell y^u somtymes in the day.

I have sent y^u a small token of amber I pray y^u were it on y^r brest for my sake wthout alteracõn. be good to Besse & Dicke, & pray to god that my lord keeper continue his honorable favours to me. I thancke god it begyns to be

excellent well. Were it not for spendinge money I would
be in Kent a little while for our work lasted till this day &
on mūday com seveñight begyns agayn. loose not the
month & season to cutt down ridde & fell all the bushes
in Brenithen wood. I hope the house is covered walled
lymed & glazed. Meete me there when I com down. I pray
yᵘ be earnest with Thomas yf he mortgage the reversion of
Trelewisdee to me I will acquitt hym for the 100ˡ he owes
me wᶜʰ he sayth is but 80. as yf he would the payinge use
to be paymᵗ of the principall. yf so then I will intreat my
sister Kempe who now hath money enough to discharge the
40ˡ to Gryffyn for hym, & pay as much more of his debts as
that Reversion is worth & any time during his lyfe he shall
redeeme it paying use. untill god send hym a sone of his
own I know noe fitter heyr for hym then my soñe yf he
marry let his wyfes portion redeem all & let hym & my
mother live out of debt.

Good sweet hart survey yʳ selfe & in this tyme let it not
be to late to weede out all presūtuouse malicious and bitter
branches of affeccon or send me word there wilbe no amend-
ment nor rest for me in Herefordsheere, & I will keepe such
a diet as by som gout or stone shall end me the sooner.
God blesse my boy & your grand-child who wilbe a meanes
that I may take away my boy the sooner. I have gotten a
day for the Doctor's cause. I will doe anythinge for any
of yᵘ all but I pray yᵘ skorne me [not?] for it. I end the
happyest mã in the world yf yᵘ love me otherwise most

miserable

J. Hoskyns.

6 June
1617.

XI

To my Mrs. Ben. Hoskyns.

Ben: I perceyve by the stile of yʳ last letter that little Ben
my sone did not dictate all to yᵘ wᶜʰ yᵘ wrote but I discover
som other phrase therein then yʳ own. and yf in things of
such privacy yᵘ are fortified wᵗʰ counsayll and assistance it

were best for me write no more. for yf I write good letters,
y^u keep them to silence me yf displeasing letters y^u reserve
them to quarrel wth me & howsoever I shalbe sure to heare
of them agayn. Only yf I send y^u gold I am suer never
to heare of it agayn therefore I send y^u by my Cosen Jones
two peeces. y^u that are so well advised need no advise of
myne, therefore looke to the mill & all y^r state yourselfe.
god geve y^u wisdom & not to think y^u have it. yf I should
say I will love y^u as well as y^u love me it were in other wives
cases happy to them. But I love y^u more and since y^u
answer it not, god helpe me, & god forgive y^u & blesse y^r
children & myne & geve us grace to place our love on hym
that never fayleth to love us though we be his enemyes.
29 June 1617.

Your poore husband
whom once y^u loved   J. Hoskyns.

XII

Sweet hart
   for gods sake be comforted in hart & assured in mynd
that I love y^u more then a thousand lives of myne own yf
I were to have thē successivelye and fram'd at my pleasure.
   My brother Doctor is cōme. My Lord Compton is Lord
president for any thinge else I have yet but seene the Citie
& Westminster hall. Deere hart intreate Thomas to cause
the bwyldinge at Brynithen to be finished & the quickset
hedges & settinge of trees to be put forward in tyme, neglect
not to bwy Hopkyns land. I will send down mony as soone
as I receive it. And let Ben learne to write & David to,
for Ben it will be of necessity for he must learne to make
a latyn vulgar or sentence shortely & that must be written.
I daylie pray for y^u & y^r little sicke daughter & for all the
family. Remember my most loving commend^{ns} to my sister
& her daughters, & forget that I was cholericke it was
nature not malice for in reason & judgem^t I am nothinge
but love and kindnesse.

y^r J. Hoskyns.

16 Oct. 1617.

XIII

God in his great mercy lyghten our hartes & cheare our souls, & make us at all hours ready for hym & graūte us lyfe everlasting in our Lord Jesus Christ. Secretary Winwood is as dead as my lord byshop. Sr James scudamore is heere I neyther know nor much care to what purpose. My brothers cause is heard & the order is enclosed in the pap^r wrapt up in this lett^r I have not receved the mony of Mr Alford as yet but shall upō the day. I supt the last week with Mr Alford & this night I sup with hym agayn. Mr Harbyn is heere in health but Sr Robert Oxenbrugge is sicke of an Ague & taketh physicke heere. Sr Guy Palmes hath payd his mony to Mr Badby (tell my sister) there is one band taken for the meane profitts wch is in Taylor's deske in y^r house wch must be sent up to Sr Guy. My brother cañot com down till about the tenth of November, for about that tyme the tenāts of the hospital are to be treated wth what they will receve yearely till the lease expire. I will send you mony & other things when I have them, in meane tyme be merry & thancke god of a poore husband that is not the

worst of husbands   J. Hoskyns.

30 Oct. 1617.

XIV

To Mrs. Ben. Hoskyns.

Sweet hart. My brother Doctor is loath to carry money but when I see what is lefte me then I will seeke som returne and coñe myselfe as soon as I can. yf there be any thinge else besides a gown for the wynter that y^u want I pray y^u send me word. I heare that my brother Thomas is so foolish as to come up in the worst tyme of the yeare to no end that I know of except it be to drincke wth Thomas Hynde. I had rather he stayed at home & procure me elmes to be sett at Brynithen and the quick sett hedge to be made that he & I talked of level from the upper gate poste at the end of the lane by the barne to the upper corner of the meadow underneath Biddlestons meadow. and to sett wallnuts, chestnutts, beechmaste, ashenkeys & akornes, & for any thinge heere I can better doe it for hym then he can for hymselfe. I am glad yf he hath bargayned wth Hopkyns for his ground but I would willingly had in som of his ground on the banke of the river to lead the other side of my ponde heade: and I would desier that David Doñe might assigne me nine shillings worth yearely of grounde for my meadow plott wch he held at his house all this while & for the acre of common ground wch he now hath held divers yeares & I have nothinge but a quarter of an acre wch I drowned wth my ponde, otherwise for that & many trespasses I must bringe down a writt. the ponde head must be lookt to otherwise it may breake at every great fludde. I am sorry to heare that y^{u} want wood, yf Thomas had ben honest of his promise it could not had [*sic*] ben so. but doe not y^{u} spare any money to keepe yourselfe & your family in health farre better to spend money & have health then have sicknesse & want money. I pray you yf y^{u} want fruit or any thinge send to me presently. I have spoken wth your new lord president. I have no ambition but to come out of debt & enjoy myne own in quiet. And whereas y^{u} write to me not to be cruell I shalbe glad to serve y^{u}, so y^{u} will not be in perpetual quarrell wth me. And I am now old & expecte to be more contemtible, & therefore to passe unmedled wth. But never looke to have any in this world love y^{u} better then

J. Hoskyns.

11. Nov. 1617.

XV

6th Feb^{r} 1617.

This is now the 8th day that I have kept my bedd. yesterday I tooke a purge by Doctor Giffords advise. he would had me this day ben let blood I would stay till this frost thaws: he would not have me stay. And I am willinge to doe as please hym for he doth all things discreetely & safely. There are but 3 ways eyth^{r} this suddayn obstruccõ will bringe death wch is most welcom of all and to speake the truth I most earnestly desire it. first to enjoy my saviour secondly I have seene enough & known enough & to much of this world: thirdly God hath led me by his hand past the difficulties of malice, misery, & debt, there is but one enemy to cõquer, death, whom my saviour hath conquerd for me, & I longe to step over his backe.

And when I am goñe an old objection will be ended, whether I wanted others or others wanted me. I shall syñe no more; I shalbe reprehended no more. the second way is yf this be but a cold it cannot be longe my strength or physicke will break it. The third is yf it grow to be a consumptiõ I shall have the longer tyme to repent but that will be the most miserable of all. I shall have them sawcy with me that ought not to be so. I shall be uprayded to be a waster of a poore estate. it grieves me of what is lost already. to save the rest & obtayn peace: it were best dye now, & best dye heere where no body dares interrupt my thoughts. To be a true Judge of myselfe I thincke the greatest part of this is Melancholy yet god graũt never worse melancholy possesse my mynde. be y^u merry for I feele no payne but a deep longe cough somtymes labour for breath wthout any payne & som daũger to be chockt when I sleepe. this ten days I have eaten once a day towards night well enough but wthout any greate desire my stomach is so full of flagme. yet somtymes I am thirsty as I drincke seldom but physicke drincke & that not 2ise a day. the losse of my pracktise makes me sadde. I know you could be contented to endure me longer wth money. yf I scape this and come home be not froward be not crosse, wthdraw not y^r hart nor coũsayll from me pracktise not upon me reprehend me no more. for then my next sicknes I will certaynly dy yf I cañ: & would now yf I could. the reasõ may be guessed: doe y^u thincke that I see not what I doe amisse. doe y^u thincke I speak not more bitterly to my own hart for every offence then you cañ? doe y^u thincke it cã be pleasinge to me to see y^u suffer such things und^r y^r eys & authority as y^u doe in others & reserve y^r gale for me? This hath made me ask, I have been somtymes stunge a fortenight to breake out in a rage. but god & y^r soule knows who begyns. Selfe & sudden will & presūtion above y^r sex in y^u: riot & misdiet in me must be amended. I by the laws of god am y^r governor you are not mine. Yf y^u desire a sole supremacy marry no more when I am dead: there be enough that cā speake y^u fair & undoe y^u, and y^u shall fynd none to deale wth myne as I have dealt with y^rs Chaūge that wicked axiom wch y^u repeat so often that y^u desire to be kyndly used though it be by a dissembler. for I dreamt I saw a dissembler pawninge y^r plate, sellinge y^r leases, feastinge in y^r house & putting my boy to keepe his hawks & dogges & y^u makinge much of hym. I will leve y^u all & therefore give me leve to leve y^u this, and I pray y^u make bett^r use of it then to grieve. For god knows I desire y^r health & contentment rather then my own lyfe. When I am goñe never doe what y^u suddaynly desire or determin, follow no counsayll of them that flatter y^u geve them good words or rather money then the governm^t of y^rselfe. be not tyed to the service of any one to much for y^u will so endure anythinge rather thē loose such a one, that y^u & y^r children will become servaūts ere y^u be aware, & therefore harken for exchaūge in tyme & use thē all well. Stuff not y^r house wth to many people. let my boy be continually kept at his booke choose an honest mā for Besse, for little Dicke neyth^r y^u nor I but god must provide an husband. It grieves me that the livinge wch I shall leve y^u is so little & that he must have a pension out of it in whom there never was courage, & now I descry snekinge lewd vices & unthriftines. I have bitterly reproved hym. I hope he will amend therefore speake not of it. Will Harbin stays heere to bringe me home yf it be gods will yf I com̄ geve me no ill words yf I come not y^u are ridde of one that offended you much. I pray you forgive hym for gods sake & he with all his soule prays for y^r health & contentment in this world & to see y^u in the kingdom of heaven longe hence.

J. Hoskyns.

God blesse the poore children.

XVI

Sweet hart. we are in health & pray for y^u. Concerning y^r resolution touching cōminge hither I leve it to god & y^r mynde. things must be as god geves occasions. Y^r daughter wrote from Ledbury that you were gone to Bath wth my sister Kempe, & Mrs. Harbyn wrote that her mother was gone & left her wth you. Yf y^u want any thinge that is to be had hence let us know we will procure it by gods helpe. Above all things make much of y^{r}selfe for y^u are the only comfort that is lefte me. I pray y^u let Ben be encouraged to learne & to write. I looke for a letter from hym. God blesse hym & Besse & Dicke & francke & Tom & all that are alive, & are to come, for when Charles died Ben succeeded when I went to Tower Dicke was geven us: and if god send us another for Oswald It is his mercyfull supply. I pray y^u keepe the stocke in lyfe & hart & branches may springe the better.

Mid: Temp. 8 May 1618.

Y^r faithfull poore
J. Hoskyns.

XVII

To Mrs. Ben Hoskyns.

Sweet hart I feare we shall not see y^u this Whitsontyde for we have not yet put of the shop & wares being a matt^r of 4000^l & above & we have great debts to pay & som to receave wch will aske continual attendaunce. Above all things take care of y^r health that shalbe the rule that shall guide my accōns & rather then y^r contentm^t shalbe trobled I will endure any thinge cōtrary to my best Resolutions. Thomas would know whether he shall receve 60^l of Maynston. I would have hym tell hym that I respect not his title to BrynIthen but his intention to quarrell & his good will wch he shews yf he refuseth to release. It were best for hym to doe soe least I put on foote a title from oth^r Maynstons to Pykefield. Notwthstandinge yf y^u neede mony doe as y^u will. The cytizens have peticōned to barre me my fees. My Lord Chaūcelour awnswerd he would geve them no helpe neyther in law nor eq̃ty. I thancke them for their good will. the und^r shieryf awnswers me it shalbe payd to whom I pleased—I say to y^u. I could doe no less then write by this good frēd of y^{rs} who is in hast so praying for y^u all I rest your loving true

J. Hoskyns.
19 May 1618.

XVIII

Sweet hart I & all the rest are in health. I perceve by franck's letters to her husband she had rather be at Ledbury then wth y^u. I pray y^u therefore love y^{r}selfe best & next love them best that love to be wth y^u. I am glad yf y^u are at Brynithen, though it seemes Francke is unwillinge to goe wth y^u. Sweet hart I never denied y^u leve to goe to Bath I rather much desired that y^u would goe, & when I heard y^u were going was sory that y^u had not servants to attend y^u & was carefull to have sent to y^u. I thincke myselfe borne to no bett^r purpose then to procure y^r cōtentm^t in all things & rather desire to dye then to fayll in it. I dare not write all the love that I beare towards y^u for feare least y^u keepe my letter as an Evidence agaynst me when y^u turne curst yet I canot forbeare to professe my selfe

Y^r truest servant
J. Hoskyns.

23 May 1618.

XIX

To Mrs. Ben: Hoskyns at Hereford.

Ben   I wrote to y^u by Moore. I am free from the cough but only in the morninge a quarter of an howre. I am faynter & weaker then ever but wth no payne. It hynders my gaigne for what wth hillary termes sicknes & the two last termes busynesse upon my brothers death & the heavynesse of my spiritts now that cañot endure to stirre abroad & meete occasions of employment, my harvest falls short of my other yeares.

God can geve a remedy for all & nothinge coms to us that can better be devised if true use be made of it, it is all good for this lyfe or another.

Good Ben when I send y^u mony let there be 20 or 30^s of it thus bestowed. for 2^d. or 3^d. a stocke there is one Lirrigo to whom Mr. Maior can direct my brother Thomas that sells younge stocks ready graft for 2^d. or 3^d. a piece. I would have so many bought of all fine fruicts as shall sett the ground called the Conigree at Brynithen all over. It is the ground eastwards the house where Thomas sayd a fine orchard would be made. Let them be sett a fair distãce asund^r that they may not shadow the ground. Let the groũd be well fenced in & let no rother beasts com̃ into it nor shall com̃ these 4 yeares. The profitt of it will be made as gaignefull by corne, at first wth oates or barly & plow it flatt & afterwards by hay for it well [*sic*] easyly be made meadow.

The carrier is goinge I cã write no more yf my sister hath a boy let hym be called John or Randolph yf a girle let it be Francke & let Francke be godmother—Godfather Mr. Clarke eyther of them Mr. Pember, Mr. Crumpe, Mr. Warden, Mr. Doctor Benson Mr. Harbyn Mr. Jefferyes or any other of no lower degree then these & I pray y^u let no sparinge be of expense to lay her down as handsomly as she was wont in this town, her own estate shall discharge it. The maydes will speake of it heere & therefore good Ben let it be well doñ. I can thincke of no more yf I could I have no tyme. Let us heare from y^u.

God keepe y^u all & blesse myne & yours & the rest of the fatherlesse. God send my sister a safe delivery. looke to her at that tyme, she may be a little out of time y^u must hier an handsom keeper, that may be Mrs. Atkyns besides her widwyfe & maydes. God send all well & have mercy upon us. Mid temp.

24 of Octob^r 1618.

> Y^r poore lazy
> J. Hoskyns.

XX

My last will & testament, J. Hoskyns.

Gracyows god I geeve thee humble thankes for all thy mercyes And I beseech thee for thy sonne Jesus Christe his sake forgeeve mee my sinnes And receaue my soule into thy kingdome. by this my last will I bequeathe my body to Christyan buryall in full Assurance of the Resurreccõn and Constant faith of my salvacõn. All my landes of any freehold estate I geeve to Benedicta my wife to take all the pfits duringe the time that shee shall continue sole and vnmaryed payinge after her maryage to Bennet my sonne yearly xvj¹ a yeare after he shall accomplishe the age of xii yeares vntill he shall accomplishe the age of xv yeares. And after xv yeares vntill he shalbe of the age of xvij^en yeares payinge vnto him xx¹ a yeare. And after xvij^en yeares of age vntill he shalbe of the age of xxj yeares payinge vnto him xxx¹ a yeare. And after he comes to the age of xxj yeares vntill he accomplishe the age of xxv yeares payinge vnto him xl¹ a yeare. And after he comes vnto xxv yeares of age vntill xxvij^en l¹ a yeare. And after xxvij^en 100 markes a yeare during her life in her coverture. The said paym^ts to be made at the feastes of S^ct Michaell tharch Aingle and Thannunciacõn of the blessed virgin S^ct Mary yearely by even porcõns. And if any of the said somes be behinde and vnpaid at any of the dayes aforesaid Then I will that my said sonne Bennet shall enter vpon all or any my said landes or ten[emen]ts and the sonne to keepe in his posson vntill he be fully satisfyed the said seu^erall somes and the Arrerages and x¹ over; I doe will that all my debtes be paid not only out of my psonall estate but out of my landes and ten[emen]ts though my sonnes Annuitye be thereby diminished. And I doe will that out of my psonall estate there be payd 200¹ to Elizabeth Boorne and 200¹ to Benedicta, my Daughter, I doe geeve to M^ris Fraunces Hoskyns my daughter in law one of my best kine; I doe geeve to my brother Mr Doctor Hoskyns the six ringes now vpon my finger And fouer of my best bookes; I doe geeve all the rest of my goodes to my sonne in law M^r: John Boorne. I doe geeve to my mother a peece of gould of xxij^s and one of my best sheets to make her a shrowde. I doe geeve to my brothers Thomas and Phillip Hoskyns my two swordes the eldest to choose; I doe geeve John Hoskyns my god sonne sonne of my said brother Phillip sixe sheepe. I doe geeve to my brother Mr Doctor Hoskyns my second best geldinge And to my sonne in law Mr John Boorne my third geldinge; I doe geeve to William Taylor iij^l a yeare for three yeares after my deathe to be receaued out of the profits of a meadow mortgaged to me by John Dunne. I doe geeve to every other of my servants xxx^s a peece; I doe geeve to my sister M^ris Elizabeth Kempe two peeces of gould of xxij^s a peece to make her a ringe. I doe geeve to my sonne Bennet Hoskyns my silver bason and Ewer my two best Coverlets and two best Carpets to be deliu^ered vnto him at the day of his maryage, And I doe geeve my said bed and furniture in my new Chamber to my daughter Benedicta to be deliu^ered vnto her likewise at her day of maryage. I doe geeve to the poore of All saints w^thin the Citye of Heref xl^s And to the poore of Lenwarne xx^s And to the poore of Lengarren xx^s. I doe geeve to my brother Mr Doctor Hoskyns the landes that I bought of Mr Thom^as Morgan to be sould to make restitucõn of the money to my brother Oswaldes Children by wch it was bought. And I doe pray him to geeve my wife good allowance for keepinge my brother Oswalds Children and widdow. And of this my last will I doe make Benedicta my wife executrix And I doe ordaine my brother Mr Doctor Hoskyns and John Bainham esqrs assistants to her and to her vse. And I doe geeve to M^r: John Bainham a smale guilte wyne boule. And I desire my wife to take care of the poore childe at Lyonhalls. In witness that this is my last will and Testament I haue herevnto put my hand and seale the xxiiij^th daye of March in the yeare of our Lord god (1618)

J Hoskyns:

XXI

To Mrs Ben. Hoskyns in Heref.

3. Feb. 1620.

Sweet hart

I have been very heavy harted and trobled in sleepe & wakinge wth imaginatiōs that y^u are sicke or dead. but yf god be so merciful to me that y^u are alive I have sent y^u all the outward & inward comforts against this miserable weather that I could suddenly prepare. scarlet kersey in a boxe, white wth direccōns on it to y^u. A capp, a wastcoate, a pair of draws for y^r thighs, a pair of germashes for y^r legges, & a pair of pantofles, a seller or cabinet of waters, six halfe pynt square glasses vizt aqua caelestis, Doctor Monfords Cordial water, lymō water, cyñamō water, worm-wood water, Rosa solis water.

Sir Walter Py is atturney of the Court of Wards. All my labour is to represse the lower house frō questionīge my comittment the last parliament & to keepe thē from revivinge the kings displeasure. I thincke whatever they doe they will not hurt me, as they promise me, but they will provide for ever agaynst the lyke as they say.

The kinge in his sollemne first speech layd all the falt of braking the last parliam^t upon the undertakers. I have my health I have no cold nor cough but seldom, but whē I doe cough I spitt blood. I am somewhat full & short breathd but better then when I parted from y^u. for gods sake & for all those childrens sakes doe what y^u can to live, and be not curst when y^u are well. medle not wth me but to provide the best things y^u can for the house & me. forbeare your censure & speeches & bestow them on y^r sone Boorne, & that servaūt that is lyke to undooe us all.

I cā & will love y^u better than they that flatt^r y^u & bett^r in earnest then any flatterer can devise to dissemble. Now doe I imagine y^u skorne this letter. I would not have y^u doe soe, but if y^u doe I will endure that & ten thousand tymes worse rather then lose y^u as curst as y^u are & I am the only old poore man on earth that truly loves y^u

J. Hoskyns.

XXII

To Mrs Ben. Hoskyns at Mounton.

Good sweet hart this is whitsonday. I had busynesse heere till friday last & must be heere agayn on friday next. this morning I promised to be at Rochester for busynesse there to-morrow. I am now goinge to the Tilt boat & my mā goes about wth my horses. Yesterday I tooke phisicke, and I am well havin [*sic*] a little remnant of the Rheume falling down on a side tooth without payne. I will see y^r 2 sisters & y^r broth^r & come up again presently. I meane to be so fine as that they shall not laugh at y^u for having a sloven to y^r husband.

I have sent down a writ by Mr Haines whereupon I would entreate my brothers to goe fetch my Cosen John Delehay & his wife to suffer a Recovery at Treraddow to cut off the Remd^rs to the sisters. I have given direccõn to whom the Recoverie shall passe & agaynst whom. I pray y^u send to Mr Rawlings at Hereford tell him I am lyke to be arrested for the liveryes wch Tom Gwillim had & shalbe driven to pay the money ere I come down. lett Tom Gwillim know the day is past.

God geve y^u health comfort & joy & god send me to sell the parsonage & so make evē god blesse y^r children & I pray y^u love y^r true poore husband who hath not an happy thought in this lyfe unlesse y^u be at one end of it most kynd vertuous lovinge Ben adieu

y^r J. H.

May 12 1621.

XXIII

To my deare Mrs Ben Hoskyns.

Deare hart

God send y^u health. y^r parliament men will tell y^u all the parliament news. For me first: for my health I thancke god I am better then I was wth you, the reason is early

risinge & somtymes fastinge one meale increaseth breath &
diminisheth fatt. Next for Mr Parry he is desperately selfe
willed. he denyeth som due reconīgs, wanteth som evidences
to make good his title, & yet would cōpell me to sett furth
his title to be good, & will have me to proceed & take what
assurāce pleaseth hym & pay what he demaūde. he will
nev̄r be in order unless his brother or som reasonable mā
were heere to over-rule hym. For my being a welsh judge
it is as constantly spoken by all great & small even to my
face as yf it were so. and every judge in the welsh circuit
& sergeāts in Westm^r would have me believe, & it is as true
a report as the commissiō for pressing mayds to Virginia.
Yet I will not say it is impossible because som of the greatest
doe warrant it, but I pray god it nev^r may be except it be
more gods will then myne. be merry & make y^r selfe stronge
to take in good part what ev^r fall. yf it be better then we
deserve y^u will rejoice the more lively yf it be but as we
deserve y^u shalbe the more contented. yf worse then we do
deserve y^u shall endure it the more courageously. be assured
the greatest preferment I looke for is to be gods servaūt &

y^r true loving J. Hoskyns.

5 Jun. 1621.

XXIV

To my Mrs Ben: Hoskyns.

Sweet hart   god graūt we may live together and all turne
to our good. god graūt we may answer every one their
own every peñy wilbe payd for morehamtō by the end of
the next moneth. proceede to goe thither. I thincke I shall
troble y^r patience wth a welsh judge, & therefore let Ben
proceede to be a barrister for John Boorne loyters.

Y^r prebendary Williams is a privie coūsaylor & not
assuredly lord-keeper. We are sealinge of writings I shalbe
ridde of Arkston only the little mañor of Meres Court stays
in pawn with me for about 300^l.

Evry mā calls for money nobody pays. god help us. God blesse y^u and all the childrē. be assured I love y^u.

J. Hoskyns.

26 June
1621.

XXV

To his very lovinge daughter Mrs Elizabeth Boorne at Morehampton give these.

My cosen Wills cause is this day ended. Mrs Morgan is to pay 200 marke fyne to the king for her selfe, & a 100 marke a peece for Sr Jasper Carpenter & Taylor & if they be not able to pay themselfs then she is to pay and all fower are committed to prison, and the pris^r and her mayd & Taylor never to be vsed as wittnes in the spiritual Coorte to proue the marriadge. And yf it proue a marriadge then Mrs Morgan is to pay a 1000 marks porcõn, and Mr Danncer & Mr Blayrich Barrys bonds are to stand for pformaunce of this decree and besides shee is to pay all the costs of suite wch shalbe allowed by the Coorte. Bid Wills sisters give thankes to god & pray for hym and for themselfs, and by this example learne to be wise, to feare god & be advised by theire best frends. Let my daughter Megg: Boorne haue any money that she shall want, for I have receaued money of hers, desire Parrot to be diligent in all husbandry. Comend mee to my Cosen Richard Hoskins and yf he want any little soñe of money let him haue it let the keep[er] be remembred to looke to the pke & to the Conyes. I am not licke to come home till the Sȳsses be past in Glouc, wch will be about the 16 of March.

My man hath written for my horses to be heere about the 3 of March, At wch tyme send word what fysh or other things yo^w will haue, And good Besse be carefull & serue god, And tell my sister Kempe I have paied the xx^li accordinge to Mr Jefferies letter & haue offerred Mr Badbey the x^li, god send vs health the fear of god, & thrift in the valley. comend mee to Mr. Hall and all other good neighbours that wishe mee well, Will & Ben & Lewis are in health & mery wth mee. Lewis shall come downe shortly, But Will & Benn may stay heere yf the sickness Increase not. pray for vs all, wee will pray for yo[w]. forgett not to put forward the gardinge. god blesse yo[w] & Dick and all the rest.

y[r] Lovinge father
J : Hoskyns.

Midle Temple this 16 of
  ffebruary. 1625.

XXVI

Pray to God to blesse us and y[r]selves. I thinck the matter to morrow wilbe so farre settled as that we shall need no other help but gods blessinge w[ch] is drawn down by the prayers of them that feare hym. Provide all things as well as y[u] can yf it please god we will be at Rosse on friday night. Thither must be brought som good coach with fower horses for I know not how we shalbe provided further. We are in hope of my Lady Comfields coach for part of the way. I had brought one downe from London had not a foolish report caused a doubtful letter to be written to me but now I will cut off all possibilities of rumours, & therefore I must make suddein provision. Sir Samuell Awbrey M[rs] Candish Sir Giles Brugges & every frend must be tried. my sister Kempe hath a good coach so hath my Lady Bodenham. but who hath horses. yf any knows any noble gentleman that now would furnish me I would truly requitt hym, & in such a case never troble frend more yf it please god, & be ever hereafter able to doe the like to another. We have somewhat to do & I cannot write much. Commend me to M[r] Howarth tell hym how yf he can help us it shalbe a worthy frendship. There must be horses sent to Oxford to be there on S[t] Thomas eve to bring down Will Hoskyns & Ben Hoskyns they meane to keepe Christmas wth us. there must be an hogshead of sacke frō Monmouth (I thincke best) or else from Hereford to walke with our Claret. take care for the coach horses to be had at this tyme and goe presently about it day & night. the rest we have more tyme to doe. Study the coach way where to breake hedges & how to avoyd deepe & dangerous ways. So god speede us and y^r

J. Hoskyns.

Mistake me not, no mā now resisteth me, we want nothing but coach & horses.

XXVII

Daughter Besse

Y^u shall have a godly worthy mother-in-law kynde & quiet. let as much be provided for her content as y^u cann, & I thancke y^u for what y^u have doñe allready. Ben woñe her for me as he came up; y^u & Dicke are her daughters she longes to see my neeces. at this tyme she brings a neece of her own & one mayde & two mē with her. I thincke y^u are every one of y^u as happy as I in the match. Comend me to my sister Kempe—tell her she wilbe a lovinge compañion for her, & is somewhat lyke her for stature & makinge. Comñend me to my daughter Margarett Boorne & tell her I hope she will thancke me for her. Let us all pray to god with thanksgevīge for the least of his benefitts & hūble supplicatiō for his pardon for our synes. Mr Edwards this bearer hath woundrously bound me to hym so hath Mr. Griffith lloyd who will come with us wth one mā only. I pray god we may be so happy as to have a coach & good horses meet us at Rosse upon fryday night. Mr Edwards will tell you the rest.

God keepe us all. Comñend me to all my Cosens

Also I rest

y^r lovinge father-in-law

J. Hoskyns.

Risingtō
11 Decr 1627.

XXVIII

To my daughter Elizabeth Boorne.

Bes

It was to much for y~ at my partinge to weepe & to write to y^r broth^er that y~ could not write for weepinge. the cause wch ȳ wept for was that all was spent, nothinge layd vp. that may be a causelesse weepinge whē I am dead. spare y^r teares the meanewhile. spend y^r care & labour rise early take an accoūpt of every bodyes worke craṁe not vp the fellowes of the basest cōpanie wth hott beef & muttō every meale, that they keepe no place cleane. I will not bwy their dunge so deare. Let the buttery be regulated. And whē y~ will let y^r Daūcer & his boy be goñe—howsoever whē I coṁe next I will neyther leve thē nor Nic Ward behynder me. Yf I fynd any stealinge it may be a iust cause to break of with two of thē. Geue Will. Hoskyns good counsell, & whē I come home I will propose more vnto you. fare well good Besse, remember now I leve ȳ none to be hiered to chargeable worke. Let my own servaūts doe the things that are downe in a note & call vpō thē to doe it daylie, it is but plantinge & only phaps Tomson may be hiered to sett stocks & John Legge to gett stocks & let the Smith fetch som frō his coūtry it may be the old stockstealer may deserue halfe a crown. farewell again. Prepare again, serue god ever, & [*sic*] will love y~ ever.

Y^r father in L

J. Hoskyns:

Send word what Arthu^r Morgā doth at Newstreet.

XXIX

To Mrs Elizabeth Bourne at
    Morehampton.

Bes. I ow fiue pound ten shillings to Mr Philips for light gold wch he returned. the doctor calls for it now as I take horse. I pray ȳ send it hym & let Pereth make hast to gett in the rents. I thancke god I am out of payne & I hope aft^r a little ridinge to be stronge again.   I had not leasure at home to thincke vpō any thinge of myne own.   now ī fynde that I shall haue occasiō to lay out much money the suiet in the Arches to reu^{er}se Will Hoskyns mariage & the fynding of the office & payinge the fine & charges for Jony Boornes wardship.   Y$\sim$ see howe the neyghbours are mynded they thincke I must serue their turnes & neglect & overthrow all my own busynesse.   take y$\sim$ heed of them & suffer thē not to incroch vpon y$\sim$.   Yf y$\sim$ geue them leve once or twise they will grow shameless & vse ov^{er} all the thinges in the house y$\sim$ will loose much by mislaying whē any thinge hath not lately ben seen it wilbe easy for any to say I nev^{er} knew what is becoīe of it a longe tyme, & so steale it.   & so I must still pay for new.   Oth^{er} things are spoyld by beinge cast in holes & corners.   Let the gentlewomē rise early & learne to know god that made not the day for sleepe & let them be sure idlenes is moth^{er} of all evill & the tyme of tēptacōn to lewdnes, & pride.   God blesse thē.   Let not Mr Richardson see what I wrote till ȳ write agayn to me. Let none be absent at prayers.   & let the gentlewomen know that I will take notice wch of them is most early riser, diligent, humble & gevē to thrive & they shall fare the bett^{er} for it though my sone & daughters haue the lesse, & they that are contrarywise gevē (wch god forbidd) I shall the lesse pytie thē whē their own rodd beats thē.   Let them looke vpon Robin Kempe & see what it is to be proude of false hopes.   God blesse & defend & guyde & p^{re}serve ȳ & them & Dicke.

Y^r father in L
J: Hoskyns:

XXX

To his loving daughter in law M^{ris} Elizabeth Boorne at Morehampton in the gilden valley—these bee dd.

Hereffshr.

Besse   I pray y^u remember there are now four of Morehampton house at London besides myselfe & three servaūts

& that the use of their portions wch is after the rate of 500^l a person must be spent heere upō them at least, wch is after the rate of eyght score pound a yeare at eyght in the hundred. & all that must be saved & spared out of the expense of Morehampton house, & y^u need not be ashamed to alleage this excuse eyther to the family or straungers. I doubt Rowland Jones is a weake bayliff or steward & can forcast nothinge for the provisiō in the house for people or abroad for cattle. let it be therefore remembered how many load of hay were provided the last yeare, & yet y^u wanted & now y^u have five coach-horses perpetually in the house. See how many cattle y^u had the last yeare what fother y^u spent how many you are lyke to wynter this yeare & let proportionable provisiō be made for them. Tell Rowland Jones that I have writtē to hym severall tymes to sort my cattle, and to keepe severall pastures for them well grown to suceed one another fresh & fresh, and to divide the kyne & the yoūge beasts the stone colts & geldings from the mares, & those that I must use to be best kept. that he very foolishly hath not doñe so but eaten up altogether. let those horses that are to be sold & be not worth the keeping be kept in som severall & made up, & packt away. Consider what corne y^u bought this last yeare above what grew at home & forecast to bring corne or teythe upon the ground. there be portions of the Prebends to be sold upon St Peter's day as Allensmore Kingston Webton & the Holdsby of these John Sheldon can informe y^u how to bargain & he will joyne wth y^u.

Tell Mr Ward that his sister & I have thought upon helpe for hym heere at London & so wish hym to take his tyme to coñe up. Tell Zachary Wilson that I myslyke his running to the Alehouse as soone as I gave hym money except he amende his falt in that & labour hard upon myne arras he shall never fynde me in that falt to geve hym a peñy. I pray y^u desier Mr Powell to put thē forward all in necessy for y^r household may breake or remove & the charge is tō greate to stand longe and learne little. Y^u must send Rowland Jones or Thomas Powell for my boards & deliver them twenty shillings & twenty pence. let old dick french provide & make a lyme kyll betwixt the parke & John Mericks ground, let stubbs be digd & lyme burnt & let Rowland Jones with the advise of John Sheldon & Robin Hughs choose ground for fallow & terne the next yere in New street ground & the furre wood. Let Lewis Powell resolve now to hold or leave his bargain and to leve me the fallow as he found it yf he leave & so resolve for so much as I hier now of hym yf he holds to leve that [... ... ...] out of his bargain and I will diminish the rent but let him looke for such peñyworths as he lets me; I must let hym of all the meadow groūnd that is as good as I rent. And with Rowland Jones & the rest of the servaūts consider whether so much be gotten in the stocke of cattle as is spent in hyringe of grounde & bringinge hay, yf there be not, sell som of the stocke to save bringinge hay & hieringe ground, keepinge only a plow of oxen and necessary kine. Let Rowland Jones lykewise consider whether there be need to put two bullocks more to the teeme for the manuringe of John Mincks ground & the further wood and whether there be any ready for the yoke. besides yf Lewis leave the farme we must needs keepe eyght oxen & som sheepe as for the meadow and pasture no doubt setting of that we can spare to grasiers & men of Madley & other parts of the country that want pasture, we shall make more of it by parcells then Lewis geveth for the whole farme. for all matters of husbandry I thincke John Hughs can geve best counsayll for he is an excellent good husband.

Daughter there are many & serious thinges to consider of, & I pray yᵘ keepe this letter and reade it dayly, for yᵘ neglect & forget many things & disappoynt me. I wonder why yᵘ never told me that Pritchard had brought some tobacco and tyffany neyther told me that you went from Glouster to Ledbury, for I had busynesse to write to my brother.

Well to conclude great payments of porcōns grow on, yʳself are one. I have no ready money it must be made out of rents & saved from expense in house keepinge or out of sales of land & if we cañot live wᵗʰ our land how shall we live without it. Where the money is there our porcõns. Doe y^r best serve god all of y^u & let y^r Girles hear the yougest childrē words & let them teach them or read to them the principles of relligion. so I most humbly beseech the great god of mercifull providence & proteccõn to compasse us wth his wisdom & mercy & to defend us & to send every one us [*sic*] such measure of fayth & saving grace as may work to our salvation in our Lord Jesus Chryst

yor poore sorrofull father in law
J. Hoskyns.

Mid. temp.
6 June 1629.

XXXI

To my Daughter Mrs Elizabeth Bourne at Morehampton this be dd.

Daughter Besse.   This gentleman was my brothers worke-man and is still for that house.   He knowes my cozens in London and I sent him by my house that he might see howe my cozens are and noetifie my cozen Mary and Magdulen of it.   I pray you bidd him heartiful welcome for indeed he is a very honest man and one that did my brother much good service.   He will convey anie letter that you will to them.   Soe praying you to be carefull of my busines at home I comit you to god and rest

yor loving father

Burnithen	If he brings anie company with him I
6 Septembris	pray you bidd them wellcome
1629	Bess I pray you doe so

J. H.

CHAPTER VIII

A Tuftaffeta Speech from *Le Prince d'Amour*

IN the Middle Temple revels in the reign of the *Prince d'Amour*,[1] Prince Martino[2] and Sir Walter Ralegh, as we have seen, successfully importuned John Hoskyns to speak. His tuftaffeta oration modestly cloaked as but a fustian answer to their importunities was one of the numerous literary parodies of the occasion. The young men who were denizens of the Inns of Court were extraordinarily self-conscious students of literary expression. Those preparing seriously for a legal career strove to gain 'store,' 'copiousness,' and 'variety' in their use of language that they might never 'faile of discourse or be left on ground for want of good invencõn.'[3] Those not primarily interested in a legal career were equally concerned in the cultivation of literary style as a social accomplishment and as a tool for advancement at court or in the household of a powerful patron. Conscious attention to tricks of style was so assiduously and generally practised in the sixteenth century that the young Templars could amuse themselves by devoting most of their Christmas revels in 1597-8[4] to elaborate literary parodies. In the realm of the *Prince d'Amour* a decree went forth that 'if any subject naturally born, for want of Wit Court his Mistris with the Fruits of Silence . . . he shall be imprisoned in the Island of Ideocy and censured by the Bishop of Saint Asses.'[5] If the young sonneteers found themselves guiltless of violating the foregoing law against silent wooing, they could hardly have failed, for some chance violation, to come under the punishment of the stern decree that if 'any man swear his foul Mistris fair, his old Mistris young, or his crooked Mistress straght . . . he shall be condemned as a forsworn Sorcerer for the one, and as a false seducer of the Innocent in the other.'[6] To ensnare in the meshes of the law those not already trapped, it was further decreed,

'If any man deprave the books of *Ovid de Arte Amandi*, *Euphues* and his England, Petite Pallace, or other laudable discourses of Love; this is loss of his Mistris favor for half a year.' Because many of the young Templars were habitually penning rimes for and about their mistresses, the tribunal set up by the *Prince d'Amour* was probably not without success as a satirical diversion.

Although the speech by John Hoskyns was not devised to ridicule the sonnets and love poems emanating from the Temple, it furnished a witty exposure of another literary fashion, the use of 'aureate' prose which, though rapidly becoming extinct, was still sufficiently common to be a fit subject for parody. The reaction against the excessive use of 'ynkehorne' terms had been well under way since the publication of Wilson's *Arte of Rhetorique* in 1553. Hoskyns' speech is one of the late parodies[7] of the affectation.

Though its author was ridiculing aureate language, he was at the same time constructing his parody on a very elaborate framework of figures which today are resorted to no more consciously than is the wealth of Latin derivatives which have long enriched the language. Sixteenth-century rhetorics indicate the conscious dependence felt at this period upon the adornments of style catalogued under the heads of *catachresis, poliptoton, epanalepsis, symploce, paralepsis, subiectio*, and the rest of the formidable array of approved figures. Hoskyns was not only aware of the absurdities attendant upon the lavish use of the aureate language, but he was also conscious of the strange effects produced by the unrestricted employment of figures, resulting sometimes in 'centuries of sentences' and other excessive ornaments. He not only parodies the 'frothy volubility of words' that results from the use of the aureate language, but he parodies as well the absurdities arising from the unrestricted use of tropes and figures. Yet the author of the 'tuftaffeta' speech would have been the last to discard the elaborate tables of figures, as is evident from his *Direccōns For Speech and Style*. He merely insists upon a judicious but still highly conscious employment of them. Thus his 'tuftaffeta' speech

is more than a parody; it is a pleasant, easy presentation of
the principles of style; and for the effectiveness of its presentation the author relied upon the principle of exaggeration.
To his listeners, it may have appeared more a *tour de force*
than we are likely to realize. With a slight suggestion of
pride in his craftsmanship, the author, more than a year
after the composition of this *jeu d'esprit*[8] for the Christmas
revel, remarked in his *Direccōns* to his younger, less experienced fellow-Templar: 'And if you will read ou^er that speech,
yo^w shall find most of the figures of Rhetorick there, meaning neither harme, nor good, but as idle as yor selfe, when
you are most at leisure.'

The modern reader will hardly encroach upon his leisure
to cull out examples of these figures; he will be content to
take the author's word that they lurk within the folds of his
'tuftaffeta.' He may, however, feel an interest in a sample
of the wit bandied about among the young Templars, which
perhaps for a moment amused a melancholy poet and ambitious courtier, colonizer, and adventurer who had persuaded
Hoskyns to display his nimble wit in the following oration:

Refused to answer at extempore being importuned by y^e
prince and Sr Walter Rawlegh. Began

Then Mr Orator I am sorry that for y^r Tufftafity speech
you shall receiue but a fustian Answer but alas* what am
I whos eares haue bin purgited* wth the tenacity of your
speeches & whos nose hath bin perfumed with the aromaticity
of y^r Sentences That I shold answer your oratiō both
voluminous and Tropical* wth a replicatiō course* & curtal
for you are able in troops of tropes & Centuries of Sentences
to muster y^r meaninge nay y^u haue such woodpiles of words
y^t vnto y^u a Cooper is but a Carpenter & Rider himself
deseru's no Reader* I am therfor driuen to say to y^u as
Heliogabalus sayd to his dear and Ho:^ble frend ffogassa* if
thou dost it* quoth he much good* do thee if wet snuff* y^e
candle for even as the snow advanced vpon ye poynts vertical
of cacuminous mountains dissolveth and discoagulateth in
self* into humorous liquidity even so by the ffrothy volubility

of y^r words the prince is perswaded to depose himself frō the regal state* & dignity to ffollow* y^r Councell wth al contradictiō & reluctatiō, wherfore I take you to be ffitter to speak vnto the stones* like Amphiō or Trees like Orpheus Then to declame to men like a crier to exclame* to boyes like a sexton. ffor what sayd Titus Situs* the sopemaker of Holborn bridge ffor quoth he since the estates* of Europe haue so many momental inclinatiōs* & the Mathematical* confusiō of theyr dominions is like to ruinate theyr subversions I see no reason why men shold adict ye selues to take Tobacco in Ramus method for let vs examine ye complotts of Polliticians frō the begiñing of ye world to this day w^t was ye cause of ye repentine mutiny in Scipios camp it is most evident it was not Tobacco w^t made me address* this expostalatiō to y^r iniquity it is plain it is not tobaco So y^t to conclude tobacco is not guilty of so many fautes as it is chargd wthal it disvnitith not ye reconciled it reconciles not* ye disvnited it builds no citties* it mends* no old breeches yet ye one or ye other* & both are not iñortal wthout reparations therfor wisely sayd ye merie conceited Heraclytas* Ho:^{ble} misfortunes haue ever an historical consideratiō.* y^u listen vnto my speeches I must needs confes it y^u harken vnto my words* I cañot deny it yo^u look for som meaning I partly belieue it but y^u find note* I do not greatly respect it ffor even as a milhors is not a horse mil, nor drink ere y^u go is not go ere you drink euen soe orator Beast* is not ye best orator The sum of al this is* I am an humble sutor to y^r excellency not only to free hī frō ye danger of ye tower wch he by his deme wits* cañot avoid but also to increase dignity vpō his head & multiply honor vpō his shoulders as well for his eloquence as for his nobility for I vnderstand by y^r Herald frō on[e] of an ancient house of ye famous Calphurnius Beastia* & so generatiō* continued frō beast to beast til this praesent beast* & y^r Astronomer hath told me y^t he hath kindred in ye zodiack I therfore in al humility* do beseech y^r excellency to grant your royal warrant to ye L^d marshal & charg hī to send to ye capt~ of ye pensioners that [he] might* send to ye capt~ of ye guard to dispatch a

CHAPTER IX

Direccõns For Speech and Style

INTRODUCTION

WHEN Benedict Hoskyns, so Aubrey tells us, asked honest Ben Jonson to adopt him as one of his sons, the poet replied: 'No, I dare not; 'tis honour enough for me to be your brother: I was your father's sonne, and 'twas he that polished me.'[1]

Whatever the extent of the 'polishing' which Hoskyns may have given Ben, we have important evidence of Jonson's admiration for Hoskyns' views on the cultivation of prose style. For, as I have pointed out elsewhere, three pages of *Discoveries*,[2] as published in the folio of 1640-41, are taken from Hoskyns' *Direccõns For Speech and Style*. The passage Jonson borrowed begins with the sentence: 'The conceipts of the mind are pictures of things, and the tongue is the interpreter of those pictures.' It continues without interruption, though with some omissions from the original, to the section 'De Poetica.'

Internal evidence makes clear that *Direccõns* was written between 1598 and 1603, with the year 1599 as the most likely date of its composition. Illustrating a figure of speech, Hoskyns remarks that one may say that 'the Earle is gone into Ireland for E: E:.' This reference to the expedition of the Earl of Essex fixes the date near if not actually during the period of 27 March to 28 September 1599, the dates upon which Essex left and returned to London. Other remarks show that the *Direccõns* was written after the quarrel between John Davies and Richard Martin, which occurred on 9 February 1598.[3] That it was written before the death of Queen Elizabeth is indicated by the fact that the young Templar to whom the treatise is addressed is referred to as a student of her Majesty's laws. Though it is not possible to date the *Discoveries* with the same definiteness, critics of that work have regarded it as the composition and compilation of Jonson's later years.[4]

It is, of course, to be remembered that the *Discoveries* is essentially a commonplace book and that it was posthumously published. However, investigations[5] suggest that it was Jonson's own wish that Sir Kenelm Digby should arrange for the printing of the material which subsequently came out in the folio of 1640-41. Several curiously inferior readings in the borrowed text indicate that Jonson had access to an inferior copy or was careless in transcribing or that his printer or Digby assumed no great responsibility for the accuracy of the text. It is also interesting to observe that Jonson indicated the source for his far from literal borrowings from Bacon's *Advancement of Learning*,[6] but made no reference to Hoskyns and his manuscript treatise. Professor Hoyt H. Hudson has suggested that the importance of Jonson's debt to Hoskyns 'may be qualified by our certainty that Jonson knew that what he copied came, in large part, from Lipsius.'[7] It is true that Jonson, like most learned men of his day, knew some of the voluminous writings of Lipsius and elsewhere in *Discoveries* quoted a sentence from him. We have knowledge, too, of one volume of his commentaries among Jonson's books.[8] Yet I know no specific grounds upon which Professor Hudson bases his assumption that Jonson recognised echoes of the *Epistolica Institutio*, the work by Lipsius to which Hoskyns' remarks on letter-writing show an indebtedness.

The *Direccōns* clarifies several readings in the *Discoveries* and necessitates the revision of certain opinions of Jonson based upon remarks that now prove to be Hoskyns'.

A collation of the corresponding passages reveals interesting differences. Hoskyns' comments on Seneca Jonson retains without change of the pronoun but omits the personal remarks addressed to the young Templar. Hoskyns explains that the vice of profusion in style may be 'eschewed by pondering yor busines well, and distinctly conceiving of yor selfe.' In the *Discoveries* we are told that the end is achieved 'by pondering your business well, and distinctly concerning your selfe.' Hoskyns elsewhere refers to 'the very strength & synnewes (as it were) of yor penning, made vpp by pithy sayings.' In the *Discoveries* the same passage reads: 'the strength and sinnewes (as it were) of your penning by pretty Sayings.' Hoskyns' phrasing in another passage is as follows: 'if you write to a man whose estate and sences yo^w are famylliar wth, Yo^w may be the bolder to sett a a [*sic*] taske to his brayne.' The same passage in the *Discoveries* is strangely garbled thus: 'if you write to a man whose estate and cense as senses,' and so on. Again, in the *Discoveries* the verb 'indangered' is omitted in the transcription of Hoskyns' statement that 'perspicuity is often times indangered by affectation.' It is at this point that Swinburne supplied the verb *lost*.[9] Although Hoskyns advised that the last item of a letter ought to leave 'the sweetest memoriall & briefe of all that is past in his vnderstanding whome yo^w write to,' the reading in *Discoveries* has become 'memoriall and beliefe.'

Since 1889, when Swinburne wrote enthusiastically of *Discoveries*, the book has been accorded a good deal of study. Hoskyns' contribution, coming in for its share of praise, has been used to interpret various aspects of Jonson's learning, humour, and judgement. Swinburne himself, for example, pointed out the richness of humour and the good sense revealed in the passage on letter-writing, which is really Hoskyns'. In the same passage he saw a suggestion of Thackeray's style.[10] Three years after Swinburne's study, Felix E. Schelling found the *Discoveries* 'attesting Jonson's unparalleled reading';[11] but certain references to Cicero, Seneca, Castiglione, and Quintilian have proved to be Hoskyns'. Remarking that Jonson does not stoop to the 'practise of wanton alliteration,' Professor Schelling found rare instances in which Jonson has fallen into this 'species of indefensible Ciceronianism' and cited as an example what is alliteration only because it is an apparently meaningless garbling of the text.[12] Maurice Castelain asserts that the passage on letter-writing 'seems more original than the rest.'

'Jonson,' he adds, 'assumes here a greater independence than usual over his model, which is all for the better.' He observes that Section 125 'contains some of the happiest traits of humour in the whole book . . . . In fact Jonson must have been desirous, not only to condense the original text, but also to enliven and relieve the dry preciseness of the great Flemish scholar.'[13]   Jonson was, however, merely inserting into his notes the informal, spirited, and practical treatise on letter-writing which one of his contemporaries had prepared with, it is true, a measure of 'inspiration from Lipsius.'   Professor Castelain[14] develops a theory that the *Discoveries* represents material for a future treatise on style in which the section on letter-writing now recognized as Hoskyns' was to be 'shoved in' between the comments on oratory and those on poetry.   Seen in its original context, the passage, it is clear, was not designed for such a position. He would also wrest the first half of the borrowed passage from what follows and insert it between the sections he calls 118 and 119; that is, just before the passage beginning 'Custome is the most certain Mistresse of Language.' Though Hoskyns' remarks on speaking would have filled in conveniently there, they were not written to stand in that context.   Professor Castelain's conjectures on what Jonson was intending to do with his material are really a revelation of the way in which he himself might have developed an essay on style out of the material at hand.

Considering the acutal purpose of the *Direccõns*, we find that Hoskyns prepared it as a gift for a young gentleman of the Temple to whose father he felt an obligation to cultivate the young man's style.   Who the Templar was for whom the treatise was to be an informal and practical guide is not known.   It is interesting to speculate, however, as to whether he may not have been Robert Harley (1579-1656). Young Harley entered the Middle Temple on 24 October 1599[15] and was bound with Hoskyns for his first instruction, and apparently they lodged in the same chambers.   Harley came from Brampton Castle, Herefordshire, and it is likely that Hoskyns knew him and his father before the young man's admission to the Temple. The tone of the *Direccõns* makes it clear that Hoskyns had such a relationship with the recipient of his gift. Apparently the young man was expected to fill a rather important place in his county at least. Harley became a knight of the Bath upon James's coronation, and later was Master of the Mint and a member of Parliament. It was his grandson who was created first Earl of Oxford of the Harley line and whose manuscripts were acquired by the British Museum. Since two of the three extant copies of the *Direccõns* (one of which is incomplete) are in the Harleian collection, the conjecture that Robert Harley may have been the young Templar is somewhat strengthened. Though in 1630 the complete Harleian manuscript, as is clear from its title-page, was in the possession of Daniel Manwaring,[16] it was not necessarily written for him. That at least one member of a Manwaring family was known to the Harleys in the seventeenth century is evident from a reference in a letter of Robert Harley's wife Brilliana.[17] Whoever the young Templar may have been, he received with the essay a marked copy of Sidney's *Arcadia* in the 1590 edition 'without Samfords Additions.'[18]

At the outset Hoskyns in a general way indicated his indebtedness to others when in the *Direccõns* he wrote: 'Yf I were not bound to yor fathers loue & yo.^rs, if I sawe not in him most kind providence, and in yo^w most willing endeavo^rs . . . I should thinke it ill manners to trouble my selfe & yo^w wth a great deale of Instruccõn, taken out of *Aristotle, Hermogenes, Quintillian, Demosthenes, Cicero,* and some latter, as *Sturmius* and *Tallaeus,* & such honest men.' Professor Castelain has pointed out the debt to Lipsius for parts of the discussion of letter-writing,[19] and Professor Hoyt H. Hudson has shown that there are echoes of Pierre de la Primaudaye's *L'Académie Françoise* in the opening remarks on the relation of thought to clear expression.[20]

To Aristotle Hoskyns refers at least five times in his *Direccõns* and declares that the 'vnderstanding of Aristotles

Rhetorique, is the directest meanes of skill to discribe, to
moue, to appease, or to prevent mocõn, whatsoeu[er]; whervnto, whoesoeuer can fitt his speech, shalbe truely eloquent.'
Though Hoskyns shows admiration for Aristotle, he seems
not to have borrowed from him specifically, unless, with
Professor Hudson, one finds a suggestion of Aristotle in
Hoskyns' discussion of metaphor.[21]   To Hermogenes Professor Hudson thinks that the discussion of the figure of
comparison may owe something.[22]   Since the printing of his
edition of the *Directions*, he has called my attention to the
possibility of Hoskyns' having borrowed from Cicero a
phrase found in the section on letter-writing; otherwise the
debt to Cicero, as to Aristotle, seems for larger principles
only.   For the whole framework of his treatise Hoskyns,
like his contemporaries, was indebted in a general way to
Quintilian, whose treatment of rhetoric furnished the Renais-
sance with what was almost a codified system.   There are
at least two instances of close parallels between Hoskyns'
work and the *Institutio Oratorio*.   Though Talaeus[23] and
others probably supplemented Quintilian as convenient references for definitions of figures of speech, Hoskyns' phrasing
is usually characterised by his own informality and freshness.
   A book which may have presented additional suggestions
as to the best method to employ is the *Arcadian Rhetorike*
by Abraham Fraunce.[24]   Fraunce's book, dedicated to the
Countess of Pembroke, is divided into two parts, the first
dealing with the art of rhetoric, the second with that of
delivery.   Hoskyns' title-page suggests that he intended to
include a section on pronunciation; but, whether or not he
wrote it, it is not found in the extant copies of the *Direccõns*.
From Fraunce he may have derived the suggestion for making his treatise a running commentary on the *Arcadia*.   In
doing so, he limited himself more than Fraunce had done,
and consequently dealt with Sidney's prose in a detailed way,
whereas Fraunce scattered his quotations over a wide range
of authors and illustrated more frequently from poetry than
from prose.   Hoskyns follows Fraunce's order of figures

fairly closely and once uses an illustration from the *Arcadia* which Fraunce had employed to illustrate the figure agnomination.

There seems to be no specific indebtedness to Sturmius. Hoskyns' debt to Wilson is slight,—merely the quotation from his own tuftaffeta speech of a sentence borrowed there from Wilson and one or two others. He may have known Fulwood's treatise on letter-writing, though no similarities are close enough to warrant regarding Fulwood as a source.[25] Hoskyns' treatise has greater informality and directness than those of Puttenham[26] and Leuer,[27] and his concern is primarily with prose.

The *Direccõns*, then, though in some measure indebted to earlier treatises of the same nature, is, so far as is now known, essentially original. Its personal tone, the immediate purpose for which it was designed, and the vigour of its style give it charm and force. A further interest may be found in the work as a kind of documentary evidence of the literary opinions, standards, and fashions prevalent at the close of the sixteenth century. For example, the *Direccõns* answers in the words of a contemporary of Sidney's one of the questions recently posed by Mr. Kenneth Orne Myrick[28] regarding the spirit in which Sidney composed his literary work. Hoskyns' opinion amply supports Mr. Myrick's conclusion that the *Arcadia*, at every point, reveals Sidney's conscious art. Indeed, Hoskyns' minute analysis gives many a clue for re-discovering the charms of Sidney's prose.

Yet Hoskyns, looking with intense admiration upon many of the already fading Arcadian graces, is at the same time an exponent of naturalness, force, clarity, and moderate though not sententious brevity. His admiration is divided between the pronounced courtly formalities of Sidney's style and the greater freedom and simplicity which were to develop in seventeenth-century prose. Like every member of the Arcadian school he admires the full rhythmic effects that we have come to associate with, for example, the richest passages of Ralegh's prose. One of the approved devices for achieving this effect was the figure of exclamation, an example of which Hoskyns quotes in *Direccōns* from his own otherwise unknown development of the theme that 'the truest mortificacōn is the study of cosmographie':

> O! endlesse endeavo[rs], & vain glorious ignorance, dost thou desire to be knowne? where in Europe how canst thou bee famous? When Asia & Africka y[t] haue thrice as many people heare not of thy Accōns, art not thou then thrice as obscure, as thou art renowned? dost thou looke that all the world should take notice of thee, when for five thousand yeares, these three parts of the world took no notice of the fourth, But Europe is the house of fame, because it is the Nurcery of Artes and bookes, wherin reports are p[re]served, O weake Imaginacōn, oh selfe pleasing fancie; căst thou expect in these parts from 40. degrees to 90.[ty] northwards such praises & hono[r] for thy name, when every mapp, or ev[er]ie wall shewes thee as much space from 40. to 90.[ty] southwards inhabited w[th] nothing, but silence & forgetfullnes.

Another example of his prose, simpler but equally forceful, may be seen in his definition of the figure *intimatio*, which Hoskyns says 'leaues the collecōn of greatnes to our vnderstandinge by expressing some part of it, it exceedeth speech in silence, & makes more palpable by a touch then by a direct handling.'

It is by illustrations like these that Hoskyns makes his analysis of figures extraordinarily palatable. At the same time he reveals himself something of a master of the rich sixteenth-century prose, but a master decidedly leaning toward a clear, moderately compressed style.

Hoskyns' remarks on his contemporaries are illuminating and indicate the independence of his judgement. His terse, just analysis of Lyly's euphuistic prose is not without interest. After defining paronomasia as 'a pleasant touch' of the same letter, syllable, or word, he remarks:

> Lilly the Author of *Euphues* seeing the dotage of the tyme vppon this small ornament, invented varieties of it, for he disposed the *Agnominacōns* in as many fashions as repiticons are distinguished by the Authors Rhetorick sometimes the first word & sometymes the myddle harped one vppon another & sometimes the first & last, sometimes in severall sentences, sometimes in one & this with a measure,

Compare a change of contention or contraries & a devise of a similitude, in those dayes made a gallant shewe, But Lilly himselfe hath outliued this style & breakes well from it.

Hoskyns also censures the popular William Warner for his excessive use of the same figure. That Hoskyns was not wrong in his judgement is evident from the following lines from *Albion's England*:

'The restlesse cloudes that mantling ride vpon the racking skie,
The scouring windes that sightlesse in the sounding aire doo flie.
The thriftie earth that bringeth out and broodeth vp her breed,
The shifting Seas whose swelling waues on shrinking shores do feede,' *etc.*[29]

On the whole Hoskyns approves of concluding a statement with a sententious clause. 'For every man,' he says, 'commonly for his paines in reading any historie of other men lookes for some private vse to himselfe like a teller whoe in drawing great somes of other mens money challendgeth somewhat in the pound for his own fee.' Daniel, he says, concludes his poems in this manner 'perpetually.' That Daniel does so occasionally at least is suggested by these lines from *The Complaint of Rosamund*:

'She set vpon me with the smoothest speech
That Court and age could cunningly deuise;
. . . .
Both were enough to circumvent the wise.
A document that well might teach the sage,
That there's no trust in youth, nor hope in age.'[30]

In one of his more discursive moments Hoskyns recalls how in the 'hands of the noble studious Henry Wotton' he came upon Sir Philip Sidney's translation of the first two books of Aristotle's *Rhetoric*.

These various observations, together with his remarks on Bacon, Spenser, Davies, and others, give us the predilections and opinions of an extraordinarily self-conscious student and assiduous craftsman engaged in the practice of the various devices of style so largely responsible for the Arcadian graces. Rather quaintly Hoskyns remarks that since he was first fellow of New College he has outworn six several styles and is still able 'to bear the fashion of writing company.' Although he was a self-conscious stylist, he was a person of great judgement, candour, and erudition who found his most approved guidance in Aristotle's Rhetoric, 'whervnto, whoesoeuer can fitt his speech, shalbe truely eloquent.'

Of the two manuscripts of the *Direccōns* preserved in the British Museum, one, *MS. Harl. 850*, is incomplete, breaking off at folio 7. b after the judgement on Lyly. In the textual notes for this chapter I have indicated its more interesting variants from *MS. Harl. 4604*, from which the present text is derived. The third extant copy is that found in *MS. Ash. Mus. d. 1* in the Bodleian Library, transcribed, as Mr. Bernard M. Wagner has pointed out, not earlier than 1621, since the references to the *Arcadia* have been changed to the pagination of the 1621 reprint. Mr. Wagner has pointed out several interesting variants in the Bodleian copy, and attention is called to others in the notes for this chapter.

In the present text I have tried to give as exact an impression of *MS. Harl. 4604* as is feasible in printed form. The contractions 'l^{tt}re' and 'l^{tt}res' I have expanded to *letter* and *letters* without further comment. As in the letters in Chapter VII, above, the initial *p*, standing for *pro, per, pre*, or *par*, has not been expanded, since, when one is aware of the scribe's practice, even the following forms are not confusing: *compisons* for *comparisons*; *pills* for *perills*; *pte, pt*, and *pts* for *parte, part*, and *parts*; *ptiallity* for *partiallity*; and *pp* for *proper*. To clarify my general procedure a representative folio is reproduced opposite page 126. In the fifth line of that folio may be observed a common device for contraction. There the flourish in the sixth word is transcribed as *er* in raised letters, and that method is followed throughout. The single hyphen is used instead of the double, and all catchwords are omitted. For divisional headings the form that happens to occur on the first page of a given section is used for that division. As in the manuscript, paragraphs are indicated by spacing, except in one instance where the scribe indented as well. Many initial *c*'s are capitals, and I fear that I have been arbitrary in deciding which ones were to remain so. The vowels *a* and *o* are frequently accented in the manuscript, but no effort has been made to indicate that fact in the following text. Hoskyns' marginal references are brought into the text in angular brackets and are placed immediately before the passage to which they refer.

At the conclusion of the notes for Chapter IX are printed a collation of the corresponding passages from *MS. Harl. 4604* and Ben Jonson's *Discoveries,* a collation of that manuscript with *MS. Ash. Mus. d. 1,* and a key to the pagination in Professor Feuillerat's edition of the *Arcadia* of 1590 corresponding to Hoskyns' references to Sidney's romance.

By comparison with Hoskyns' letters, none of the three manuscripts of the *Direccõns* seems to be a holograph, although all three may be in the careful, conventional hand of a single scribe.

THE TEXT

D. M.

Dan: Manwaring's

Booke.

A Domini
MDCXXX

To the forwardnes of many virtuous hopes in
a gent of the Temple by the Author. /

The Conceipts of the minde are pictures of things and the
Tongue is Interp^reter of those pictures; The order of gods
Creatures in themselues is not only admirable & glorious but
eloquent, then hee that could app^rehend the consequence of
things in their truth and vtter his app^rehensions as truly,
were a right Orator, therefore *Cicero* said much when hee
said *Dicere recte nemo Potest nisi qui prudenter intelligit.*

The shame of speaking vnskillfully were small if the tongue
were only disgraced by it, But as the image of the kinge in
a Seale of waxe ill rep^resented, is not soe much a blemish to
the waxe or the signett, that sealeth itt, as to the king whome
it resembleth, Soe disordered speech is not soe much iniury
to the lipps wch giue it forth, or the thoughts wch put it forth,
as to the right pporcõn & Coherence of things in themselues
soe wrongfully expressed, Yet cannot his mynde bee thought
in tune, whose wordes doe iarr, nor his reason in frame
whose sentences are p^reposterous nor his fancie cleare and
pfect, whose vtterance breakes it selfe into fragments, and
vncertaintyes; Were it an honor to a Prince to haue the
maiestie of his Embassage spoyled by a carelesse Embas-
sado^r? And is it not as great an indignity y^t an excellent
Conceipt & Capacitie, by the indilligence of an idle tongue
should be defaced? Carelesse speech doth not onlie discreditt the personage of the speaker, but it doth discreditt
the oppinion of his reason and iudgment it discreditteth the
truth, force, & vniformity of the matter & substance; if it
be soe then in wordes wch fly and escape censure, and where
one good phrase beggs pdon for many incongruities & faults,
howe shall he be thought wise whose penning is thinne &
shallowe? how shall yo^w looke for witt from him, whose
leasure & whose head (assisted wth the examinacõn of his
eyes, could yeald yo^w noe life & sharpnes in his writing; I
never flattered yo^w, and now methinkes I terrify and threaten
yo^w, for yo^w see my oppinion of yo^w, if yo^w should not write
well. nay yo^w were happie if I should thinke soe favo^rably

of yo^w, I knowe how farr yo^w are stept into the iudgment
skill, & practise of a good style, yo^w cannott but make
[f. 2. b] a most shamefull retreat to the ordinarie fashion of
penning; Yf I were not bound to yor fathers loue & yo^{rs}.,
if I sawe not in him most kind pvidence, and in yo^w most
willinge endeavo^{rs} to make somewhat more of yo^w. then one
of my yonge maisters of the Temple, I should thinke it ill
manners to trouble my selfe and yo^w wth a great deal of
Instruccõn, taken out of *Aristotle, Hermogenes, Quintillian,
Demosthenes, Cicero,* and some latter, as *Sturmius* and
Tallaeus, & such honest men, whoe (but for yor sake) had
never renewed their accquaintance wth me nor had not
become Clyents to any student of her Ma^{ts} Lawes; well
what I haue done he that reades will knowe (if he hath
read much) I did it most willingly & I dedicate it to yor
future discrecõn. /

The dearest lover of yor well-doings

Jo: Hoskins. /

For Penninge of Letters

[f. 3. a] <Invencõn> In writing of letters there is to be regarded the *Invencõn* & the fashion, for the invencõn that ariseth vppon yor busines whereof there can be noe rules of more Certainty or precepts of better direccon given yo^w, then Coniecture can lay downe of all the seu^{er}all occasions of all pticuler mens lives & vocacõns. /

But sometimes men make busines of kyndnes, as, I could not satisfye my selfe, till I had discharged my remembrance, and charged my letter wth comendacõns vnto yo^w., my busines is noe other then to certify my Love towards yo^w. & to put yo^w in mynd of my willingnes to doe yo^w all kinde offices, Or, Haue yo^w leisure to discend to the remembrance of that assurance, wch yo^w haue long had in me, and vppon yor next oppertunity to make me happie wth any imployment yo^w shall assigne me, or such like wordes, wch goe a begging for some meaning, & labo^r to be deliu^{er}ed of the great burthen of nothing, when yo^w haue invented (if yor busines be matter, & not beare forme, nor meere Ceremonyes, but some earnestnes) then are yo^w to pceed to the ordering of it, & the disgestion of the pts wch is sought out of Circumstances, One is the vnderstanding of the pson to whome yo^w write, the other is the Coherence of the sentences for mens capacity & delight; yo^w are to weigh what wilbee app^{re}hended first wth great delight & attencõn, what next regarded & longed for especially, And what (last) will leaue most satisfaccon & (as it were) the sweetest memoriall & briefe of all that is past in his vnderstanding whome yo^w write to, The rules of Decency follow after in a Chapter by it selfe; ffor the consequence of the sentences, yo^w must see that euery clause doth (as it were) giue the Q: to the other, and bee (as it were) spoken before it come. / This for Invencõn & order. /

<2 fashion> Nowe for fashion it consisteth in 4 things or quallities of yor style, The first is *Brevity*, for letters must

not be treatises, or discourcings, except it be amonge learned
men & eaven amongst them, there is a kinde of thrift or
saving of words.   Therefore are yoᵂ to examyne the clearest
passages of yoʳ vnderstanding, & through them to convey
yoʳ sweetest & most significant *English* wordes, that yoᵂ can
devise, yᵗ yoᵂ may the easier teach them the readyest way to
another mans conceipt, & to penn it fully, roundly, & distinctly, soe as the reader may not thinke a second viewe cast
away vppon yoʳ letter, But though respect be a pte after this,
yet nowe still must I here remember it, if yoᵂ write to a man
whose estate & sences yoᵂ are famylliar wᵗʰ, Yoᵂ may be the
bolder to sett a a [*sic*] taske to his brayne; yf to yoʳ Superioʳ.
yoᵂ are bound in him to measure .3. further points, yoʳ
interest in him, his Capacitie of yoʳ letters, & his leisure to
pvse them.   ffor yoʳ interest & favoʳ wᵗʰ him, yoᵂ are to be
the shorter, or longer, more familliar or submisse, as hee
[f. 3. b] will afford yoᵂ tyme; for his Capacity, yoᵂ are to
be quicker or fuller of those reaches, & glaunces of witt, or
learning, as hee is able to enterteyne them; ffor his leasure
yoᵂ are comaunded to the greater briefnes, as his place is of
greater discharges and cares; With yoʳ better yoᵂ are not to
put riddles of yoʳ witt, by being too scarce of wordes; nor
to cause the trouble of making *Breviats*, by writing too
plenteously & wastingly; brevity is attayned by the matter in
avoyding idle complemᵗˢ., places, ptestacõns, penthesis,
supfluous & wanton Circuits of figures, & digressions, by
the composicõn omitting coniunctions, not only but alsoe;
both one, & the other; whereby it cometh to passe & such
idle pticularities, that haue noe great busines in a serious
letter. By breaking of Sentences as oftentymes a longe
Journey is made shorter by many baytes, but as *Quintillian*
sayth, there is a briefenes of ptes sometymes that make the
whole longe; as; I came to the staires, I tooke a paire of
Oares; they launched out, rowed apace, I landed at the
Court-gate, I payed my fare went vpp to the Presence, asked
for my lord, I was admytted, all this is but I went to the
Coʳt & spake wᵗʰ my lord, this is the fault of some lattin

writers (wthin this last hundred Yeares) of my reading and phaps *Seneca* may be appeached of it, I accuse him not. /

<Perspicuity> The next good pptie of Epistolarie style is perspicuitie & is often tymes indangered by the former quallity (*Brevity*) oftentimes by affeccõn of some witt ill angled for, or ostentacõn of some hidden termes of art; few wordes they darken the speech, & soe doe too many, as well too much light hurts the eyes as too little, & a longe bill of Chauncery confounds the vnderstanding, as much as the shortest note; Therefore lett not yor letter be pennd like an English statute, This is obteyned, & their vices eschewed by pondering yor busines well, and distinctly conceiving of yor selfe, wch is much furthered by vttering yor thoughts, & letting them as well come forth to light, & iudgm^t. of yor owne outward sences, as to the Censure of other mens eares; That is the reason why many good schollers speake but stumblingly, like a rich man that for want of pticular note & difference can bringe yo^w noe c^{er}taine ware readily out of his shopp, ffor this reason talkatiue shallow men doe often content the hearers more then the wise; But this may finde a speedier [f. 4. a] redresse in writing, where all comes vnder the last exaiacõn of the eyes, first minde it well, then penne it, then examine it, then amend it, & yo^w may bee in the better hope of doing reasonable well.   <Plainnesse> vnder this virtue may come Plaiñess, wch is not to be curious in the order, as to answeare a letter as if yo^w were to answeare Interogatories, to the first, second, &c: But both in method & word to vse (as Ladies vse in their Attyre) a kinde of dilligent negligence, & though wth some men yo^w are not to ieast or practize tricks, yet the deliu^{er}ie of most weighty & important things, may be caryed wth such a grace, as that it may yeald a pleasure to the conceipt of the reader, There must be store, (though not excesse) of Termes, as if yo^w are to name (store) sometimes yo^w may call it Choice, sometymes plentie, sometymes copiousnes, or variety, & soe that the word wch comes in leiw haue not such difference of meaning, as that it may put the sence in hazard to bee mis-

taken. / Yo^w are not to cast a ring for the pfumed Termes
of the tyme, as App^{re}hensivenes Complem^{ts} Spirrit accomõ-
date &c: but vse them pplye in their places, as others;
Thereof followeth liffe wch is the very strength & synnewes
(as it were) of yor penning, made vpp by pithy sayings,
symillitudes, conceipts, Allusions to some knowne history, or
other comõon place, such as are in the *Courtier* & the .2^d.
booke of *Cicero de Oratore*.   <Respect> Last is respect to
discerne what fitts yor selfe: him to whome yo^w write: &
that wch yo^w handle, wch is a quallity fitt to include the rest,
& that must pceed from ripenesse of Judgm^t wch as another
truly sayth is given by 4. meanes, God: Nature:, Dilligence,:
& conversacõn; Serue the first well & the rest will serue
Yo^w. /

For Varyinge.

[f. 5. a] A *Metaphore* or Translacõn is the friendly & neigh-
bo^{r}ly borrowing, of one word to expresse a thing wth more
light & better note: though not soe directly & proplie as the
naturall name of the thinge meant would signifye; As feyned
sights [*sic*] the nearest to fayning; is streching an imytacõn
of truth by Art & endeavo^r.   Therefore Sr Phillip Sydney
would not say vnfeyned sighes, but <341> vntaught
sighes: 341 desirous) nowe desire is a kinde of thirst, &
not much different from thirst is hunger, & therefore for
(swordes) desirous of bloud, hee sayth hungry of bloud,
where yo^w may note .3. degrees of Metaphors in the vnderstanding, first that the fittnes of bloudshed in a weapon
vsurpes the name desirous, wch is pp to a living creature, &
then that it pcedeth to thirst, & then to hunger; The rule
of a Metaphor is that it be not too bold nor too farr fetch't,
& though all Metaphors goe beyond the significacõn of
things, yet are they requisite to match the compasinge
sweetnes of mens myndes that are not content to fix themselues vppon one thinge but they must wander into the
confynes like the eye that cannot chuse but view the whole

knott, when it beholds but one flower in a gardin of purpose, Or like an Archer that knowing his bowe, will ou^{er}cast or cary too short, takes an ayme on this syde or beyond his marke. /

Besydes a *Metaphor* is pleasant because it enricheth o^r knowledge wth two things at once wth the truth and wth simillitude as this, <268> Heads disinherited of their naturall seignioryes, wherby we vnderstand both beheading, & the goverm^t of the head over the body, as the heire hath o^{er} the Lordship wch hee inheriteth, 268 of the same matter in another place <331> to divorce the faire mariage of the head & body, where besides the cutting of the head, we vnderstand the coniunction of head & bodie to resemble mariage 331, The like in concealing loue vttered by these wordes <244> to keep loue close prisoner 244 & in nomber of places in yor booke wch are all noted wth this letter (M:) in the margent; there came alonge the streets a whole ffleet of coaches, for a great nomber. /

[f. 5. b] An *Allegory* is the continuall followinge of a *Metaphor* wch before I defyned to be the translacõn of one word & pþortionable through the sentence, or through many sentences, as *Philoclea* was soe envyroned wth sweet rivers of virtue, as that she could neither bee battered nor vndermyned, where *Philoclea* is exprest by the simillitude of a Castle, her Nature (defence,) by the naturall fortificacõn of a River about a Castle & the metaphore continewes in the tempting her by force or craft exprest by battering & vndermyning; another, But when that wish had once his ensigne in his mynd, then followed whole squadrons of longing that soe it might be a mayne battell of mislikings & repynings against their creacõn, Ensignes, squadrons mayne battell metaphors still deriued from the same thing at first warr, As I said before that a metaphor might be too bold, or too farr fetcht, Soe I nowe remember, that it may be too base; As, ye Tempest of Iudgm^t. had broken the maine mast of his will, a goodly Audience of sheepe, shoulders of friendship &

such like too base; as in that speech Frittor of Fraude, & seething pott of iniquity, & they that say a red herring is a shooeing horne to a pott of ale; But they that speake of a scornefull thinge speake grosely; Therefore to delight gen^{er}ally take those Termes from ingenious & seu^{er}all pfessions from ingenious Acts [*sic*] to please the learned, & from seu^{er}all Arts to please the learned of all sorts, as from the Meteors, Planetts, & Beasts in naturall philosophie from the starrs, spheres, & their mocõns in Astronomie, ffrom the better pte of husbandry, from the politique gou^{er}ment of Citties, from Navigacõn, from millitary pfession, from Phisick, but not out of the depth of these misteries but euer (unlesse yor purpose bee to disgrace) let the word be taken from a thinge of equall or greater dignity, as speaking of virtue, the skye of pfect virtue, euer clouded wth Sorrow, where he thought it vnfitt to stoope to any metaphore lower then heaven; yo^w may assure yor selfe of this observacõn & all ye rest if yo^w but compare those places in yor booke noted wth this note (M) & in truth it is ye best flower growing most plentifully in all *Arcadia.* /

[f. 6. a] An *Embleme*, an *Allegory*, a Simillitude, a fable, & a *Poets* tale, differ thus an Embleme is but the one pte of the Simillitude, the other pte videlicet: the Applicacõn expressed indifferently & ioyntly in one Sentence, wth wordes some pp to the one pte, some to the other; A Simillitude hath 2 sentences of Sev^{er}all pp Termes compared, A fable is a simillitude acted by fiction in beasts, A Poets tale for the most pte by gods & men, In the former example, plant a castle compast wth rivers & let the word bee (*Nec obsidione nec cuniculis*) neither by siedge nor vndermyning, that is an Embleme, the pp termes of the one pte, lay it as it is in Sr *Phillip* S: *Philocleas* virtue, the pper termes of the one pte environed rivers, battered, vndermyned: the termes of the other pte, All these termes in one sentence & it is an Allegorie, Let it be this, there was a lambe in a castle, & an Elephant: & a fox besiedged it, The Elephant would haue assayled the castle, but hee would not swiñe ouer the river, the fox would make a hole in the earth to gett vnder it, but he feared the river would haue suncke in vppon him & drowned him, then it is a fable. Let Spencer tell yo^w such a tale of a ffaery Queene, & *Ovid* of *Diana* & then it is a poets tale, but vtter it thus in one sentence (Even as a Castle compased about wth rivers cannot be battered or vndermyned,) & this in another (*Philoclea* defended round about wth virtuous resolucõns could neither be forced nor surprised by deceipt,) then it is a simillitude in his owne nature, wch is the ground of all Emblemes, Allegories fables and fictions: /

Metanimia is an exchange of a name, when one word comes in lieu of another not for simillitude but for other naturall affinitie & coherence, as when the matter is vsed, for that wch thereof consisteth, as I want silver for money, when the efficient or author is vsed for the thinge made, as my blade is a right *Sebastian*, for of *Sebastians* making; the thing conteyning, for the thinge or pson conteyned, as the cittie met the Queene, for the cittizens, The adiunct, pptie, quallity, or badge for the subiect of it [f. 6. b] as deserts are preferred for men deserving: Giue roome to the coyfe, for the s^ergeant, noe doubt better examples of this sort are in *Arcadia*, if I had leisure to looke soe lowe, as where they are. /

Synechdoche is an exchange of the name of the part for the whole, or of the name of the whole for the part, There are 2. kindes of totall comp^rehencõns, as an entire body, & a gen^erall name, As I my name is tost & censured by many tongues for manye men <1> where the part of an entire bodye goes for ye whole, <2> contrariwise, Hee carryes a Goldsmyths shopp on his fingers, for rings; Hee fell into the water & swallowed the Thames for the water, <3> Soe the gen^erall name for the speciall put vpp yor weapon, for yor dagger, <4> And the speciall for the perticuler, as the Earle is gone into Ireland for, E: E: The pticuler for the speciall, as I would willingly make yo^w a Sr *Phillip Sidney* for an

The eares of men are not onlie delighted wth store & choyse of diverse wordes, but feele great delight in repetition of ye same wch because it begynneth in the middle, & in the end, & in sundry sortes spendinge & care of their place, out to another, it happeneth, therefore, it hath purchered severall names of figures: as a repetition of the same word, or some immediatly or wthout interposition of any other is called *Epizeixis*. Flie not, fly not from yu hee powred upon me distresse. Tormented, tormented, torment of my soule *Philoclea*, tormented. This figure is not to be usd but in passion.

Anadiplosis is a repetition in the end of the former sentence & beginning of the next, as shall Erona dye? Erona dye? Braue men: And *Cecropias* diserciuall: pouring spite? You shore least yu should offend because shee doth grieve and doest by any tooth, & could laugh, say why liued I? alas! alas! wth liued I? to dye: wisheged & to be the example of the heavens hate, & hate & spare not, for the worst that is is pardon. And as not *India* is sicke in it self upon out tonge: but for some what more or distresse. For in spring after it nor repetition wthout important.

Climax is a kind of *Anadiplosis* leadinge by degrees and makinge the last word a step to the further meaninge, if it be turned to an Argument it is a *Sorites*, a singe made of great beautie, beautified wth great force, forced by great vallo: for yu could not enioy ye goodnes wthout gouernmt nor gouernmt wthout a magistrate, nor magistrate wthout obedience, & not obedience where every one upon his priuate passion doth interpret the doings of the duste. Now to make it a *Sorites* or stynning Argument, ioyne ye first & the last wt an Egg: so, Egg yt raine it enioy ye owne good where every man upon his priuate passion doth &c &c: thus in vtround spending too Arede heirtall: but in discourse most visible & plausible, seeing so like, likinge to soue: for use &c. *Item* 21. 4. Iorealde not, after discourse, abused mens affections forsaken men, what doth become wisemen better then to discerne what is worthy the louinge, what is most agreeable to goodnes, then to loue it soe discerned, & what to greatnes of heart, then to be constant in it out louied. The like so a where the last word or some out word in ye last sentence begytte the next clause. This signet usde in times when yu are well entred into discourse & haue yu mind vpon matter meant to rise & amplifie.

eloquent learned valliant gent., <6> One for many as the Spaniard they say comes against vs, for the Spaniards & such like, wch because they are easy, I haue exemplyfied familliarly, both these figures serue well, when yo^w haue mencōed a thing before for variety in repeticōn, & yo^w may well obserue better instances in yor reading then my interrupted thought can nowe meet w^th.

Catachresis (in English *Abuse*) is nowe growne in fashion (as most abuses are,) It is somewhat more desperate then a *Metaphore*, it is the expressing of one matter by the name of another, wch is incompatible wth it, & sometimes cleane contrary as I gaue order to some servaunts of myne, (whome I thought as apt for such charities as my selfe) to lead him out into the forrest & there to kill him; where charitie is vsed for crueltie, but this may alsoe be by the figure *Ironia*, And the abuse of a word drawne from thinges farr different, as <51. a> A voice beautifull to his ears, <67. b> Accusing in himselfe noe great trouble in mynd, by his behaviour or Action; <920. a> doe yo^w grudge me pte of yor sorrowe, being sister in nature, I would I were not soe farr of a kynne in fortune, this is a vsuall figure wth the fine conv^ersants of o^r tyme, when they strayne for an extraordinary phraze, as I am not guilty of those phrases, I am in danger of preferm^t. I haue hardly escaped good fortune, he threatens me a good turne all by the contrary, and as he sayd that misliked a picture wth a crooked nose, affirminge the elbowe of his nose to bee disproportionable: /

[f. 7. a]   <Epizeuxis> The eares of men are not onlie delighted wth store & exchange of divers words, but feele greate delight in repeticōn of the same wch because it beginneth in the myddle, & in the end, & in Sundry Correspondencies of each of their places, one to another, it happneth, therefore, it hath purchased seu^erall names of figures as a repeticōn of the same word, or sound imediatly or w^thout interposicōn of any other is called *Epizeuxis*, <178. a> O let not, Let not from yo^w bee powred vppon

me distruccõn, <342. b> Tormented? Tormented? torment
of my soule *Philoclea* tormented? This figure is not to be
vsed but in passion. /

Anadiplosis is a repeticõn in the end of the former sentence
& beginning of the next, as, <136. b> shall Erona dye?
Erona dye? o heaven &c: And *Cecropias* Rhetoricall seduc-
ing speech, < 313. b> Yo^w feare least yo^w should offend
because shee doth denie, denye? nowe by my troth I could
laugh &c: <336. a> why lived I alas? alas wch loved I!
to dye wretched, & to be the example of the heavens hate,
& hate & spare not, for the worst blowe is stricken. / And
as noe man is sicke in thought vppon one thinge, but for
some vehemency or distresse, Soe in speech there is noe
repeticõn w^{th}out importance: /

Climax is a kinde of *Anadiplosis* leadinge by degrees and
makinge the last word a stepp to the further meaninge, if it
be turned to an Argum^t it is a *Sorites*; <349> a yonge
man of great beautie, beautified wth. great hono^r. honored
by great vallo^r. &c: <259> yo^w could not inioy yor goodnes
w^{th}out gou^{er}ment, nor gouerment w^{th}out a magistrate, nor
magistrate w^{th}out obedience, & noe obedience where every
one vppon his private passion doth interpret the doeings of
the Rulers, Nowe to make it a *Sorites* or Clyming Argument, ioyne the first & the last wth an *Ergo*, as *Ergo* yo^w
cannot enioy yor owne goods where euery man vppon his
private passion doth &c: this in pennd speech is too
Accademicall, but in discource more passible & plausible,
<230. a> seeing to like, likinge to loue, lovinge &c: *Idem*
21. 45. Deceaved me, after deceipt, abused mee, after abuse
forsaken mee, what doth become wisdome better then to
discerne what is worthy the lovinge, what is more agreeable
to goodnes, then to loue it soe discerned, & what to greatnes
of heart, then to be constant in it once loued. <150. a>
The like 150. a. where the last word or some one word in
the last sentence begetts the next Clause, This figure hath
his tyme, when yo^w are well entred into discource, & haue
pcured attencõn & meane to rise & amplifie. /

[f. 7. b] *Anaphora* is when many clauses haue the like beginning <178. a> whome virtue hath made the Prince of felicitie, be not the minister of ruyne, yo^w whome my choice hath made the gods of my safetie, yo^w that nature hath made the loadstarr of comfort, bee not the rocke of shipwracke, this figure beates vppon one thinge to cause the quicker feeling in the audience, & to awake a sleepie or dull pson. /

Epistrophe is contrarie to the former, when many clauses end wth the same words, <263. b> where the richnes did invite the eyes, the fashion did entertaine the eyes, & the devise did teach the eyes, <337. a> And all the night hee did nothing but weepe *Philoclea,* sigh *Philoclea,* & cry out *Philoclea* &c: 45. either arme their liues or take away their liues 356a. this figure is rather of narracõn, or instruccõn then of mocõn.

Symploce or *Complexio* is when seu^erall sentences haue the same beginning & the same ending, <119. a> The most covetous man longs not to get riches out of a ground wch can beare nothing, whye? because it is impossible. The most Ambitious weight vexeth not his witts to clyme into heaven, why? because it is impossible, this is the wantonest of repeticõns, & is not to bee vsed in matters too serious, yo^w haue an example of it in fustian speech about Tobacco in derision of vayne Rhetoricke. /

Epanalepsis is the same in one sentence w^ch *Symploce* or Complexio, is in seu^erall sentences, as severe to his Servants; to his children severe, or the same sound reitterated first & last in a sentence, as his Superio^r in meate, in place his Inferiour, In sorrowe I was borne, & must dye in Sorrowe, vnkyndnes moued mee, & what can soe trouble my courses or wracke my thoughts as vnkyndnes, This a mylde & sweet figure of much vse though single & by it selfe, not vsuall in the *Arcadia,* & therefore vnnoted but .359. b. <359. b> ouerthrowe of my desires, recompence of my overthrowe. /

Epanados is when the midst & the end, or the midst & the
the [*sic*] beginning are the same, as if there were any true
pleasure in Sleepe and Idlenes, then noe doubt the heathen
Philosophers would haue placed some pte of the felicity of
their heathen gods, in sleepe & idlenes, yor dilligence to
speake well must be great, but yo^w shalbe abundantly recom-
penced for the greatnes in the Successe (pswasion) if I euer
wish for the perfeccõn of [f. 8. a] eloquence, it is for yor
Instruccõn, & for yor benifitt, I would wish I were eloquent,
this kinde of repeticõn & the former *Epanalepsis* are most
easily admitted into discourse, & are freest from the oppinion
of affectacõn, because wordes received at the begining of
many sentences or at both ends of the same are more
notorious. /

Antimetabole or *Commutatio*, is a sentence invers'd or turned
backe, as <286. a> if any for loue of hon^r. or hon.^r of
loue <261. b> that as yo^w are child to a mother, soe yo^w
may bee mother to a child; <323. b> They misliked what
themselues did, & yet did still what themselues misliked,
<322. b> if 'before he languished because he could not
obtaine his desire, he nowe lamented because he could not
desire the obtayning, either not striving because he was contented, or contented because he would not striue, <294>
Just to execercise [*sic*] his might mightie to pforme his
Justice; Our learned knight skipt often into this figure, as
2. a. & b. at the very begining 116. a. & b. 137. 219. a. 205:
yet he conceived the pticularity of his affeccõn by this, sometimes by not turning the words wholly backe as they laye. /
<218> To account it not a purse for Treasure; but as a
Treasure it selfe worthy to be pursed vpp &c: <9> men
venter liues to conquer, to conquerrers liues wthout ventur-
ing, shewed such furie in his force, such stay in his furie,
wch is rather *Epanados*.   Sometimes the same sence must be
in contrarie wordes, as <20. b> *Parthenia* desired aboue all
things to haue *Argalus*, *Argalus* feared nothinge but to miss
Parthenia, where feare to misse, is put in stead of desire to
haue, <37. a> neither could yo^w haue thought soe well of

me if extremity of loue had not made yor iudgment ptiall,
nor yo^w could haue loved me soe intirely if yo^w had not bin
apt to make soe great vndeserved Iudgm^t of me, where he
returnes, (for extremity of Loue,) loving intirely, & (for
ptiall Iudgm^t.) great vndeserved Iudgm^t. /

And notwthstanding that this is a sharpe & wittie figure &
shewes out of the same wordes a pithy distinction of meaning, very convenient for schoolemen, yet M^r. P. did wrong
to tyer this poore figure, by vsing it 30 tymes in one Sermon,
ffor vse this or any other point vnseasonably, it is as ridiculous as it was in the fustian oration, horse mill, mill-horse
&c: but let Discrecõn bee the greatest & generall figure of
figures. /

[f. 8. b] *Paranomasia* is a pleasant touch of the same letter
Sillable, or word, wyth a different meaning, as for the ruñing
vppon the word (more) this very little is more then too much
Sr *Phillip Sidney* in *Astrophell* & *Stella* calls the *Dictionary*
method, & the verses soe made rymes running in ratling
rowes, wch is an example of it. There is a swynish poem
made thereof in Lattin called *Pugna Porcorũ*, & L Lloid in
his youth tickled in fashion of a *Poets Dictionary*. /

> *Hector, Hamo, Hannibal*, dead *Pompey, Pirhus* spild
> *Cirus, Sipio, Caesar*, slayne & *Allexander kild*

The *Author* of *Albions England* hath set forth good invencõn
too often in this attire, in those dayes Lilly the Author of
Eupheus, seeing the dotage of the tyme vppon this small
ornament, invented varieties of it, for he disposed the
Agnominacõns in as many fashions as repiticõns are distinguished by the Authors *Rhetorick* sometimes the first word
& the myddle harped one vppon another, sometymes the first
& last, sometimes in severall sentences, sometimes in one &
this wth a measure, Compare a change of contention or
contraries & a devise of a simillitude, in those dayes made a
gallant shewe, But Lilly himselfe hath outliued this style &
breakes well from it. /

An agnominacõn of some sillables is sometimes found in *Arcadia*, as <199. b> Alas, what can saying make them belieue whome seeing cannot pswade? <271. a> And whist [*sic*] hee was followed by the valiantest hee made away for the vilest, <284. b> whoe went away repyning, but not repenting, his mynd, her merritt, loving, living, not only Lilly, whose *Poesie* at the begining of his booke, was stampt wth cognizance, Commend it or Amend it, but euen wth Doctor Mathew this figure was of great Accompt, & he lost noe estimacõn by it, our Paradice is a paire of dice, or almes deeds are turned into all-misdeeds, our praying into playing, o[r] fasting into feasting, but that kinde of breakinge wordes into another meaning is prettie to play wth amonge gentle-women, as yo[w] will haue but a bare gaine, of this bargaine, otherwise it will be best become the tuff taffata Orato[r.s] to skipp vpp & downe the neighbourhood of these wordes, that differ more in sence, then in sound, tending neerer to meeter, then to matter, in whose mouth [f. 9. a] longe may that phraze psper, A man not onlie fitt for the gowne, but for the gunne, for the penne but for the pike, for the booke but for the blade, See to what p[re]ferm[t]. a figure may aspire, if it once get in credit in a world that hath not much true *Rhetorick*. That was the cause that S[r] *Phillip Sidney* would not haue his stile be much beholding to this kinde of garnish, And of a truth if the Tymes giues itselfe too much to any one florish, it makes it a toy & barrs a learned mans writ-ings from it, least it seeme to come more of the gen[er]all humor then the private Judgment. /

Polliptoton or *Traductio* is a repeticõn of wordes of the same lynage, that differ only in Terminacõn as <332> exceedingly exceeding that exceedingnes, <183. b> by this faultie vsing of o[r] faults; sometime the same word in seu[er]all cases, as <266> for feare hide his feare sometime the same verbe in seu[er]all voices, as <268>forsaken by all friends and forsaking all comfort; Sometymes the same adiectiue in seu[er]all comparisons, <54. b> much may bee saide in my

defence, much more for Loue, & most of all for that divine
creature wch hath ioyned me & Loue togeather. /

This is a good figure, & may be vsed wth or wthout passion,
but soe as the vse of it come from some Choice & not from
Barrennesse. /

To Amplifye

[f. 10. a] To *Amplifye* and *Illustrate*, are two the chiefest
ornam^{ts}. of eloquence; & gaine of mens myndes two the
chiefest advantages admyracon & beliefe, for how can yo^w
comend a thing more acceptably to o^r attencõn, then by
tellinge vs it is extraordynary, and by shewing vs that it is
evident, There is noe lookinge at a Comett if it be eyther
little or obscure, & wee loue & looke on the sun aboue all
starrs for these 2 excellencyes, his greatnes, his cleerenes,
Such in speech is Amplificacõn & Illustracõn./

Wee amplifye .5. wayes, by *Comparison, Division, Accumil-
lation, Intimacon,* & *Progression.* /

<Equall> *Comparison* is either of things contrary, equall,
or things different, Equall, as Themistocles & Coriolane,
both great statesmen, both of great Deserts to their countryes
both bannished, both dead at one Tyme, Themistocles his
councell could not prevaile against the Ingratitude of the
Athenians, nor Coriolanus discrecõn ouercome the vnkindnes
of the *Romans,* The one was to excellent the other too
noble for the envious of their countrymen to endure, Such
is the force of virtue (aboue all quarrells of nacõns &
divisions of Allegiances, that their exiles were ho.^{blye} enter-
teyned Coriolanus by the *Volsci,* Themistocles by the *Per-
sians,* both by their enemyes, and both leading great Armies
against those countries wch soe ingratfullie expelled them,
were soe inwardly restrayned wth a conscience of sackinge
their natiue soyle, That they chose rather to offer violence
to their owne lives, then to the liues of their fellow cittizens,

And tooke it for a sufficient revenge, to showe that it was euident they might haue bin revenged. /

But this not soe forcible an Amplification of things equall indeed, wherein (as yo^w see) there are to be searched out all the seu^erall points, of a consorted æquallity, as when things seeming vnequall are compared, & that in simillitudes as well as examples, as in my speech of a widdowe, compared to a shipp, both aske much tackling & sometimes rigging, & yo^w shall most of all pfitt by inventing matter of agreem^t. in things most vnlike, as London, and a Tenis Court, for in both all the gaine goes to the hazard, *Pollicie* is like the Sea, it serues for intercourse of proffitts, for defence ag^t invasions, [f. 10. b] There are both Ebbings and flowings, calmes & Tempests, the observacõn whereof may make a man first wise, then rich, But as the water serues for many outward vses, soe can it not please inwardly swallowed, if yo^w saile vppon it it will carry yo^w whither yo^w will desire, but if yo^w drinke it, it doth not satisfy but increase a desire, Againe for examples, *Eriphile* and *Tarpeia* both women in whome nature should gou^erne loue, & loue warrant fidellity, were both easily seduced to be false wth trifling temptacõns, they both betrayed not one friend to another, nor the dearenes of loue, for the highnes of p^referm^t. but their most assured louers to their most deadly enemyes, for toyes, Jewells & for braceletts. *Eriphile* her husband *Amphiorames*, (the stay of her life) to *Adrastus* his professed foe; *Tarpeia*, the capitoll (the stay of her country) to the Sabines that besiedged it, yet neither can remaine vnto posteritie, as an inticement, (much lesse as an incouragm^t.,) to treason. ffor *Eriphile* was slaine by her sonne, whome nature should haue bound to her defence, & *Tarpeia* by the *Sabines,* whome her deserts should haue wonne to her safeguard. /

In comparing two, when yo^w should praise the pson or thing whome yo^w intend to make excellent, yo^w must take the meanest pte of greater examples, & match them wth the best of yor purpose, & by such ptiallity, yo^w shall grace & extoll yor subiect wch yo^w handle, as *Isocrates* doth in his comparisons of *Cirus* & *Thuagoras*, otherwise for vnptiall compisons, wch not wthstanding doe amplifie, read the matches & incounters of the most famous Grecian & Roman examples in *Plutarch*. /

<Different> Comparisons of thinges different in ye form^{er} compisons is a composicon, of the history on both sydes, to be fauorable vnto yo^w by reading, but if I were to marshall histories wherof both, or either, were not sufficiently knowne, then had I need to begin wth single relacons, As if a man would compare *Vastus Gama* wth S^r ffrauncis Drake, hee might say S^r ffrauncis Drake indeed travailled round about the world in 2 yeares, sawe divers nacōns, indured many pills att sea, & retourned laden wth great treasure, and *Vastus Gama* first searched the coast of *Quilon*, *Moramba*, and *Calicut*, & opened a passage to the east [f. 11. a] Indias, But it was easie for Drake to pceed further in discoveries, when hee had an entrance made by *Columbus*, Soe was it most dangerous & difficult for *Gama* to adventure a course wthout example & direccōn Drake scoured the coast wth a sufficient companie of ships, made pillage of others & therby furnished his owne enterprises, *Gama* went but weake at the first, lost most of his small fleet, & mett nothing at sea, but Tempests & famyne, Drake invaded vppon oppertunities hazarded but his owne fortune, & retyred to sea vppon all advauntage, *Gama* had in charge an expedicōn of his Sou^{er}-aignes comaundem^t., was constrayned to victuall himselfe amongst barbarous nacōns, & not only to buy pvision in their continent, land wth the price of his bloud, but durst not dept wthout leaving his king pclaymed & possessed in their Terri-tories, divers places of strength established to his vse, Soe that if *Gama* had bin to pvse the example of Drake, as Drak had the light of *Columbus*, & *Magellus* travayles, *Vastus Gama's* spirrit was as likely to haue conquered the whole world, as Drakes fortune was to compasse it. /

And where yor ptes of collacōn are more obscure, then yor *Narration* must be the longer, as *Cicero* in comparing *Mar-cellus* & *Verres* makes a longe recitall of the acts of *Marcellus* to acquaint the hearers wth them before comparison, in some cases after good confidence of proofe yor examples may come in more quicke, hott, & plentifully as, if to ptract battaile vppon advise bee Cowardice, then *Phocion*, then *Metellus*, then *ffabius*, then all the valliantest captaines of all ages were Cowardes; if to displant the rebellious natiues of Ireland, & to roote them out of the Iland be cruelty, then colonies translated into ffraunce, into Scicily, into seuerall coasts of Itally & divers other places by the Romans testify great cruelty. /

But nowe in comparison of things different [it] is most comendable, where there seemes to be great affinity in the matter conferr'd, as in the Kinge of Spaines assistinge ye Irish, the Queene of Englands ayding the *Netherlands*. ye Spaniard, prepared helpes for a people vntrue in their treatises, vncivill in their manners, for them wch haue trayterously rebelled w^thout pvocation, & fled out contrary to their owne submission, breake their owne peace, & wasted their owne country; The Queene did but lend some few voluntaries to ye ptection of a nacõn, peaceable in their liues, free by their priviledges, a people denying noe clayme of any true prince except ppetuall servitude of their bodies & insupportable exactions in their goods. /

[f. 11. b] Another example of thinges different compared The mariages of heads of houses & colledges, is not as lawfull as the mariage of the *Doctors* of the *Arches*, or Clarkes of the Chauncery, both were interdicted by the same lawe, & yet I take it not indifferent that both should (by the abbrogacõn of the same lawe) be equally repeald, The one hath his living casuall by his temporall paines, the other his maintenance certaine by Ecclesiasticall pvision, the one may purchase by his annuall revenewe, and soe may raise a patrymonie lawfully to mainteyne his posterity, the other can by noe thrift vppon these common goods gather a living for wife & children w^thout imbeselling from the poore, deducting from hospitality, defrauding the intent of the giuer or defrauding his successo^rs. lastly the one hath all to the vse

of his office, the other is owner of nothinge but to his owne
behoofe & disposicõn. /

In these two sorts of Amplyfying, yo^w may insert all figures
as the passion of the matter, shall serue & for the pper season
& state of each figure, looke in the end of their pticuler
Treatises. /

<Contrayes> *Comparison* of contraries is the third (&
most florishing) way of comparison, Contraries are sometymes arranged togeither by payres one to one, as compare
the ones impatience to the others myldnes, the ones impeni-
tency wth the others submission, the ones humillity wth the
others indignacon, & tell me whether hee that conquered,
seemed not rather confounded, That hee wch yielded vnto
him, not any thing discouraged   Compare not mynd w^th
mynd, least it seeme fantasticall, & beyond the tryall of o^r
senses, but sett the ones tryumph against the others captivitie,
losse against victorie, feasts against wounds, a crowne ag^t
fetters, misfortune ag^t. felicity, & the maiesty of courage
wilbe found in the ou^erthrowe, more examples of this yo^w
haue in the figure Contentio, wch is one of the instrum^ts. to
aggravate by way of comparison, Yet one example more hee
that preffers wealthy Ignorance before chargeable study
p^referrs contempt before hono^r, darkenes before light, death
before life & earth before heaven, thus are contraries
arranged one waye. /

[f. 12. a] There is another way of ordering them wth inter-
changeable correspondencies in sentences, that though each
touch not the other, yet each affronts th' other, as, shall a
soldier for a blowe wth his hand given in warr to a captaine
bee disgraced, & shall a lawyer for the bastinadoe given in
a hall of court to his companion be advanced? we that pfesse
lawes maintaine outrage? & they that breake all lawes, yet
in this obserue civillity? where yo^w may obserue euery word
in the latter sentence aggrauated by oposicõn to eu^erie word
in the former.   Another, did the most innocent, vouchsafe
it as a pte of his glory to pray for his enemyes, and shall we

the most sinfull esteeme it a blott to our reputacõn to be vnrevenged on oᵉ brethren, of this yoᵘ shall haue more examples in the consorts of figures, especially where *Compar* & Contentio meet, but vnless it be for declamatorie exercise, yoʷ are to avoide too great swelling wᵗʰout substance in the figure *Compar*: yoʷ shall haue examples of this out of *Arcadia*: /

<Division> Division the second way of amplyficacõn, wᶜʰ *Bacon* in his first colonie tooke out of the *Rhetoritians*, a way to amplify anything (quoth he) is to breake it & make an *Anattomie* of it into seuᵉʳall pts, & to examine it, according to seuᵉʳall circumstances, he said true, it is like the shewe wᶜʰ Pedlers make of their Packes. when they display them contrary to the German magnificence, that serues in all the good meate in one dish, But whereas he sayes, that this Art of amplifying will betray it selfe in method & order, I thinke that it rather adorneth it selfe, for instead of sayinge he put the whole Towne to the sword, let men reckon all ages & sortes, & say, he neither saved the yonge men, as pittyinge the vnripe flower of theyr youth; nor the aged men as respectinge their gravity, nor children as pdoning their weaknes, nor women as having compassion vppon their sex, Soldier, Clergy-man, Citizen, armed or vnarmed, resisting or submittinge all wᵗʰin the Towne, destroyed wᵗʰ the fury of yᵗ bloody execution. /

Note that yoᵉ. divisions here are taken from, age, profession Sex, habitt, or behaviour, & soe may be from all circumstances this only tricke made vpp J: Ds poeme of dauncing, All daunceth, yᵉ heavens, yᵉ elemᵗˢ., mens myndes, comõnwealths, & soe by pts all daunceth, Another example varied, he appelleth himselfe wᵗʰ great discrecõn thus amplified by circumstances for yᵉ stuffe, his clothes were more rich then glittering, as for fashion, rather vsuall for his sorte then fantasticall for his invencõn, for coullor more graue and [f. 12. b] vniforme, then wylde, & light, for fittnes, made as well for ease of exercise as to set forth to the eye those pᵗˢ

wch in him had most excellency; Soe to say hee would take
any occasion of discource wth a gentlewoman, first, wth yonge
witty ladyes, from their behavio^r, if she said nothing, he
would pretily quarrell wth her silence if she smyled, he would
gather out of it some interp^{re}tacõn of her praise & favo^r, &
of his owne ioy & good fortune, if she frowned hee would
both moue her to mirth, & denie that she would be angrie in
earnest; if she were scornefull he would conforme his speech
& action in that sobernes to her humo^r, as might beguile her
passion by way of false confederacy: if she walk't or playd
the secret praise her face, her eyes, her haire, her voice, her
bodie, her handes, her gate, wth the applicacõn of other conceipts, what euer gaue the ground of them, yet wth such
dissembled Arte, as if forgetfullnes or Loue alluded in them,
not cunninge, or want of varietye. /

Soe yo^w may devide by the formes of speech in gen^{er}all, as
hee was never to seeke howe to ppose, or invert, to raise, or
maintaine, reconcile, or distinguish an argum^t., histories,
simillitudes, pverbs, iests, attended him in greater plenty then
he needed to imploy; he could offer weightie reasons cleerly;
& choyce wordes smoothly & vnaffectedly, he vsed a sporting
wisdome & eloquent pratlinge, but wth matrons & ladies of
better respect, & less curiosity, his dutie, their kindnes, their
comõn acquaintance, the occasion of his coming, the remembrance of his last conferrence, the place, the tyme, the last
newes of fforreigne lands, the court, the countrie, the cittie,
fed his Invencõn, satisfyed their eares, all this is but division
of the persons, wth whome yo^w meete, their manners cariage,
the fashions, & ornam^{ts}, the matter & subiect of discourse,
this in some sorte vsed, is more pplie called dilacõn then
Amplification, & being often practised will enable yo^w to
discourse almost of anything wherein yo^w are not p^{re}cisely
tyed to the exact manner of division, wth [f. 13. a] vse, but
yo^w haue libertie of seeking all thinges, compased wthin the
sence of yor gen^{er}all Theme, differ they essentially or in any
notable pptie, but yo^w may alsoe if yo^w please run ouer the
intire pte of comparison as, the shipp was blowen vpp, (ffor

the shipp,) yo^w may say the mast, sayles, tackling, keele,
Prowe, sterne, (for blowen vpp) rent, torne, smothered,
scattered in the ayre, sunck vnder water, and all the circumstances of blowing vpp, Soe in sayinge a faire tree, yo^w may
devide it into the rootes, bodye, branches, & fruite, & fairenes,
into tallnes, straightnes, fresh coullo^r. & such thinges, as are
faire in a tree, in discribing a valliant man, yo^w may talke of
his mynd, body, his attempting, psecuting, finishing of an
enterprise. / but therof more in the art of invencõn, only
note this that this amplificacõn hath in it more credibillitie &
instruccõn, for it makes instances of that wch being generallie
spoken would seeme, but a florish & giues more especiall
note, of that wch vniu^ersally could not be conceipted w^thout
confusion & dullnes; This kinde of *Amplificacõn* is more
taken vpp by *Cicero* then *Demosthenes*, for *Demosthenes*
never vseth it, but it followes his way. /

<Accumilacõn>   The third   kinde   of   *Amplificacõn*   is
Accumilacõn wch is heaping vpp of many termes of praise
or accusing, importing but the same matter w^thout discend-
ing to any pte, & hath his due season after some Argument
or proofe, otherwise it is like a schoolmaister foaming out
<Synonyma*> Sinonymies* or wordes of one meaning, &
will sooner yeald a coniecture of supfluity of wordes, then
of sufficiency of matter, But let us giue some example to
amplyfye a sedition, Tumults, mutinyes, vprores, despate
conspiracies, wicked confederacies, furious comõtions traiterous rebellions, associations in villanye, distraccõns from
allegiance, bloody garboyles, & intestine massacres of the
cittizens, but this example is somewhat too swelling, nowe
to talke of one (wth mild lookes) yo^w may say he hath a
sweet countenance a most pleasant eye, a most amiable presence [f. 13. b] a cheerfull aspect, he is a most delectable
obiect &c: Yo^w will be well stored for this purpose, when yo^w
haue made vpp yor Synonyma booke after my direction, the
tast of former tymes hath termed it sweet to bring in 3
clauses togeather, of the same sence, as yor beautie (Sweet
Ladie) hath conquered my reason, subdued my witt, &

maistered my Judgment, howe this will hold amongst o^r curious Successo^{rs}. in their tyme I knowe not He that lookes on the wearinge of it will finde it bare, howe full (of stuffe) soeuer it appeareth for it passeth for parts of a division, when indeed it is but variacõn of an English, yet not wthstanding the practise of it will bringe yo^w to aboundance of phrases wthout wch yo^w shall never haue choice (the mother of pfeccõn) *Cicero* (in his *oracons*) vseth it oft. Some others follow it to foure clauses but he seldome exceedeth three; But it hath this certaine effect, that it will sufficiently testifye yor vayne not to be drye & spent. /

And to retourne to our first sort of Accumilacõns, & fetch it wth this vnder one precept, I take the vse of this amplificacõn to bee in Anger, detestacõn, cõmisseracõn & such passions as yo^w seeming throughly possest wth would willingly stirr in others.

The 4th. way of *Amplifying* is by *Intimation* that leaues the colleccõn of greatnes to our vnderstandinge, by expressing some marke of it, it exceedeth speech in silence, & makes our meaning more palpable by a touch, then by a direct handling, as he that should say (yo^w must liue many yeares in his companie, whome yo^w shall accompt for yor friend) sayth well, but he that saith yo^w had need eate a bushell of sault wth him, saith more, & giues yo^w to reckon more then many yeares. /

[f. 14. a]   It savoures somtymes of *Hiperbole*, that a man is growne grosse, he is growne from a bodie to a corporacõn againe for a little man on horsebacke (as the tale is) that he was mistaken for a hat ridinge on the pomell of a saddle, of this sort yo^w haue examples in yor *Paragnomies*, soe honest a wrangler, that his nose beinge betwixt, was the onlie cause his two eyes went not to lawe, &c: for the highnes of a gyant is expres'd by saying his skull held halfe a bushell of wheate; this may be done wth *Ironia*, or deniall he was noe notorious malefactor, but hee had bin twice on the pillorie & once burnt in the hand for tryfling ov^{er}sights; soe

by the ambiguitie of the word, hee drawes his sword oftener
then hee drawes his purse, this fashion of *Amplificacõn* I
terme *Intimacon,* because it doth not directly Aggrauate but
by consequence & pporcõn, & intimateth more to yor mynd
then to yor eares. /

<Progressio> *Progression* is the last kinde of amplificacõn
wch by stepps of comparison stores euerie degree, till it come
to the topp, & make the matter seeme the higher advaunced,
sometimes descends the lower; it is a bad grace in dancing
either to shrinke much in, or sincke farr downe, that yo[w]
may rise the higher caper, But it is an ornam[t]. in speech, to
begin att the lowest that yo[w] the better aspire to the height
of amplyficacõn; for example in reprehendinge the pdigallity
of monuments in the speech of .D.H. I beginn wth the
excesse of *Alphonsus* on his fathers funerall, Thence to
Allexanders pfusion on his friends Tombe, Then to *Vrbinus*
towards his servant, thence to Caesar on his horses buriall,
after that to the *Mollosians* on their doggs, thence to the
Ægiptians that charge themselues wth the sumptuous Buryall
of a Crocodile, Soe seeminge in some sort to admitt the first
but lesse, the second, & soe growing weaker in the excuse of
euery one, as I pceed the last will seeme most ridiculous if
not odious, Soe *Cicero* against *Verres,* meaning to amplifie
his briberie & extorcõns, It is a rigorous accõn (quoth hee)
not to absolue the Innocent w[th]out money; [f. 14. b] great
crueltie to comitt him till hee ransome himselfe, but not to
suffer the parents to come vnto him w[th]out a reward is
lamentable coueteousnes to sell the egresse & regresse of
them that bringe him victualls, nay to take money that hee
shall haue but an easie death, to put a price on the stockes
that shall execute him, soe much that hee shalbe beheaded
at one blowe. /   Soe much that at two, this is beyond devise
of most barborous & intollerable extorcõn, Soe in another
example, hee was carelesse of welldoeing, a loosenes of
youth, hee was inclyned to ill, a weakenes of fflesh, his minde
consented to offend, a shrewd temptacõn, he comitted the
act, an vnhappie fall, hee accustomed himselfe to the abuse,

a lamentable ouerthrowe, but hee did not only this, but infect others wth his pswasions & seduced them by his example not that onlie, but held in those (whome hee had caryed away) wth fresh invencõn; & disgraced the modestie of them who risisted his corrupcõn, and scornes their admonitions, wch would argue noe lesse in him then a most reprobate & damnable resolucõn. /

The rule of this is when yo^w would praise or dispraise anything to consider howe many lesse things there are of that kinde, to wch notw^thstanding yo^w would giue shew of importance; as he that could make sleepe haynous may shewe that Idlenes wch is lesse (by *Dracoes* lawes) was a fellonie, or to giue that Bisp. his right, that built 2 absolute colledges att his owne charges; & endowed them wth landes; looke downewards howe rare it is in these dayes, for a Prelate not to graunt longe leases, diminish the revenues of his fee [*sic*], howe laudable it is but to repaire the Ruynes of his owne decayed Pallaces & Churches, how magnificent a thinge it is thought for a Noble-man to build an hospitall, howe royall for .2. or .3 Princes to erect one colledge, & can there bee such vnthankfullnes as to beare but one ordynary remembrance of him that [f. 15. a] enriched his Bishopwricke, built 2 of the most famous Nurseries of Learning in the land, was liberall to all wants in his life, & left worthie bequests to all degrees at his death, In like sort in this example to abuse the name of god, to make table talke of a meane man's name wronge, to run vpon a noblemans tytle were a great scandall, to play wth a Princes name were a treason, & what shall it bee to make a vanitie of that name, wch is most terrible even to tirants & divells, & most reu^erende euen to Monarchs and Angells. /

There be 2 contrarie ascents to the topp of this forme either by extenuating the meanes, as in the former example of D: H, or by aggravating them, as by this last of swearing, and may not a matter bee as well amplified in this forme, by examyning the comparison in euery pticular circumstance, that the whole may seeme the greater, in this example, it is lamentable that yonge man should be offended wth the advice of his experienced friend tending to his proffitt; first it is a hard case that councell, should be neglected, but harder that it should offend, it is woefull to see any man displeased wth good admonicõns; but more woefull to see a youth soe affected, whoe would not grieue to haue his advice ill taken? but whoe would not grieue to see his owne experience controlled, vnhappie is that youth that listens not to good exhortacõns of his skilfull friends, he is miserable & infortunate that quarrels wth the sound precepts of his discreet friends, but more miserable & vnfortunate he that mislikes direccõns giuen for his owne good advantage. /

This is a most easie cleere and vsuall kinde of amplificacõn, for it giues more light & force out of euerie circumstance, the circumstances are these, the psons whoe, & to whome, the matter, the Intent, the tyme, the place, the manner, the consequences, & many more, out of eu^erie one of wch any thing may be made more notable [f. 15. b] and egregious, by way of compison, & because I would leaue it fresh in yor. memorie, let this bee yor last charge to inquire in euerie controu^ersie for the circumstances, & compare them wth other lesse matters, & yo^w shall hardly faile of discourse or be left on ground for want of good invencõn. /

There is richer shew in this kind of amplificacõn by euerie circumstance then in any other. first y^t yo^w must begin euerie circumstance wth a figure, Sometimes wth affirmacõn, sometimes wth interrogacõns sometimes wth admition, sometimes wth Ironia, And secondlie that when yo^w vppon euerie circumstance vrge the whole sence, yo^w are for eu^erie circumstance almost to vary the wordes, as here, for lamentable, vnhappie, vnfortunate, heavie case, woefull, grievous; Soe for councell, admonicõns, Instruccõns p^recepts, direccõns, againe I say remember this kinde of pgression by circumstances & vrging & aggravatinge all the points of a Sentence,

for yo^w shall see it handled most com̃endably by any Coullo^r
in Rhetoricke by all good speakers & writers:

Figures Serving for
Amplificacõn. /

Here are figures that make a faire offer to set forth a matter
better then it is. /

<Hyperbole> The first of them in single wordes & phrases
as Hyperbole wherein I will giue yo^w. some such examples,
as by my once readinge long since I observed in *Arcadia*,
sometimes it expresseth a thinge in the highest degree of
possibillitie, beyond the truth, that it descendinge thence may
finde the truth, Sometimes in flatt impossibillitie, that rather
yo^w may conceaue the vnspeakeablenes, then the vntruth of
the relacõn (Possibly) as for an hipocriticall host, <136>
he gaue as pleasing intertainm^t. as the falsest heart could
giue him that he meanes the worst vnto, <318> That euer
eye sawe or thought [f. 16. a] could ymagine, for delight,
<293> enquirie making their eyes, eares, & tongues, serue
for nothing els but that inquirie, this is the vttermost that is
possible; but in the frontiers of possibilitie; <321. a>
accustomed to vse victorie as an inheritance, wth more impossibillitie, thus <99. a> though a thousand deathes followed, & eurie death followed wth a hundred shames,
<21. a> the world sooner want accusacõns, then he vallo^r
to goe through them, wordes & blowes came soe thicke
togeither, as the one seemed lightning to the others thunder./

Sometimes there is a certaine quantitie of a thinge set but
plainely & ingeniously told, vnenarrable, as <254> beyond
the bounds of conceipt; much more of vttering & this figure
is more creddit to yor wit then to yor speech: /

Correctio having vsed a word of sufficient force, yet p^{re}tend-
ing a greater vehemencie of meaning, refuseth it, & supplies
the place wth a greater, as I pswaded yo^w not to loose hold
of occasion, whilst it may not onlie be taken, but offers, nay
sues to be taken, where the first rising of the matter is vppon,

(not onlie but alsoe; then vppon the correcting, nay againe yo^w must be content, nay yo^w must be desirous to take paines, if yo^w will write well it is the only quallitie wch in all accons in yor shiere will winne yo^w praise praise (q^d I) nay hono^r & admiracõn. /

This figure is to be vsed when yo^w would make the thinge more credible it selfe, then in the manner of yor vtterance, it is sometimes vsed vppon passion wth an intent to amplify, as <129. a> yo^w starrs! yo^w doe not succo^r me, noe noe yo^w will not help me, <295> o! *Parthenia*! noe more *Parthenia* what art thou; there are 2 contrary wayes to these former & both lead to amplificacõn, but in dissemblinge sorte, <Ironia> the first is *Ironia* wch expresseth a thinge by contrary by shewe of exhortacõn, when indeed, it dehorteth as yet a while, sleepe a while, fold thine armes a while &c: & soe shall necessitie ouertake thee like a travailler & poverty set vppon thee like an armed man, or as if a man should say, It is [f. 16. b] simple creditt that the dilligent man shall come to, when he shall stand before Princes, It was but small charge of idle money that the *Ægiptians* bestowed vppon the erecting of a *Piramis* of bricke, when the expence in Onions & garlike for workmens dyett in the buildinge of it, came to aboue 238. thousand pounds of money, *Milo* had but a slender strength that caried an oxe a furlonge on his backe, & then killed him wth his fist & eat him to his breakfast, *Titerinus* had a reasonable good arme, that could hold 2 bulls by the tayle the one in one hand, the other in the other & neuer be stirred out of the place by their violent pulling, here, small, slender, reasonable, amplifie as much as if yo^w had said great, exceeding, incredible. /

Paralepsis the second counterfeit of Amplificacõn, is when yo^w say yo^w let passe that wch not wthstanding yo^w touch at full, as I account not my hindrance in others, the direct studyes of my course, I vallue not my paines in collecting these observacons, I will forget that I denied the earnest intreaties of many kindes of gent: that sued vnto me for such helpes, I am loth to tell yo^w they are notes of whome (yor maisters of the vniversities haue thought) the author, as great a reader & a greater observer thereof then them-selues, I desire not that yo^w should make any greater esti-macon of them, then as a testimonie of my loue to yo^w & a pledge of my resolucõn to encourage those liuely sparkes of invencõn wch if yo^w smoother or quench, yo^w comĩtt a kind of intellectual murder, the like is often vsed in pgres-sion, But another, I vrge not to yo^w the hope of yor friends, though that should animate yo^w to answer their expectacõn, I lay not before yo^w the necessitie of the place wch yo^w are to furnish, wherein to be defectiue & insufficient were some shame. /

[f. 17. a]   I omit the envious concurrencies & some p^{re}pared comparisons in yor countrie, wch haue some feeling wth yonge men of fore-sight, I onlie say howe our owne promises shall giue Judgm^t. ag^t vs, how shall we discharge o^r owne ingagem^{ts}. to yor father, if this tyme hath not taken full effect of pffitt in our labour & indeavo^{rs}. /

Two figures pperlie belonge to these kinds of *Amplificacõn*, wch I called accumilacon & division, the first is a round dis-patching of much disiointed matter, not plainlie & simply the same in sence, yet tendinge to the same end, as <52. b> Loues companions, be vnquietnes, longings, fond comforts, faint discomforts, hopes Jelousies, vngrounded rages, causeles yealdings &c: spite, rage, disdaine, shame, revenge, came vppon hatred, theise examples are out of *Arcadia*; Yo^w may frame one thus, all men exclaime vppon these exactions, nobles, gentlemen, comunaltie, poore, rich, scholler, merchants, peasants, yonge, old, wise, ignorant, high, lowe, & all cry out, vppon the hard imposicõns of these burdens, this (in one word) is but all men, & therefore appteines to accumilation, but is expressed by seu^{er}all degrees, and pffessions of men, & therefore belonge [*sic*] to division. /

The second figure differs not much from the first but that
the first is a sodaine entrance into a confused heape of
matter, This is a wild & dissolute repeticõn of all that went
before, as yo^w haue heard of his pride, ambicõn, cosenage,
robberies, mutinyes in the cittie, in the campe in the countrie,
what kinsman of his vnabused what friend vndeceaued, what
companion vncorrupted can speake for him, where can he
liue wthout shame? where can he dye wth hono^r.? /

These .2. figures doe not only make yor cause seeme better,
but (skillfully & fittly) vsed, doe amase an adversarie of
meane conceipt. /

[f. 17. b]   There are other figures that fitly come in after
Amplificacõn, or any great heate iustly inflamed. <interoga-
tion> *Interogatiõ* & Exclamacõn, *Interogation* is but a
warme proposicõn, & therefore often times serues more fitlie
then a bare affirmacõn, wch were but too gentle & harmeles
a speech, as, the credit of behavio^r is to couer impfeccõns &
set forth yor best ptes, better thus vttered, is it not the
chiefest credit of behaviour to set forth yor good pts fairely,
and cleanly to couer yor impfeccõns; The most pte of men
are ignorant, & there fore by shewes (wthout vaunting &
impudencie) yo^w should gaine a more gen^{er}all oppinion, then
by sufficiencie, smoothered into a modest disposicõn.   by
interrogacõn thus, are not the most pte of men ignorant?
shall yo^w not then by meere shewes, that are not too grosse
& vauntinge, please more, & gett a more gen^{er}all good
oppinion, then by great sufficiencie darkened by yor owne
shamefac'dnes; To retire & dissemble excellencies is onlie
good pollicie, in him whome his course must at length
necessarily drawe into light & proofe, & then all that hee
showes wilbe admirable, because expectacõn forestalled
nothing of his worth wch sentence may likewise turne
Interogatio, it is verie fitt for a speech to many & indiscreet
hearers, & therefore much vsed in Pirocles oracõn to the
seditious multitude, & then it may welbe frequented &
iterated, <219.> Did the sun euer bringe fruitfull harvest,

but was more hott then pleasant? haue yo^w any of yor
children that be not sometimes cumbersome? haue yo^w any
fathers that be not sometimes warish? shall we therfore
curse the sun? hate o^r children or disobey o^r parents? the
like 338. b. & in many places in like sort; an example of
many interrogacõns of myne, haue yo^w not seene a stately
kind of curtesie? & proud kind of humillity [f. 18. a] Haue
yo^w not seene a wise man drawe himselfe from meane companie, wth a better grace & more kindnes, then some silly
gent that bestowed himselfe vppon fooles, throwne himselfe
downe into the middest of his miseries, doth not a comen-
dacõn a capp, a good word, a good morrow purchase more
hearts, then a monthes familliar pratling, wth a flocke of
rude people, doe not yo^w converse wth yor Superio^rs to learne
them, & to be able to iudge of them & benifit yor selfe? &
shall not yor Inferio^rs do the like wth yo^w. Is it not a safer
gaine of popularitie wth ceremonies then wth disclosing of
yor nature, Another, shall hee bee a badd husband, whoe
having all his wealth abroad in stockes doth not oftentymes
survey it? And shall hee bee a discreet gent, whose creditt
consisting in acquaintance of great psonages, & doth not
often visitt them since they accompt it their hono^r to be
visited? I could here write a whole life of interrogacõns,
But let it suffice that it is easie and sweet to receiue the flatt
style of affirmacõns to a downer right telling of tales: /

Exclamacõn is not lawfull, but in extremity of mocõn, as
Pirocles seeing the milde *Philoclea* innocently beheaded,
cryed out, <335. a> oh Tyrant heaven. Traito^r earth,
blind pvidence, noe Justice, howe is this done? howe is this
suffred? hath this world a goverment, The like in the
beginning of the second booke of *Arcadia*, in the pson of
Gynecia tormented in mynd, oh Sun, o yo^w heavens, deserts,
o virtue, o impfect pporcõn; & in my booke of charity and
resignacõn of the chapter that the truest mortificacõn is the
study of cosmographie, o! endlesse endeavo^rs, & vayne
glorious ignorance, dost thou desire to bee knowne? where
in *Europe* howe canst thou bee famous? when *Asia* &

Affricka y^t haue thrice as many people heare not of thy Accõns, art not thou then thrice as obscure, as thou art renowned? dost thou looke that all the world should take notice of thee, when for five thousand yeares, these three pts of the world took not notice of the fourth, But *Europe* is the house of fame, because it is the Nurcery of *Artes* [f. 18. b] and bookes, wherein reports are p^reserved, O weake Imaginacõn, oh selfe pleasing fancie; cãst thou expect in these pts from 40. degrees to 90^ty northwards such praises & hono^r for thy name, when euery mapp, or eu^erie wall shewes thee as much space from 40. to 90^ty southwards inhabited wth nothing, but silence & forgetfullnes. /

Acclamacon is a sententious clause of a discourse or report such as Daniell in his poems concludes wth ppetually. It is a gen^erall instruccõn for euery man comonly for his paines in reading any historie of other men lookes for some private vse, to himselfe like a teller whoe in drawing great somes of other mens money, challendgeth somewhat in the pound for his owne ffee, It serues for Amplificacõn, when (after a great <*> . . . or desert, exclaymed vppon or extolled,) it gives a morall note worth creditt & observacõn, As after the true relacon of *Scipio Affricanus* his course, whoe having bin chiefe gen^erall of the greatest Armyes in the world, having (all hisi life tyme,) kinges suto^rs. for his favo^r. & nacons kept in awe of his name, yet in 56. yeares, never bought or sould, goods or landes newe built any house or castle of his owne, left not aboue 40^li in gold & 6^li in silver behinde him at his death. /

It may be folded vpp in this *Acclamacõn* soe little need hath hee to stoope to private cares that thriues vppon publique victoryes, & soe small leisure hath hee to be desirous of riches, (being but the meanes) whoe hath bin soe longe possest of hono^r wch is the mortall end of mortall Accons, Such notes are these scrappes of pollicie wch men nowe adayes gather out of *Polibius* & *Tacitus,* & not vnlike are those morralls that hange vppon *Æsops* fables. /

This Acclamacõn expresseth sometimes the cause & reason
of a former narracõn, as a story of one whoe being a
servant of a familye & of many quallities wonne the doating
loue of a wittie Lady in the house whereas shee never lookt
vppon the humble suites the cuñing insinuacõns, the worthie
deserts of [f. 19. a] manie lovers of higher degree, but w^{th}
ffree Judgm^t. & carelesse censure, this clause may followe
soe hard entrance hath liking into a heart p^{re}pared to suspicõn especially in the weakest natures, whose safeguard is
mistrust, Soe easie is the increase of loue by insensible stepps
when the service yo^w offer seemes to issue out of the goodnes
of yor owne disposicõn, wch women expect to be pmanent,
& not out of the necessity of yor suite, wch may frame yo^w
for a tyme to vaine difference from yor pp hono^r.; yet if
this be too much vsed, it is like a note booke gathered out of
histories /

<Diminucõn>   Contrary to *Amplificacon*, is *Diminucõn* &
descends by the same stepps that Ampli: ascends by, &
differrs noe otherwise then vpp-hill, & doune-hill, wch is the
same way begun at severall tymes, yet some examples in
yor *Arcadia* giue yo^w to obserue 2. wayes of diminuishing
single termes, one by denying the contrary, as if yo^w should
say reasonable pleasant Arcadian speech is, <38. b> not
vnpleasant, hardly liked, <67. a> not misliked, <128. b>
not vnfitt, not altogeather modest, <125> not deny, <249>
but why should I giue examples of the most vsuall phrazes
in the English tongue, as we say not the wisest man that
euer I sawe, for a man of small wisedome, the second way
is by denying the right vse of the word, but by erro^r. of some
as, <38. a> those fantasticall mynded people, wch children
& musitians call lovers, <392. b>   This coullor of myne
wch shee in the deceavable style of affeccõn would intitle
beautifull, that in misfortune of letting fall his dagger, w^{ch}
the rude swagg^{er}ers of o^r tyme call disarmed That oppinion
of honestie, wch hath lately bin soe proudly translated by
Souldiers into the word hono^r. & such like, But the former
fashion of diminucõn sometimes in erroneous sort goes for

amplificacõn as speakinge of a great psonage, noe meane
man. &c: This is an ordinarie figure for all sorts of
speeches but these figures are but counterfeits of
Amplificacõn. /

> These figures following serue properly for
> Amplification. /

Synœceosis is a composicõn of contraries, & by both wordes
intymateth the meaning of neyther p^recisely but a moderacõn
& mediocrity of both, as brauerie & raggs are contrary, yet
somewhat better then both is <314> braue raggednes, the
like, <248. b> wanton modestie, inticing [f. 19. b] Sobernes, <340> And wth that shee pretilie smyled, wch mingled
wth her teares, a man could not tell whether it were mourning
pleasure, or delightfull sorrowe, wittie ignorance It was an
excellent pastime to those that would delight in the play of
virtue, wth what a witty Ignorance shee would not vnderstand, impatient patient 183. absented presence .49. well
willing spite 213. vnkynd carefulnes. /

And one contrarie is affirmed to be in the other directly by
making one the substantiue, the other, th' adiectiue as aboue
in the examples: or indirectly, as in these words following,
<321. a> seeking hono^r. by dishonoring, & buildinge safetie
vppon ruyne, <281. a> O foolish woman, & most miserablie
foolish, because witt makes thee foolish; <284> captivitie
might seeme to haue authoritie over captivitie. /

This is a fine course to stirr admiracõn in the hearer & make
them thinke it a strange harmonie wch must bee exprest in
such discords, therefore this example shall conclude, <288>
There was soe pfect agreem^t. in soe mortall disagreem^t, like
a musicke made of cunning discords; This is an easie figure
nowe in fashion not like euer to be soe vsuall. /

Contentio is contrarie to the former, That was a composicon
of <*> *Hernies* [*terms?*] disagreeing, this is an opposicõn
of them as <359. a> there was strength against nimblenes,

rage against resolucõn, furie against virtue, confidence ag^t. courage, pride against noblenes, he is a swaggerer amongst quiett men, but a quiett man amongst swag^{er}ers earnest in idle thinges, idle in matters of earnestnes where there is both *Antimetab*: for the turninge of Sentences backe & *Contentio* respecting the contrarieties of things meant thereby, <177. a> could not looke on, would not looke of; <176. a> neither the one hurt her nor the other helpe her; iust wthout ptiallitie, mighty wthout contradiccõn, liberall wthout loosing wise wthout curiositie;

This figure Askam told Sturnius [*sic*] y^t he taught the queene of England, & that shee excells in practize of it & indeed it is a figure, fitt to set forth a copious style, this figure serues much for amplificacõn; for comparison : /

[f. 20. a] *Comparison* is an even gate of sentences, answearing each other in measures int^{er}changeably, such as in S^t. *Augustine*, but often in *Gregory* the divine, such as in the Bi^{pp} of W : his bookes wch he hath written in English & manie places of Euphues, but that S^t. Austine Bilson & Lillie doe verie much mingle this figure wth *Agnominatio*, & *similliter Cadens*, it is a smooth and memorable style for vtterance, but in penning it must be vsed moderately & modestlie, a touch of *Agnom*: of the letter is tollerable wth a comparison as in the first wordes of *Philanax* his speech, If euer I could wish my faith vntryed, & my councell vntrusted, & where there is a *similiter cadens*, but a more eminent falling, alike in this, <327> my yeares are not soe manie but that one death may conclude them; nor my faults soe manie, but that one death may satisfie them, wthout consonancie of fall or harping vppon letter or sillable; & yet a *Compar*. because they say the wordes match each other in ranke, <375> saue his gray hayres from rebuke, & his aged mynd from dispaire, answeare each other, againe <277> rather seeke to obtaine that constantlie by courtesy wch yo^w cannot assuredly enioy by violence, verbe to verbe, adverbe, to adverbe, & substantiue to substantiue lonelynes can neither warr^t. yo^w from suspic$\tilde{o}$n in others, nor deffend yo^w from Melanchollie in yor selfe, <Syndeton> In some place there is a shorter compison, where substantiue to substantiue, or word to word are ioyned, & yet wthout coniunction wch is a *Syndeton*, <111. b> her skull wth beautie, her head wth wisedome her eyes wth maiestie, her countenance wth gracefullnes, her lipps wth lovingnes where many (ands) are spared, some places only the coniunction is put in, in the last, In a compar of 3. as, <236. a> her witt indeed by youth, her affecc$\tilde{o}$n by byrth, & her sadnes by her beautie, <219> A faire woman shall not onlie com̄aund wthout authoritie, but pswade wthout speaking, this is an excellent figure in noe place vntymely, if not too often, It fits well the eaven plawses, & int^{er}pretacons of an [f. 20. b] eloquent tongue that seems to bee rich & wise, & to conteine many parts, whereof each wth a tedious man would make a sentence sticke in the hearers sences thereof, I called it smooth & memorable, It hath bin in request euer since the daies of *Isocrates*, whose oracc$\tilde{o}$ns are full of them, This figure belonges more pplie to that pte of *Amplificacon*, called division, then to Accumulac$\tilde{o}$n. /

Sententia (if it be well vsed) is a figure (if ill & too much) it is a style, whereof none that writes humorously or factiously nowe adayes can bee cleare, for nowe there are such schismes of eloquence, that it is enough for any i0 yeares that all the bravest witts doe imitate Some one figure wch a criticke hath taught some great psonage, soe it may bee wthin this 200 yeares, wee shall goe through the whole bodie of *Rhethorick*. /

It is true that we studie accordinge to the p^{re}dominancie of courtly inclynac$\tilde{o}$ns, whilest mathematiques were in requests all o^r simillitudes came from lynes, circles, & Angles, whilest morall philosophie is nowe a while spoken of, it is rudenesse, not to be sententious, & for my pte, I'le make one, I haue vsed & outworne 6 severall styles, since I was first fellowe of newe Colledge, & am yet able to beare the fashion of

writing companie, let oʳ age therefore onlie speake morally,
& let the next age liue morrally. /

It is very true that a sentence is a pearle in a discourse, but
is it a good discourse that is all pearle? It is like an eye
in the bodie, but is it not monstrous to be all eyes? I take
Ciclops to be as handsome a man as *Argus,* & if a sentence
were as like to be an hand in the text, as it is cõmonlie
noted wᵗʰ a hand in the margent, yet I should rather like the
text that had noe more hands then *Hercules,* then that wᶜʰ
had as many as *Briarcus;* But these short breathed gent:
these Judicious myndes, will shewe mee in their workes,
Intᵉʳogacõns, Agnominacõns, Correccõns, & all the figures
of *Rhetorique,* I yeald to it, & yet will they shewe me
nothing but sentences, vnles there be some difference betwixt
writing all in sentences & writing all sententiouslie, this is a
sentence <267> mans experience in womans best eye sight;
There is small difference betweene a pposicon & a question
if [f. 21. a] I forget not *Aristotle* lº Topic: <230> since
length of Accquaintance, mutuall secrecies nor height of
benifitts could bynd a savage mynde, There is a Sentence
& in it *Asyndeton, Zeugma,* & *Metaphors* <289. b> Hee
felt valueing money higher then æquitie that guiltynes is
not alwayes wᵗʰ ease oppressed where there is *Moiosis,* not
always wᵗʰ ease, for euer & hardly <154> whoe stands
only vppon deffence, stands vppon noe deffence, wᵗʰ *Synoec*:
& *Epanados,* <419> vnlawfull desires are punished after
the effect of enioying but impossible desires are punished
in the desire it selfe, a sentence wᵗʰ *Distinctio,* & *Contentio,*
<78. b> Loue to a yealding heart is a kinge, but to a
resisting is a Tirant, *Compar*: & *Contentio,* It is a foolish
wittines to speake more then one thinkes, *Synoec*: neither is
this sentence wᵗʰout a *Compar*: & is a double sentence (as
they call it) <58. a> to a heart fullie resolute counsaile is
tedious, but repʳᵉhension is loathsome & their is nothing
more terrible to a guiltie minde then the eye of a respected
friend. /

There be alsoe sentences pticuler to some men as well, as
<309. b> *Amphialus*, to whome abused kyndnes became
spitefull rage, fearefullnes (contrary to all other vices)
making *Clinias* thinke the better of another, the worse hee
found himselfe, <127> *Evarchus* making his life the
example of his lawes, his accõns arising out of his deedes,
wch all may be taken for rule, & cõmonplaces, by putting
the gen^{er}all name for the speciall (as they say) drawing it
a Thesi ad Hipothesin; from a position to a supposicõn. /

Theise examples may make yo^w belieue that a sentence may
be <*> course,* through the whole figure booke, & it shall
appeare in a sett treatise that many figures may easily
assemble in one clause, & any figure may sorte wth any, a
slender reason to ground vppon any one figure the frame &
fashion of yor whole style, in o^r pfession there are not many
(if 2 were many) whose speeches relye vppon this figure,
And in my Judgm^t. *Sententia*, is better for the Bench then
the Barr, then of all others why would the writers of these
daies, imprison themselues in the straightnes of these maximes [f. 21. b]   It makes there stile like *Arena sine calce*,
(as one saith) of such a writer, & doth not he vouchsafe to
vse them that* <*> [called] them poesies for ringes; If it
be matter of short dirreccon for life & accõn, or notes for
memorie, I intend not to discreditt this newe tricke, But otherwise hee that hath a longe Journey to walke in that pace, is
like a horse that overreacheth & yet goes slowe; S^t. *Ambrose*
sanctifies this figure. /

To Illustrate. /

[f. 22. a]   Illustracõn consists in thinges or wordes, In the
discription of thinges living or dead; of living thinges, either
reasonable, as of men & of psonages, & quallities, of
vnreasonable, as of horses, shipps, Ilands, castles & such
like. /

Men are discribed most excellentlie in *Arcadia, Basilius, Plexirtus, Pirocles, Musidorus, Anaxius* &c. but hee that will truely set downe a man in a figured storie, must first learne truely to set downe an humo^r. a passion, a virtue, a vice, & therein keeping decent pporcõn add but names, & knitt togeather the accidents & incount^{ers}: The pfect expressing of all quallities is learned out of *Aristotles* io. bookes of morrall *Philosophy*; but because (as *Machiavile* saith) pfect virtue, or pfect vice is not seene in our tyme, wch altogeather is humorous & spirting, therefore the vnderstanding of Aristotles *Rhetorique*, is the directest meanes of skill to discribe, to moue, to appease, or to prevent any mocõn, whatsoeu^{er}; whervnto, whoesoeuer can fitt his speech, shalbe truely eloquent. This was my oppinion ever; & Sr *Phillip Sidney*, betrayed his knowledge in this booke of *Aristotle* to me, before euer I knewe that hee had translated any pte of it, for I found the 2 first bookes englished by him in the handes of the noble studious *Henry Wotton*, but lately, I thinke alsoe that he had much helpe out of *Theophrasti imagines*, for the webb (as it were) of his storie hee followed three *Heliodorus* in greeke, *Sanazarus Arcadia* in Itallian, & *Diana* de montemaior in spanish, But to o^r purpose what psonages & affeccons are sett forth in *Arcadia* for men, pleasant idle retirednes in kinge *Basillius*, & the dangerous end of it, vnfortunate vallo^r in *Plangus;* courteous valo^r in Amphialus, proud vallo^r in *Anaxius* 305. hospitallitie in *Kallander.* / The mirro^r of true courage & friendshipp in *Pirocles* & *Musidorus*, miserablenes & ingratitude in *Chremes*, 188. feare & fatall subtiltie in *Clinias*, 299. feare & rudenes wth ill affected civillitie in Dametas 84, & through the storie mutuall virtuous loue, in mariage, in *Argalus* [f. 22. b] And *Parthenia* 291. out of mariage in *Pirocles* and *Philoclea*, *Musidorus* and *Pamela*, true constant loue vnrespected in *Plangus* <*> and* Helena 47, In the true Zelmane 200. inconstancie & envie, suspicõn & Tirannye in a kinge & his councello^{rs}. 139. generally false loue in *Pamphilus* 185. & light courage & credulity in *Chremes* daughter, base dotage on a wife in *Plangus* father, But in

women a mischievous seditious stomacke in *Cecropia* 25i
wise courage in *Pamela*, mylde discrecõn in *Philoclea*,
Pamela's praier, 264 her discourse 28i squeamish cuning
vnworthynes in *Artesia*, respectiue & restles dotage in
Gynecia's loue, proud illfavoured sluttish simplicity in *Mopsa*,
nowe in these psons is euer a stedfast decencie & vniforme
difference of manners observed whereever yoᵂ finde them,
& howsoeuer each interrupt the others storie & accõns, And
for *Accõns* of psons there are many rarely discribed, as a
mutinye & fire in a shipp 210.   causes of an vprore 223.
2i8.   the garboile 215, and armed skirmish 268. 27i pollicie
& preparacõn 286.   but pollicy genᵉʳally in all pticuler accõns
is noted in yoʳ booke &c: managing a horse is discribed i22
tilting shewes from 69. to 72 many other notable & liuely
portracts are, wᶜʰ I will not lay downe to saue yoᵂ soe
sweet a labour, as the reading of that wᶜʰ may make yoᵂ
eloquent, & wise Sʳ *Phillip Sidney's* course was (besides
reading *Arle* and *Theophrastus*) to imagine the thinge pnte
in his owne brayne, that is [*sic*] pen might the better pnte it to
yoᵂ whose example I would yoᵂ durst followe till I pulld
yoᵂ backe. /

This haue I written of illustracõn in conveyance & well
gayning of the substance of a treatise where evident &
liuely discripcõns are in *Arcadia* [f. 23. a] Yoᵂ haue this
noate des: where the pson is aptly fitted with speech &
accõn :dc: both these giue light to the handling, & growe
into very pleasant acquaintance wᵗʰ the vnderstanding &
memorie of the reader, for speciall lights in euery sentence. /

<Distinctio> There are other sparkes of figures, first if
there be any doubt or ambiguity in the wordes, it is better
left out then distinguished, but if yoᵂ are to answeare any
former speeches, yoᵂ may disperce all cloudes, & remoue
all scruples wᵗʰ distinction as being charged that yoᵂ haue
brought very light reasons, yoᵂ may answeare, if by light,
yoᵂ meane cleare I am glad yoᵂ doe see them, if by light
yoᵂ meane of noe weight, I am sory yoᵂ doe not feele them,

Soe yo^w may expresse yor selfe, a man of hidden learning, hidden, as well for the obscure & meane estate of his pson as hidden for the vnvsuall & intricate conceipt of the matter : /

But as *Ambiguity* is not onlie in wordes but in matter, soe both wayes it is taken away by distinction, Sometimes it is in single wordes, as in theise former (light & hidden) sometimes in coherence of sentences by relation of each word to each, or by reason of change of the pointing wch is opened by vtterance, yo^w haue many examples thereof in the *Courtier*, the second booke of *Cicero de oratore*, & in *Quintillian*, where there is mencõn of (Jocus and Ambiguo) and yo^w may satisfie yor selfe at full, if yo^w search but the margent of *Erasmus Apothegmes* where *Ambigus* is written./

Distinction of *Ambiguity* in matter is a det^{er}minacõn of the truth of generall pposicõns, to tell wherein they are certaine, & wherein they are not, as travayle in forreigne countreyes, setleth a yonge mans humo^{rs}. If it be taken in this sorte, It will inforce him to warynes & secrecy, & restrayne him from powringe forth his counsailes; It is verie pfitable, for he shall [f. 23. b] haue fewe friends to put confidence in, & fewe companions to prattle wth, vppon whome he might bestowe his idle tyme, or idle thoughts, But if yo^w intend that by travailling all vanities should be taken awaie, It seems not soe likely, & admyttable, because hee shall walke through many ill examples & great libtie : /

Another pposicõn distinguished, They are but fraile merritts, wch yo^w shall bestowe vppon yongue mens friendshipp It is true if yo^w please those desires wch are like to depte wth their youth, as gaming, feasting, & idle sportings, yo^w are like to bee cast of wth those toyes and forgotten, But if yor deserts of yongue men bee in honest exercise, learned conferrence, and civile friendlie offices, the remembrance thereof will increase, and growe as fast as their discrecõn. Soe much for distinction. /

Next followes deffinicõn wch is the shortest & truest expo-
sicon of the nature of any thinge, hereof yo^w haue examples
of virtues & vice in *Arles* morrals, of passions in his
Rhetorick, both in *Thomas Aquinas Secunda* of many
affeccons & pturbacõns, in *Tusculans* questions and *Cicero
de finibus*, The gen^erall *Diffinition* of Virtue is this *Virtus
est habitus rationi consentaneus*, virtue is a quallitie setled
in reason, feare is an app^rehension of future harme, Thrift
is a moderate & lawfull increase of wealth, by carefull
gou^ernem^t. of yor owne estate. /

Complem^t. is pformance of affected ceremonies in words,
lookes, or gesture, where *Diffinition* runs into *Division* of
7 or 8 wayes of *Diffinition* reade *Valerius Logique*, But
to be most pfectly instructed reade the sixt booke of Arles
Top: yor diffinicõns need not to be strictly tyed to the rules
of Logicke, nor yor *Divisions*, the matter is sometimes illustrated by *Paraphr*, as spurd his horse apace, <309> made
his spurrs clayme hast of his horse, A man not to be contemned, <262> a man against whome contempt might make
noe Just challendge, snorting aloud, <148> snorting soe
loud that noe man might lay the stealing of a Napp to her
charge, but of paphr. & periphr is a seu^erall chapter. /

[f. 24. a] *Sometimes Parenthesis*, makes yor discource faire
& more sencible, as <140> hee (swelling in their humble-
ness) like a bubble swolne vpp wth a small breath, broken
wth a great) [*sic*] forgetting (or not knowinge) humanity;
caused their heads to be struck of; <58. b> That what
his witt could conceiue (and his wit can conceiue as far as
the limitts of reason can stretch;) was all directed to the
setting forth of his friend Till the next morning (better
by the howre-glass; then by the dayes clearenes) having
run fortune &c: & indeed all penthesis [*sic*] are in extremi-
ties, either graces or disgraces, to a speech; if they be longe,
the[y] seeme int^errupcõns & therefore at the end of them
there must be a retreyt to the matter, called *Antanoclasis*,
as assure thyselfe (most wicked woman! that hast soe

plaugely a corrupted mynd, as that thou canst not keepe thy
sicknes to thy selfe, but must most wickedly infect others)
assure thy selfe I say &c: Shall that heart (wch doth not
only feele them, but hath all the working of his life placed
in them) shall that heart I say &c:

Diuision is a severing of the whole into pts, as of tyme into
that past, pnte, & to come, wch is rather a breaking then a
division, of *Magistrates* into supreame, or subordinate from
their order, of *Beasts* or vnreasonable creatures into those
of the aire, water, earth, *Love* is either of *Beauty*, or *Virtue*,
from the obiect: Study is of lib^erall or mechanicall Sciences;
from the Subiect, & soe yo^w may divide as many wayes as
things may differ, as by their beginnings, endings, ppties,
markes, effects, Tymes, places, formes, & psons, in whome
they are & howsoeuer, whereof the pp treaty belongs to
Logicke. & something is spoken thereof in the second way
of *Amplification*. /

Out of *Division* arise 3 seu^erall inforcem^ts. & manifestacõns
of yor purpose, w^ch (though they are by *Rhetoricians*
diversely termed) yet are in effect grounded vppon one *Art
of Distribucõn*

The first is expedicõn wch reckoning vppon div^ers pts
distroyes all but that one wch yo^w meane to rest vppon, as
one of these courses must be taken, eyther yo^w must dilli-
gently obserue, or practise these rules, or denie that euer
yo^w received instruccõns, or alleadge want of capacitie in
yor selfe, or want of vse of them in yor life, [f. 24. b]
that they are vnnecessarie yo^w cannot saye, ffor what more
necessarie in yor life then to write well; that yo^w are vncap-
able is a slaunder & contradiccõn to yor owne conscience, &
my experience that haue seene such faire essayes & beginning
of yor endeavo^rs. & to say, yo^w had never any directions,
were to giue yor 2. eyes the lye, & to make me·belieue that
I did never but dreame yo^w good, Therefore must yor labour
conspire wth my invencõns, & soe must yo^w vnexcusablie
become skillfull, this enumeracõn & inferrence therevppon

is that wch the Logitians call induccõn, as in reckoning vpp, it is neither this nor that, therefore it is this, & (as one merrily sayth) it is the doggs *Syllogisme* in a crosse way, that sayth my M^r is gone this or that way, but I smell him not this way, nor this, therefore he runs on his conclusion wthout smellinge. /

The seacond of this sort is *Prosopoesis*, that ou^{er}throweth noe pte of the *Division*, but returneth some reason to each member; in *Arcadia*: <39. b> Heretofore I haue accused the sea, condemned the *Pirats*, & hated my evill fortune that depriued me of thee, But nowe thy selfe art the sea, thy selfe the *Pirate*; & thy will the evill fortune, Tyme at one instant seeming short & long to them short in the pleasingnes of such presence, longe in the stay of their desires; yor silence must carrie wth it a construccõn of contempt, vnkindness or displeasure, If yo^w take me not for yor friend, yo^w offer vnkyndnes, if yo^w deeme me vnworthie of an answeare it comes of contempt, if yor passion differrs a reply, it argues yor displeasure. The first of this sort denyed all pts saue one, this affirmes & keepes all sides vpp: /

The last is *Dilema*, wch proposeth 2 sides & ou^{er}throwes both, yo^w must haue both abillity & will to write well, for to say I cannot is childish, & to say I will not, is womanish:

Periphrasis, & Paraphrasis. /

There is in the best writers sometymes a vaine of speech, wherein the vulgar conceipts are exceedingly pleased, ffor they admire this most, that there is some excellencie in it & yet they themselues suspect that it excells their admiracõn, in some examples I [f. 25. a] would gladlie discouer the reason thereof, It cannot bee but (if either the meaning or the wordes be obscure or vnfamilliar vnto a mans mynde,) that the speech soe consisting should be much accepted, & yet it is impossible that there should be any extraordynarie delight in ordinarie wordes & plaine meaning, howe then

shall we determine? It is as it is in many dishes at oᵣ
tables, our eyes & tast giue them comēndacōn, nor for the
substance, but for the dressing & service, what playner
meaning then sleepe amongst theeves, & verily sleepe, life,
trust, are comōn English wordes, yet it is not a comōn fashion
of speech to say <187. b> trust a sleeping life amongst
theeves; in the same sence, when they had slept a while is
ordynary, but <42. a> when they had a while hearkned to
the pswasion of sleepe is extraordynarie; though all the
wordes of it by themselues, are most knowne & famylliar,
yet the bringing in & fetch of it is strange & admyrable to
the Ignorant, we therefore call it Periphrasis, or circumlocu-
tion, & it is much helped by metaphores as before, inclyned
to sleepe is expressed by a metaphore taken from an *Orator,*
whoe moues & inclynes by pswasion & to be soe moved it
is to hearken: In this sort Sᵣ P.S: being to speake his
vsuall meanings, yet notwᵗʰstanding shunned vsuall phrazes,
as (for it is absurd,) in my conceipt (saith hee) it hath a
great incongruitie; but let us haue one boute more wᵗʰ (oᵣ
advᵉʳsary) sleepe, for having risen early, he saith <200>
having stryven wᵗʰ the suns earlynes, Instead of *Mopsa*
wept illfavouredly,* <249*> *Mopsa* disgraced weeping wᵗʰ
her countenance; Instead of saying they that guarded
Amphialus, were killed themselues, it is said, seeking to
saue him they lost their fortresses wᶜʰ nature placed them
in, instead of *Plangus* speech began to bee suspected It is
sayd <169> Plangus speech began to bee translated into
the language of suspicōn, & this of purpose did he write to
keepe his style from basenes, as being to name a thresher,
he calls him <171. b> one of *Ceres* servants, Instead of
his name was knowne to high & lowe, he sayth that
<208. b> Noe *Prince* could pʳᵉtend height nor *Beggar* low-
nesse to barr him from the sounds thereof, ffor old & yonge
malecontents, hee saith such whome youthfull age or youthfull myndes had filled [f. 25. b] wᵗʰ vnlymmitted desires, &
this is by goeing *a Concreto ad abstractum,* & divᵉʳˢ others
[*sic*] wayes. /

If a short ordinarie sence bee odly expressd by more wordes it is (*Periphrasis*) but if by as manie other, it is *Paraphrasis*, as many false oathes, plentifull piurye, to make a great shewe of himselfe, to make a muster of himselfe, in the Iland, for kill any maryed man, <298. a> make his sword accursed by any widdowe, wch is by consequence seeking by courtesie to vndoe him, making courtesie the outside of mischiefe, by simillitude or metaphore, Soe then the course is insteed of any ordinarie wordes importing any trivyall sence, to take the abstract, or some consequente, simillitude, note, pptie, or effect, & thereby declare it, These 2 figures serue for Illustracõn. /

It is most convenient, sometimes for the bringing in of life & lustre, to represent some vnexpected straynes beside the teno^r of yor. tale, & act (as it were) yor meaning wch is done either by feighning the presence or the discourse of some such psons, as either are not at all, or if there be, yet speake not, but by imaginacõn, the first is by *Apostrophe*, or *Prosopopeia*. /

Apostrophe, is a turning of yor speech to some newe pson, as to the people, when yor speech before was to the Judge, to the def^t. to the adv^ersary to the witnesses, as, & herein yo^w wittnesses are to consult wth yor owne consciences, & to enter into true examinacõn of yor memorie, did yo^w. marke his lookes did yo^u note his speeches, did yo^w. truly obserue the pticuler pceedings of the accõn, To the people thus, Nowe let me intreat any man here p[rese]nte that thinkes himselfe not exempted from misfortunes, & privilledged from all mischaunces, to imagine himselfe in my case, & to vnder-take for my sake, but some fewe thoughts of my distresse, Sometymes the occasion is to some quallitie, or thing, that yor selfe giues shewe of life to as <336. a> hope tell me, what hast thou to hope for? Loue be ashamed to be called Loue. /

Occupatio as this, yo[w] will say to me, that in a factious
countrey it is the only pollicie to stand newtrall, I say noe
vnless many circumstances helpe yo[w], *videlicet* these, If none
of those friends by whome yor loue is scan'd be entred into
a quarrell, If yo[w] bee [f. 26. b] assured, that yor wealth
& discrecõn is æquall to the best, if there be likelyhood of
scatteringe the reliance of both sides & making a newe packe,
then is it wisedome to stand aloofe off a while, that if yo[w]
please yo[w] may add the victorie to w[ch] side yo[w] will, but
having vndertaken a side, if yo[w] intend to bee vpright, yo[w]
will growe contemptible; yo[w] offer reconciliacõn, yo[r] strength
will forsake yo[w], if yo[w] dispraise yo[r] adv[er]sary, yo[w] wilbee
deemed envious, if yo[w] coñend his wisedome yo[w] betraye
yo[r] owne weaknes, Praise then his wealth, his Auncest[ors].
his beautie, his pleasantnes, but praise not his foresights, nor
his valo[r]. Are yo[w] Judge amongst yo[r] neighbo[rs]. & inferio[rs].
be precisely iust & equall, are yo[w] assistant to yor friend,
Be advisedly, but throughlie piall; Yo[w] would be accompted
liberall, testify seldome, but publiquly & worthily; Yo[w]
would thrive in bargaining doe it not in many matters
covertlie, for manie small breaches of confidence, are more
infamous then one great one, But offend not yo[r] conscience
wittingly, to be Tre[asure]r of all the *Indian Mines*: /

Thus yo[w] see howe Counsayle, Precepts, or Sentences may
be translated into the forme of *Occupatio* & *Subiectio*.
Sometimes *Occupatio* is left out & argum[t]. brought to the
contrary, as *Cecropia* pswading her sonne *Amphialus* to offer
violence to *Philoclea*, presupposed that he would say he must
be modest, shee replies <313> each virtue hath his tyme,
The soldier that should march formost, must not giue the
waie for modestie, There is *Occupatio* & *Subiectio* in
Arcadia 112. If shee contemned me then thus; if then &c:
The like is 25i did I goe to charge them. &c: did I walke
abroade to see any delight, my walking was the delight
itselfe, he sawe her aliue; he was glad to see her aliue,
He sawe her weepe, hee was sorye to see her weepe; hee

heard her comfortable speeches* <*> nothing more glad-
some, This figure cannot bee out of season but of purpose as
was in the fustian speech, yo^w listen to my speeches I must
confesse it, yo^w hearken to me I cannot denie it, yo^w looke
for some sence I ptly belieue it, but yo^w finde none, I doe
not respect it, And if yo^w will reade ou^{er} that speech, yo^w
shall find most of the figures of *Rhetorick* there, meaning
neither harme, nor good, but as idle as yor selfe, when yo^w
are most at leisure. /

There is another figure called *Concessio*, But I meane to
mistake *Occupatio* & *Concessio*, one for another till I knowe
them better, The forme of *Concessio* is this, I admitt yo^w
are resolute, I graunt yor det^{er}mynacõn is im̃oveable, but it
is in things against yor fryendes Judgment, & things against
yor owne praise & pffitt. /

Figures in varying. /   fol.

Metaphora
Metonimia
Synechdoche
Catachresis
Epizeuxis
Anadiplosis
Climax
Anaphora
Epistrophe
Symploce, Complexio
Epanados
Antimetabole, *com̃utatio verborũ manente sensu*
Paranomasia, agnominatio
Poliptoton
Epanalepsis

In Amplification. /

Hyperbole
Correctio
Paralepsis
Accumilatio
Divisio
Interogatio
Exclamatio
Acclamatio
intimatio

figures more prop for
Amplifying. /

Synœceosis, *quae docet diversas res coniungere,*
et communi oppinioni cum ratione adversari

Contentio
Sententia

In Illustration. /

Distinctio
Deffinitio
Parenthesis
Divisio, Prosopoesis, Dilema
Periphrasis, & Paraphrasis
Apostrophe, *aversio*
Prosopopeia, *sive confictio personae*
Deliberatio
Preventio { Occupatio
           { Subiectio

CHAPTER X

VERSES

POETRY, in this latter age,' remarks Ben Jonson in *Discoveries*, 'hath proved but a mean mistress to such as have wholly addicted themselves to her, or given their names up to her family. They who have but saluted her on the by, and now and then tendered their visits, she hath done much for, and advanced in the way of their own professions. . . .'

John Hoskyns, in his relation to poetry, could scarcely be better described than as one who 'but saluted her on the by' and now and then tendered his visits. Though his suit to poetry was never ardent, it was paradoxical, gay, and mercurial in its 'reaches and glaunces of wit.' What he lacked in profundity he compensated for, in a measure, with his gaiety; and undoubtedly even the verse that now seems wholly trivial was not without point and timeliness for his fellows at the Mitre and the Mermaid. Today his nonsense verse on 'waues of brainless buttered fish . . . fuming vp flounders like a chafing dish' scarcely overwhelms the reader by its cleverness. Yet one can hardly fail to relish his coinage of a Latin verb, *Fleet-streetare*. Suitability to the occasion, aptness in the turn of thought, deftness of personal allusion, and critical good humour made him 'able to bear the fashion of writing company,' as he himself says in his *Direccōns*. In what may at first glance seem a strange clutter of verses, there are indeed several charming lyrics and numerous witty and sententious epigrams.

The ensuing collection has been gathered from such varied sources that a short bibliographical and textual notice for each of the poems will be round in the notes for this chapter. Some of the lines have appeared in print before; others are taken from manuscript sources. Except in the few instances noted, the text has been reproduced exactly as found in the source of the present transcription.

I

Effigiem Servi si vis spectare probati,
    Quisque es, haec oculos pascat imago tuos.
Porcinum os quocunque cibo jejunia sedat,
    Haec *sera* consilium ne fluat arcta premit.
Dat patientem *Asinus* Dominis jurgantibus aurem,
    Cervus habet celeres ire, redire, pedes.
Leva docet multum tot rebus onusta laborem,
    Vestis munditiem, dextera aperta fidem.
Accinctus gladio, clypeo munitus, et inde
    Vel se vel Dominum quo tueatur, habet.

II

In Syllabam *Cos*; in Pentecost Dom.
in Schola Wintoniensi.

Dic mihi Semesas Lipsi serutate figuras
    Qui de Romano marmore mira sapis
Cos positum nostris an sit pro Consule fastis
    Vtq*ue* sit hoc cuius Consulis acta notet.
Tu deleta reples mutili vestigia verbi,
    Et rara est apicem, quae tibi blatta rapit.
Arte tua sensusq*ue* redit chartaeq*ue* per aequor
    Litera naufragio Sparsa priore coit.
Non ita Theside discerptos junxerat artus
    Docta vel a Phoebo patre stupenda manus
Non humerus Pelopi melius, non Vita reposta est
    Seq*ue* peregrinum viuere sensit ebur.
Dic mihi namq*ue* potes de Vocibus omnia Lipsi
    Dic mihi quid Vox haec Cos sibi sola velit?
Sic tibi Serrani monumentum rastra vetusti
    Dentur, & a prisco pocula fracta Numa,
Diues et inscriptis, milleno [*sic*] Caesare nummis
    Restituas formis amphitheatra suis.

FIGURE AT WINCHESTER COLLEGE

The Trusty Servant at Winchester

Sic ego, sic moto responderat, ille cucullo
    (Namque Ita Lovanii non benè Justus agit)
Serius, erecta transacta in Saecula vulta.
    Ante datos visus sis dubitare sonos
Hoc recte, Minus hoc, sed castigatiùs illud,
    Verum ego de veteri codice muto nihil.
Si Capitolinae memini bene nomina chartae
    Ecce puer quid Cos Wintoniense velit.
Æmilius Lepidus, Laetus Pomponius, anni
    Signant auspiciis tempora fausta suis.
Siccine? An hoc ipso fortasse Domitius anno
    Militibus missis imperat ire domum.
Anne ita? Romanos acuit Cos iusta secures
    Publica cum vetitum vindicat ire scelus.
Hoc quo*que* enim dubito, Ratio sin prima coacta est,
    Nescio quid vox haec Cos sibi sola velit.
Huic ego, dulce domum nimium placet omen eundi
    Nec prior inscitus, Consul vter*que* iocus.
Da mihi Laetitias Lipsi, Da Juste Lepores.
    Tu tibi detritae cotis acumen habe,
His aliena mihi quamuis oracula Chalcas
    Pandat, Cassandrae sunt habitura fidem.

III

Here lyeth the bodie of Hugh Poache
Bellied like a herringe headed like a Roache
God of his mercy send him his grace
for he never had heare, growe one his face.

IV

Here lyes the man w^{th}oute repentaunce,
whose death hath lost him much acquaintaunce

V

Hic jacet Egremundus Rarus,
Tuendis paradoxis clarus.
Mortuus est, ut hic apparet:
At si loqui posset, hoc negaret.

VI

Song vppon a bellowes mender

Here lyes Tom short ye king of good fellowes
Who in his time was a mender of bellowes
But when he came to ye howre of his death
Hee that made bellowes could not make breath.

VII

Vppon on of the Mayds of Honor to Queen Elizabeth

Here lies, the lord haue Mercie vppon hur!
on[e] of hur Ma:^tis mayds of Honor
She was younge slender and prettye
and died a Mayde, mor's the pittye.

VIII

Here the bodie of that man lyes
Whose actions all were Histories
Noe Epitaphe can make him knowne,
nor add one prayse more then his owne.

IX

Of ye losse of time.

If life be time that here is spent
and time on earth be cast away
Who so his time hath here mispent
hath hastned his owne dying day
So it doth proue a killing crime
to massacre our living time.

If doing nought be like to death,
of him y^t doth Camelion wise
take only paines to draw his breath
the passers by may pasquilize
not here he liues: but here he dyes.

X

Mr Hoskines, his own Epitaphe
when he was sicke beinge fellow
in New Colledge
in Oxford

Reader I wold not haue the[e] mistake
deade or alive I deserve not thy knowledge
onelie but this that my bones may make
parte of the dust of soe worthie a Colledge/

XI

Of Swifte

Here lyes Swifte that swiftlie fledd
all company alive, and lived as deade
when death cam for Swift he was verie glad
that so might he shifte of those fewe freindes he hadd
  Always he wo'ld in hast, noe man could intreate him
  Yet nowe here he lyes, yf the wormes haue not
    eate him.

XII

An Ep: one a man for doyinge nothinge

Here lyes the man was borne and cryed
tould three score yeares, fell sick and dyed.

XIII

Of Sr Tho. Gressam

Here lyes Gressam under the ground
  as wise as fifty thousand pound
  he never refused the drinck of his freind
drincke was his life and drunck was his ende.

XIV

HEVS PERIPATETICE

Conde tibi tvmvlvm nec fide haeredis amori
    Epitaphivmque compara
Mortvvs est nec emit libris haec verba dvcentis
    Woodgatvs hic sepvltvs est

XV

Ph. Sidnæi Peplus

[1]

Tandem orata, diu vix exorata Thalia,
    Iamqué satis rauco sollicitata sono:
Surda quidem semper, sed & hoc quoque tempore pauló
    Surdior, ad nostras, quàm solet esse, preces,
Aduenit: & quamuis dea sit iuuenilibus annis,
    Nec iuuenis tardo nec dea visa gradu.
Quærenti quæ causa moræ, nec ad hoc mihi proratè
    Audit, & in gelida lumina figit humo.
Fare precor, dixi, si fas cognoscere, causam,
    An quia non audis, an quia raucus ego?
An quia, quæ quondam tetigit vos gratia nostri,
    Incipit in vestro vilior esse choro?
An Deus Harpocrates Pharia delapsus ab vrbe
    Nunc Heliconiadas iure coërcet aquas?
Illa oculos ab humo paulatim erecta verendos,
    Ah nihil istorum me retinebat, ait.
Sidnæus, Sidnæus, & hoc bis nomine dicto
    Plura locuturæ comprimit ora dolor.
Mox vbi conualuit, Scio quid mediteris; & idem
    Cur vocer, in causa est, curqué vocata morer.
Audiui, veniqué libens, tibi nota Thalia,
    Sum tamen ex animi tarda dolore mei.
Quæ siturus eram, cùm narratura dolorem,
    Tu tace, ait. Tacui. Sic prior illa refert.

Tu quoniam celebrare paras, ego flere, *Philippum,*
    Et mea cum causa iuncta querela tua est:
Audi igitur nostramqué moram, mortemqué *Philippi,*
    Quam quærendo petis, quamqué tacendo cupis.
Ille modò inuitis (ita se bene gesserat) Anglis,
    Ipse nec inuitus, *Belgica* regna petit.
Atque vtinam studio coluisset bella minore,
    Aut minus hoc vno bella gerenda loco.
Nec tamen inuideo laudem quamcumque *Philippo,*
    Sed male quód cedant optima facta, queror.
Hic igitur *Flandris* nimium citó redditus oris,
    (Namqué breuem fecit, me comitante, viam)
Erigit alloquio iam pænè emortua *Belgis*
    Pectora, laturus postmodo rebus opem.
Ecce Dei *Hispanus* veros vi tollere cultus
    Pugnat, vt hoc leue sit quód vetet arua coli.
Non tulit oppressos virtus *Sidneïa Flandros,*
    Non tulit hic spretos mens generosa Deos.
Induit arma Deo plenus, studijqué tenaci
    Me quoque præcipitem traxit in arma manu.
Hîc modó vibratas hastas, modò plumbea furtim
    Miror in incertam tela rotata necem.
Hic bombarda tonat, sera post vulnera voce,
    Terret & ad Stygias quem modò misit aquas.
Ast illic subitô visæ se attollere turres,
    Quodqué fuit tellus antè, fit arte fretum.
Hic facit ingentes in terram turba recessus,
    Inqué suum sese protinus abdit opus.
His, puto, si vera est, onerata est Ossa lacertis,
    Hæc, puto, diuulsus brachia sensit Athos.
Hortatur comites *Sidnæus* in hostica *Belgas,*
    Et docet exemplo vincere castra suo.
Sic pro Romana fertur pugnasse salute
    Tusco Tyndarides auxiliaris agro.
Non ego facta oculis dicam *Sidnëia* nostris
    Cognita, non mæstis facta canenda modis.
Sed cadis, heu, *Sidnæe,* cadis, Miracula nulla
    Terra tulit multos conspicienda dies.

Impius ignauum prædo in te destinat ictum,
  Crusqué venenato figit equestre globo.
At neque tu læsam sentis, Fortissime, partem,
  Nec tibi pars corpus creditur esse tui.
Descensurus equo, data tandem vulnera cernis,
  Cùm negat officium pars tibi læsa suum.
Cernis, & irato suspiria pectore ducis,
  Non quia pes tibi, sed quód pedis vsus abest.
Deficeret corpus, gereres sine corpore bellum,
  Corpore si quisquam militet absque suo.
Quærebat sibi virus edax in corpore vires,
  Nec tabes medicam lenta ferebat opem.
Atque ita *Sidnæus* tot noctes anxius egit,
  Quot tibi non simplex, Regule, pœna foret:
Cum Deus hunc vigilem seruatas linquere terras
  Iussit, & æternum perpetuare diem.
Scilicet hunc rapitis super astra, nec amplius alter
  Quem, Superi, terris inuideatis erit?
Tanti erat hunc vnum miseris donasse Camœnis,
  Gaudia Pierij nec rapuisse chori?
Quis mihi Danubius miseræ satis ora rigabit,
  Aut satis in lacrymas quis mihi Nilus erit?
At ferus ille mei Mars causa caputáue doloris,
  Hunc Parnassiacis egit in arma iugis.
Nec satis hoc fuerat, raptum quoque luget ab armis,
  Et partem luctus pugnat habere mei.
Sint lugenda licèt, recreant me fata *Philippi,*
  Fata quòd Æmonij sint imitata ducis.
Missilibus telis transfixus vterque: sed ille
  In templo: hic, acie, cæsus: vterque dolo.
Viuit vterque tamen moriens: Heroïbus alter,
  Alter Dijs superis iunctus, vterque polo.
Quid quòd Alexander Farnesius alter, & alter
  Troïcus, occultam struxit vtrique necem.
Sed quid agis?   Frustra quid fles ingrata Thalia?
  Flebile Achilleo credis obire modo?
Marte obijt, decus est ipsi: clàm, dedecus hosti:
  At iuuenis, iuuenis corpore, mente senex.

Ergo venenata perijt quia glande, dolebo:
    An latet, ad cælos esse venena viam?
Trita via est, æuo saltem tritissima nostro:
    Gallia Medeam, si dubitatur, habet.
Hoc, fatum est Troiæ fatis, occumbere fato:
    Nec virtus nisi per virus obire potest.
Senserat Alcides, Alcidæ senserat hæres;
    Sensit Phyllirides, Phylliridæqué puer.
Si, quæ *Sidnæum*, non abstulit omnia nobis,
    Tristis & ex fastis eijcienda dies:
Si quid adhuc animi mihi restat, & vnica tantæ
    Integra iacturæ mens superesse potes:
Mens age & Hispanos saltem aspice læta dolores,
    Et minuant luctus hostica fata tuos.
Auguror en: dabitis pœnas Hispana iuuentus,
    Et tu sub Parma dux male tecte tua.
Manibus innumeris *Sidnæum* optabitis vnum
    A fatis redimi: nec redimendus erit.
Interea hunc titulum rapti super astra *Philippi*
    Felix subiecto corpore marmor habe:
Qui iacet hîc, non ille iacet, sed ad astra volauit:
    Ista sequi vellet pars, nisi clauda foret.
Est bene quòd partem patriæ, *Sidnæe*, relinquis,
    Vt neque totus abis, sic neque totus obis.

Ph. Sidnæi Peplus

[2]

Celebrate funeratum
Hilares Deæ *Philippum.*
Videóne vos Camœnæ,
An iniqua fascinatis
Species obest ocellis?
Aganippides-né veræ,
Mihi numen expetitum?
Aganippidum-né talis
Lacerata turba crines,
Caperata turba frontem,

Oculos, genas, labella,
Misero rigata fletu,
Venit ad suos poëtas?
Aganippides profectò:
Nimium tamen seuera
Facie, sed vnde vobis
Nebulosa frons paternum
Didicit referre fulmen?
Vbi splendor ille vestri,
Vbi lux serena vultus,
Satis ausa prouocare
Veneremque Gratiasque,
Hyperionisque nato
Medio inuidenda cœlo?
Ego me nitore tanto
Comitante, non grauarer
Stygijs datum tenebris.
Heliconios in agros
Ego vos sequens, negarem
Rhodios vel esse solis
Radijs, vel esse famâ
Nisi mentiente, claros.
Nitor iste quò recessit,
Et amabilis venustas?
Redeat vetusta forma,
Mihi grata, cariorque
Maris Indici profundo
Rutilantibus lapillis.
Remouete iam dolores,
Gemitusque pertinaces:
Satis est, satis, superque
Cineri datum *Philippi.*
Lacrymis quousque vestris
Heliconis vnda notas
Superabit aucta ripas?
Sale fons coinquinatos
Latices, nec eliquatis
Niuibus, nec imbre factos

Stupet alueus tumores.
Stupet ecce fons, fugamque
Meditatur Hippocrene.
Moderatiore fletu
Nepheleïs expetita est.
Quoties opaca mater
Mare turbat, atque mersam,
Sua damna, quærit Hellen:
Freta cum Leander audax
Putat excitata ventis,
Lacrymis sed illa crescunt.
At vt huic nihil citato
Licet inuenire ponto,
Nisi triste nomen Helles:
Ita vos nihil, *Philippi*
Nisi nomen hoc in orbe,
Et in orbe nil celebre
Nisi nomen hoc *Philippi,*
Reperire fas putetis.
Aliud nihil Pelasgæ
Nisi te, *Philippe*, Musæ,
Aliud nihil Latinæ,
Nisi te, sonare norunt:
Latioque iam potita
Decus agri turba Tusci
Proprium silet Petrarcham,
Tibi carmen ore fundit.
Neque Galla, nec Britanna,
Nec Ibera siqua Clio est,
Alium virum canendum
Nisi te, *Philippe*, sumit.
Licèt hostis ipse, fusi
Sibi conscius cruoris,
Renuat, tuas vel aure
Bibit abnuente laudes.
Alemanicæ Camœnæ,
Facilesque iam Sycambræ,
Sibi militem ducemque

Doluere morte raptum.
Et Aramicam *Philippi*
Tetigere fata Musam:
Nisi forte Musa nulla est,
Quia Musa nota paucis.
Sed in his, *Philippe*, paucis
Quis inesse te vetabit?
Tibi nulla pars peractæ
Fuit vsitata vitæ.
Tua qui sequendo viui
Potuit referre facta;
Nimis ille, si quis ille est,
Ioue natus est secundo.
Tua qui cadendo in armis
Potuit referre fata;
Nimis ille (sed quis ille?)
Nimis ille nemo certé;
Nisi Iupiter sit ipse.
Celebrate funeratum
Nouies nouem Camœnæ.
Celebrate quotquot vsquam
Heliconidum sororum
Varias soletis artes
Varia docere voce.
Reticetis? impeditné
Dolor has, an ira, laudes?
Vetat ira; nam dolorem
Doluistis antè totum.
Nihil est quod antè fusis
Lacrymis quis alter addat
Gemitus: sed ira, Musæ,
Iubet ira vos tacere.
Scelus ecquod est Philippi,
Sibi quod priùs secundum
Rear excitare numen?
Scelus esset hoc putare.
Grauis at rapina, nuper
Fugientis hinc Philippi,

Tulit hinc in astra, quidquid
Helicon scientiarum
Peperit: suisqué Tempe
Vacua artibus reliquit.
Fruitur sed ille tantis
Opibus; colitqué cœlos
Spolijsqué tecta partis
Iouis ornat alta victor.
Pater annuit Deorum,
Neque lętior putatur
Statuisse, post Gygantes
Superûm labore cæsos,
Medio tropæa cælo.
Inopes dolent receptum,
Et amant tamen receptum,
Superis Deæ *Philippum.*
Sed vt inuicem profari
Dolor, ira, amorǘque pugnant,
Faciunt silere mœstas
Dolor, ira, amorque Musas.
Mea quisquis (vt merentur)
Malè nata verba culpas,
Reticentibus memento
Domino excidisse Musis.

Ph. Sidnæi Peplus

[3]

Mors grauis nimis, ah, nimis grauis mors,
Quæ cunctis animam suam Britannis
Rapis, totǘque homines necas in vno:
Quod crudele satis, satisǘque longum
Facto supplicium tuo precabor?
An, qua tu reliquis soles nocere
Morte, illam capiti tuo precabor?
Vt fiat tibi pœna talionis.
At mors non poterit nocere Morti,
Serpentem citiùs venena perdent.

Ergo (Dij iubeant valere vota)
Vitam perpetuam tibi precabor.
Vt sis ipsa tuæ molesta vitæ
Mors grauis nimis, ah, nimis grauis mors.

Ph. Sidnæi Peplus

[4]

Vt inexorabile texi
Vidit Tritonia fatum,
Neque Mauors cætera discors,
Sed in hoc concordibus vno
Studijs, fera flectere posset
Auidarum corda sororum,
Fratrisque suasque Minerua
His verbis prodidit iras:
Solus-né Coronide natus
Superas reuocabit ad auras
Thesiden; solus Apollo
Immensos fata per annos
Poterit proferre Sibyllæ?
Igitur dea nulla Minerua est,
Et Mars sine numine nomen:
Et quisquam é plebe deinde est,
Qui nostris credulus aris
Imponet thuris honores?
Et quisquam credet habere
Diuinas carmina vires,
Aut fortis robora dextræ?
Noster iacet, ecce, *Philippus*,
Nec dos fugat vtraque mortem.
Neque sustinuere sorores
Dare tempora iusta senectæ,
Viridis sed fila iuuentæ
Placet immatura secari.
Sed & hoc fortasse verentur,
Ne, cum stata venerit hora,
Instantia fata repellat,

Qui tam iuuenilibus annis
Studet immortalia tantùm.
Properant quoque stamina Parcę,
Ne, si mora parua supersit,
Fatorum à legibus ipsam
Redimat virtute iuuentam.
Impunis cætera turba
Quæ sicut corpore curuo,
Ita spectat pectore terram,
Digitis, iam mente labante,
Transactos computat annos,
Primis neque rapta sub ausis
Moritur lugenda propinquis:
Tu, cuius cœlica virtus
Ad lucida nititur astra,
Cadis immaturus, & in te
Miseri spes occidit orbis.
At nil nisi corpus iniqua
Mors deletura *Philippi* es,
Pulchro adiungetur Olympo
Nostri pars altera iuris.
Dixit Dea, at inuida Clotho
Fusum aptat, & altera telam
Quærit, vix Atropos illam
Patitur sua ducere fila,
Sed in ipso stamina fuso
Scelerato pollice rumpit.

Ph. Sidnæi Peplus
[5]

Collis ô Heliconij
Cultor, ô modó Belgicæ
Grande militiæ decus,
Nunc poli rutilans iubar,
    Gaudiumq́ue Deorum,
An-né de supera vacat
Arce, funeris irritas
Cernere exsequias tui,

Vt locum lacrymis rigent
    Myrrhinis*que* suis*que*
Nobilis procerum cohors,
Sordida*que* Academia
Veste? tu tamen omnium
Rides stultitiam piam,
    Et stultam pietatem.
Aula quem pia Principis,
Quem parens Academia
Mortuum putat & gemit,
Non ibi positus iacet,
    Sed cum Dijs agit æuum.
Luctus hic tibi cognitus
Anté, non animum mouet,
Videras quot amantibus
Funderent lacrymas genis,
    Astra te petituro:
Hoc stupes tamen vnicum,
Quid velit sibi fæmina,
Quæ flet ad tumulum tuum,
Sic tumens, quasi viscera
    Rumpi tota minentur:
Corpus est macie obsitum,
Recta nusquam acies stetit,
Carpit, ipsa*que* carpitur,
Est*que* supplicium suum,
    Felle pectora squalent:
Vulgus Inuidiam vocat.
Non flet illa, quòd occidis
Morte, sed lacrymas ciet,
Quòd tam fortiter occidis
    Morte non lacrymanda.

Ph. Sidnæi Peplus

[6]

Qvi iam fato meliore viges,
Acie*que*, vides præsente Deos,

Tætra mundi fæce solutus,
Pæné in primo limine vitæ,
Quemq́ue, imprudens fecerat hostis
Terras supero mutare polo,
Si modó rursus patrijs esses
Redditus oris, rursusqué suo
Hæc gestiret terra *Philippo* :
Quid tibi tandem prius optares,
Quàm, si posses, occidere vt priùs?
Si Nestoreos Dij tibi vellent
Iterum viuo donare dies,
Pro Nestoreis tu tamen annis
Toties peteres, vt prius, emori,
Quoties Pylius musta quotannis
Bibit autumno redeunte senex.
Si quid Superos velle putarem
Potius fieri quàm superos Deos,
Tecum rerer velle perisse
Funere parti nominis æmulos.
Hoc officium nunquam potuit
Pro Dardanidis præstare suis,
Cætera præstans omnia, Apollo :
Nec pro Troia sustinuit mori
Licèt *Æneæ* saucia mater.
Tam præclaro licèt inuideant
Numina facto, numina tale
Edere facinus natura vetat.

Ph. Sidnæi Peplus

[7]

Reddita cognato proles Sidneïa cœlo,
    Quem tenet in vobis, Numina summa, locum?
An nouus in cœlo fidicen stellisq*ue* coruscus
    Temperat Orpheæ fila canora lyræ?
An-né, fatigato post tot modó secla Tonante,
    Pro Ioue nec dextra debiliore tonat?

Sic licèt hic vates, quo nemo doctius ipsos
  Detineat cithara carminibusque Deos:
Non tamen Ismario est dignus succedat vt Orpheo,
  Et cui non primo sit lyra danda loco.
An iaciet fulmen? dilectas fulmine terras
  Lædere tam mites non didicere manus.
Atqui aliquod munus, Superi, præscribite: munus
  Desidiam virtus nescia ferre, petit.
Spreta (videtis enim) Phœbeæ fræna senectæ
  Igniferos ægrè iam moderantur equos.
Huic date soliferos currus, nec ab igne timete;
  Nouit quas habeat terra polus*que* vias.
Nec nouus hic fuerit Phœbus; nam munera Phœbi
  Inter Castalias gesserat antè Deas.

Ph. Sidnæi Peplus

[8]

Thalia debet omne, quod potest, bonum
  Carmen *Philippo* soluere:
Nihil Thalia carminis boni potest;
  Persoluit hoc totum Nihil.

XVI

[Epitaph on Anne, Countess of Oxford]

Anna Vera uxor Eduardi Veri Comitis Oxoniæ, filia Guil.
Burghlæi summi Angliæ Quæstoris, mulier pietate, prudentia,
patientia, pudicitia & in Coniugem amore singulari, principi,
parentibus, fratribus & universæ Aulæ regiæ admodum chara.
Obiit in Aula regia Greenwici. Tres filias superstites
reliquit.

Anna

Anna soror soror Anna suae charissima Elisæ
  Dum fugit hostiles per $\begin{Bmatrix} mare \\ freta \end{Bmatrix}$ fratis opes:
Itala naufragio felici littora tangit
  Et potitur Latia numen et exul humo

Invenit et nomen, templum invenit, invenit aras,
   { Pigmalionææ sic nocuere minæ
   { Pigmalionæis nuper abacta minis
Sors ea Phoenissæ: sed Romæ traditur Anna
   Culta suburbanis altera diva locis.
Namque sacro dum plebs dubitavit monte, Tribunos
   An penum potius posceret, illa dedit.
Has sua seu pietas seu munificentia divas
   Effecit, certe fecit utramque deam
Nec satis esse deas, voluit quoque fama Perennas
   Addere, ne titulis posset obesse dies.
Tertia si nostro nondum cognoscitur æro
   Anna, poetarum nunc ego pace canam.
Non hanc suppeditant vatum mihi somma: Vera est:
   (Id quoque quod verum est esse perenne solet.)
Sive amor in reliquos ab eodem stemmata natos
   Efficiat numen, sive benigna manus;
Quin Veræ fers thura Deæ? Nam fratribus eius
   Notus amor satis est, pauperibusque manus.
Scilicet Anna Dea est: nondum tamen Anna Perenna est:
   Vita dare id nequiit, mors id honesta dedit.
Exulat a patria veluti Phœnissa, simulque
   Invenit exilio gaudia vera suo.

Vera

Vera fuit: satis hoc: nec fas superaddere, falsum
   Quicquid id est vero quod superaddis erit.
Et tamen insignis sub Verae nomine splendor
   Conditur & plus quam Penelopea fides.
Penelopen etenim potuit locus ipse pudicam
   Reddere & absentis cura metusque viri.
Thracis equi terrore animum tenuere pudicum,
   Et referens madidas Hector ab hoste manus:
Et Læstrigoniæ memorata pericula terræ
   Atque premens rabidos Scylla proterva canes:
Oraque Cyclopis crudo eructantia tabo
   Semibolosque pedes, semipedesque bolos.

Et Circe et plures quam finxerat illa figuræ
    Sollicitam nuptæ continuere fidem.
Et merito: sed quæ gaudet præsente marito,
    Et facie fruitur non fruitura toro.
Hæc si casta manet votis operata pudicis,
    Continet hæc omnis unica Penelopas.

Uxor Eduardi Veri Comitis Oxoniæ.

Dat Comes a nostris socium: tibi nomen Athenis
    Ingenii Actæas tu superaddis opes.

Filia Guilielmi Burghlæi summi Angliæ
Quæstoris.

Cui Deus hanc terram thesaurum credidit orbis,
    Et cui thesauros hæc quoque terra suos,
Qui fit ut amittas hanc (prudentissime) gemmam?
    Scilicet illa Dei non tua sola fuit.
Hanc dedit hanc rapuit Deus, æquum fecit uterque
    Tu quod habes grates, iusque quod ille suum.

Mulier pietate

Quæ superis dignam te fecit, & abstulit istinc,
    Plura mihi dolor hac de pietate loqui.

Prudentia

Fata Sibylleum pectus tribuere, sed eheu
Fata Sibyllæos non tribuere dies.

Pudicitia patientia & in Coniugem amore singulari

Fida viro (licet hoc mihi dicere) Vera fuisti,
    Cætera mitto satis nota, probata nimis.
Hæc tua posteritas dictum est, quando putabit
    Nemo suum laudi crimen messe tuæ.

Principi, parentibus, fratribus & uniuersæ
Aulæ regiæ admodum chara.

Quæ nunquam nocuit sciens amicis
    Et sueta est inimicum habere nullum
    Omnes illa sciens volensque amicos
    Læsit, nempe sciens volensque obivit.

Obiit in Aula regia Greenwici.

Quo Regina loco nata est & mortua Vera,
Hic satis absque suo nomine notus erit.

Tres filias superstites reliquit.

En Veri et Verae, Jovis Eunomiæque putăris
    Tres natas totidem credideris Charitas
Vatibus hinc hinc est quod gratia nulla supersit
    Hinc est carminibus quod gratia iusta negatur
    Tristantur Charites Occidit Eunomia.
Calliope his inquis nulla est in versibus erras.
    Ipsa est, quam raptam defleo, Calliope.
          vel sic
Par sine Calliope numeris hæc verba ligari
    His ego Calliopen occubuisse fleo.

Qui doctis oculis soles
    Cœli convexa tueri
Accipe nunc quare latitârit septima Pleias?
    Scilicet hoc *quare* latuit quoque sæculo priori.
Atlantis illa filia est.   Atlantis at Britanni.
    Polus hanc nec ante texit, nec enim polus habuit.
    Sed illa fecit ut Britanniæ solum
    Non invideret Pleiadas suas cælo.
    Tanta coruscantis gloria lucis erat.
    Cladis Hispanæ tamen illa nuper
    Abit ad superas nuncia sedes.
    O quam nunc vereor ne placeat Jovi
    & ne recursum protervus
    Invideat teneatque cælo.
Digna quidem cælo est Atlantis, dignus et Atlas.
Onus ille grande regni validis tulit humeris.
Feretque spero longius: diesque quos negavit
In terris natæ, volet addere Juppiter parenti.

Arguis obscurum verbis qui struxerat aram?
Nimirum lapidas debuit ille loqui.

Ara quidem non est tamen aram carmina credunt,
    Cernis enim ut spreto huc ordine conglomerent.
                sive ita
Spectârunt aram versus, fierique putârant
    Sacra, & cuiusvis ordinis irruerant.
Ne lege, nam flebis, dubitas? prædico ego, flebis,
    Nec siccis oculis ista videre potes.
Nam tu materiam si non fles, carmina flebis,
    Condidimus vitiis carmina flenda suis.
                    V. M. Pergamam
                    Joh. Hoskins.

XVII

From

Oxoniensivm Στεναγμός siué   Carmina . . . in
obitum . . . Christophori Hattoni

    Si mens, si virtus, si gratia principis ornant
        Hattone nec tenuis nuda nec umbra iaces.
Occidis exesos renes torrente lapillo,
    Nunc tibi sub lapidum mole beata quies.
Cum generi humano lapis intra viscera crescat,
    Quis poterit tumuli non meminisse sui?

XVIII

[Commendatory Verses for William Gager's
Vlysses Redux]

Ibis, Homere, foras, venias si nudus, Homere,
    Spernit inornatum Scena superba senem.
Texuit auratum tua Musa, Gagere, cothurnum,
    Credo equidem iam non ibis, Homere, foras.

Cum iam cicutam Socrates haustu vltimo
    Sumpturus esset, lætius mortem tulit,
Campis quod Ithacum mox in Elysijs Ducem
    Videret; atqui Socrates iam viueret,
Campis*que* vellet credo ab Elysijs gradum
    Referre, vt Ithacum videat in Scenâ Ducem.

XIX

Of the B. of London.

I was the first that made Christendom see
a Bishop to marry a Ladie, Lady
the cause of my death is secreat and hid
I cryed out I dyed and soe I did

XX

Of One y^t kepte runinge Horses

Here lyes that man whose horse did gayne
the bell, in race one Salisburye playne
Reader I know not whether nedes it,
Yo^u or the horse rather to reade it.

XXI

On Dreames

Yo^u nimble dreames wth cob webb winges
   that flie aboute from braine to braine
   and rep^{r}sent a world of thinges
wth much adoe and little paine

Yo^u visitt Ladies in their bedds
   and are most busie in their ease
Yo^u putt such fancies in their heads
   that makes them thynck on what yo^u please.

Howe highelie am I bound to yo^u
   (Safe Messengers of secresie)
   that made my M^{rs} thynke on mee
iust in the place where I would bee.

O that yo^u would [me] once preferr
   to bee in place of one of yo^u
that I might goe to visitt her
   and shee might sweare here dreame was true.

XXII

Loue is a foolish melancholie
    Leading mens Minds w^t false persuasion
Else why should I not see my folye
    That loose whole times to gaine occasion

My loue is almost Lunacy
    Mee thinkes my hart is so on fire
    That though my mistrisse sent for mee
I dare not for my life com nye her.

Mee thinkes loues sparkles so would starte
    And at her sight giue forth such flame
That standers by would see my hart
    And by the light cleare read my name.

Then best to single her alone
    Though to encounter shee be loth
The match is equall one to one
    And solitud will right us both

Alone or elsewhere else in vaine /
    For evrye time that yet wee met
Was but a cause to meet againe /
    for some what that I did forget.

I will not loue and yet I will
    for feare lest I leaue off a looser
I will not let my sute lye still
    lest man speed besyde that wooes her.

Let loue the God or Loue the Boy
    Make her to loue me if he can
Let God or Boy teach her that Toy
    Ile say at least he is a Man.

XXIII

The Dying Louer

Some powers Regard me or my hart will burne
Till it conuert my bosome to an vrne
I call for no physitians how you Spread
You fatall Carryons of a Sick mans bed
Stand frō about mee hearbs nor mineralls can
Cure yᵉ Consumption of a loue-sick man
You Climbing waues if happily at this hower
you haue Some New Leander in yʳ power
Oh let his Voyage Calmer fortunes try
T'is pitty yᵉ belou'd againe should die
But well you may my Scorn'd breast ouerflow
yet would my heart make yoʳ Cold billowes glow
you Rude winds troublers both of Seas & Skies
before whose wrath yᵉ white wing'd Vessell flye's
leaue persecuting wretches on yᵉ maine
and Coole mee wᵗʰ a Storme but t'were in Vaine
I sprinkle Teares & wᵗʰ full Sayles I breath
Doe fanne flames only to bee quench'd by death.
And See hee Comes how pale! how far unlike
to her yᵗ sent him to mee! wouldst thou strike?
T'is done all readie: Look upon my hart
Alas! Thou knewst not when shee threw yᵗ Dart
Shee makes both Loue & you not as you will
but as Shee guides yʳ hands to saue or kill
perhaps you raign'd in times past but in mine
her Smiles were Loue's darts & her frowns were thine
I'ue Seen her mix a Sad look wᵗʰ a Sweete
Then Life & death All Ioyes All torments meete
like twilight as her Louer could not Say
whether his feares brought night or hopes brought day
Which I must see no more tis her decree
That add's one Sister to yᵉ fatall three
Another to yᵉ Muses if Th' enquire
What wonder this may be please yoʳ desire

It is a beauty such as might giue breath
to Senseless pictures and to me giues death
Muses farewell: Your friendes death deplore
Whom you are not Medeas to restore
Loue let me kiss thy hand by whō I fall
Yet thou hast kill'd mee wth a Cordiall
Death cry thee mercie Loue's Cōmand extend's
soe farre I Saw not thine; yet wee'l meete friends
I feele thee, in my marrow, Thy Shaft lurkes
wth a cold poyson Typt; now now it workes
What Ague's this? but now my heart did glow
Ætna was not soe fiery no^w I grow
more Cold then are ye Alpes I am like one
Toss'd from ye torrid to ye frigid Zone
A winter's in my blood my Veins freeze ore
It Snows upon my heart I Can no more
moue my contracted Sinews If there bee
mongst those y^t in theyr teares would burie mee
Some poore forsaken Virgin y^t did meane
All faith & found no Iustice let her gleane
The ruines of my hart, ye rest Convey
Into Some Sad groue where ye Turtle may
Mourn out my Elegie   write on my Tombe
I had a faire Iudge but a Cruell Doom

XXIV

Absence

That time and absence proves
Rather helps than hurts to loues.

Absence heare my protestation
Against thy strengthe
Distance and lengthe,
Doe what thou canst for alteration:
For harts of truest mettall
Absence doth joyne, and time doth settle.

Who loves a Mistris of right quality,
      His mind hath founde
      Affections grounde
Beyond time, place, and all mortality:
      To harts that cannot vary
      Absence is present, time doth tary:

My Sences want their outward motion
      Which now within
      Reason doth win,
Redoubled by her secret notion:
      Like rich men that take pleasure
      In hidinge more then handling treasure.

By absence this good means I gaine
      That I can catch her
      Where none can watch her
In some close corner of my braine:
      There I embrace and there kiss her,
      And so enjoye her, and so misse her.

XXV

[From

*Oxoniensis Academiæ Funebre Officium in memoriam
Honoratissimam Serenissimæ et Beatissimæ Elisabethæ,
nvper Angliæ, Franciæ, & Hiberniæ Reginæ*]

Nascenti, Regina, tibi Lucina favebat;
      Quæ daret ingenii dona, Minerva fuit:
Corpus, ut excrevit, voluit Venus esse venustum
      Fortunis forma conveniente tuis:
Et Fortuna etiam studuit non cæca videri,
      Dum tulit in summas non nisi summa manus.

Mars animos, varii cultum sermonis Apollo
    Tradidit, & dotes Numina quæque suas.
Sic utinam his donis posses Pandora vocari,
    Ut, pro parte sua, nil Libitina daret.

Miraris tanta saturari pace Britannos
    Per totidem fragili sub muliere dies?
Mireris potius mulierem posse putari,
    Cui præter corpus nil muliebre fuit.

Qui fuerat morbus Reginæ immissus ab alto
    Nobilis ut posset nuncius esse necis
Callidus obstruxit guttur, linguamque ligavit,
    Ne cuperet summum flectere lingua Deum.

Dum cecidere alii, lacrymæ cecidere: nec unquam
    Bis, semel abruptus, flebilis esse solet.
At quoties quotiesque unam meditamur Elisam,
    Efficit ut toties visa sit illa mori.

O quæ tam sacræ resecabas stamina vitæ,
    Siue dea es, veri sive ministra dei;
Anglica te potuit Reginæ lingua movere,
    Ausoniâ potuit lingua movere prece,
Te potuit verâ Gallorum voce rogare,
    Nec non Cecropiis sollicitare sonis:
Quin, sermone tuo si forte imiteris Iberos,
    Hac didicit quamvis hostis ab hoste loqui.
Sed tu, Parca, omnes superabas, barbara, Gentes,
    Nam tibi, quo loqueris, nil nisi culter erat.

Ex quo legitimum sumpserunt brachia sceptrum,
    Estque adeo puras nacta Corona cornas,
Cura fuit semper divini gloria cultus,
    In terris cœlum condere cura fuit:
Dic mihi, num cœlos, ubi sunt non invenit illa,
    Quæ voluit cœlos ædificare solo?

XXVI

[From
Academiæ Oxoniensis Pietas Erga Serenissimvm
Et Potentissimvm Iacobvm AngliÆ Scotjæ Franciæ
& Hiberniæ Regem, Fidei defensorem, Beatissimæ
Elizabethæ nuper Reginæ legitimè & auspicatissimè
succedentem]

Vt quondam Isacus, proli benedixit Elisa:
    Relligio est proles, tùm benedicta, minor;
Ille vetustatis fingens sibi nomina, parces
    Papicola est, Esau qui senioris agit.
Ille dies luctus fatum*que* precatus Elisæ
    In fratrem statuit tela faces*que* suum;
Ecce dies luctus; quia fata subivit Elisa
    Nunc Abrahæ Isaco proxima tecta sinu.
Nec scio quid tantis Esau profecerit ausis:
    Hoc scio, iam verus sceptra Iacobus habet.

Regia secretos nescit fortuna recessus,
    Stat quasi conspicuo Pyramis illa situ;
Oderit hanc regni malè parti conscia lucem
    Oderit hanc furijs mens agitata suis:
Sed tibi maior eo surget, (sanctissime Regum)
    Spectari possis quo magis intus, honos.

Maxime rex de te scribuntur magna, nec Orbis
    Scribere, vt haud possit plus superesse, potest:
Tu lege, de meritis proprijs & amore tuorum,
    Quæ scribunt alij, verùm ego quæ taceo.

XXVII

To Rowland Vaughan

In praise of the VVorke
and Author.

My little ROWLAND you may looke that I
    (All things considered) MVCH should say of you:
    Then, this your WORKE (to say that MVCH in few)
Shall worke the Workers endlesse Praise: and why?
    „A worldly *WITT*, with Heau'nly *Helpes* indow'd,
    „Getts *Ground*, and *glory* of the *Multitude*.

XXVIII

Convivium philosophicum

Quilibet si sit contentus
Ut statutus stet conventus
    Sicut nos promisimus;
Signum *Mitræ* erit locus,
Erit cibus, erit jocus,
    Optimatatissimus.

Veniet, sed lente currens,
Christoferus vocatus *Torrens*
    Et Johannes *Factus*,
Gruicampus et Arthurus,
Ante coenam non pransurus,
    Veniet primo exactus.

Robertus *Equorum amicus*,
Ne vile æstimet Henricus
    Dignabitur adesse,
*Cuniculus*que *quercianus*,
Caligula occurret Janus
    Si modo sit necesse.

Et Richardus *Guasta-stannum*
Et Henricus *Bonum-annum*
    Et Johannes *Occidens*
Et si quis desideretur
Protinus amercietur
    Pro defaulto fourty-pence.

Hugo *Inferior-Germanus,*
Nec indoctus nec profanus
    Ignatius *architectus*
Sed jocus, nisi invitatus
Veniet illuc *Coriatus,*
    Erit imperfectus.

Nam facete super illum,
Sicut malleus in anvillum,
    Unusquisque ludet.
Coriatus cum potavit,
Lingua regnum peragrabit
    Nec illum quicquam pudet.

Puer fuit expers artis
Et cum fabis et cum fartis
    Somersetizatus.
Vir cum Scotis et cum Anglis
Et cum scarfis et cum spanglis
    Est accommodatus.

Si Londinum,
Si Latinum,
    Amas, te amabit.
Sive Græcum,
Ille tecum
    Sir Edward Ratcliffabit,

Hic orator aratores,
Studens meliorare mores,
    Ubi congregavit,
Rusticos et Corydones,
Fatuos et moriones,
    Dis-coxcombiavit.

Ultra littus, ultra mare,
Per Europam Fleetstreetare,
 Res periculosa.
Idem calceus hunc revexit,
Eadem camisia texit,
 Res pediculosa.

Quisquis hunc ecavilat,
Garretando squabberizat,
 Et pro hac injuria
Disrespectus ambulabit,
Cum bonis sociis non cœnabit
 In urbe vel in curia.

Hic in stolidum elatus,
Ut mountebankus hic effatus,
 Haranguizans bene.
Quisquis hic vult esse prudens,
Adsit, nihil aliud studens,
 Quam potare plene.

Quicquid agis, quicquid dicis,
Jocundando cum amicis,
 Eris fortunatus.
Hunc secundum rectum stampum,
Qui non vivit rampum scrampum
 Nemo est beatus.

Rex religionem curat,
Populus legianciam jurat,
 Cives fœnerantur;
Miles et mercator clamant,
Puer <i> et puellæ amant,
 Fœminæ mœchantur.

Princeps nescit otiari,
Cupiens materiam dari
 Propriæ virtuti.
Carolus, imago patris,
Imitatur acta fratris,
 Prælucens juventuti.

Cancellarius juvat multos,
Prudentes juvat, juvat stultos,
   Humillime supplicantes.
Thesaurarius juvat summos;
Sed quoniam non habet nummos,
   Invident mendicantes.

Northamptonius, nunquam satis
Literis et literatis
   Juvandis, delectatur.
Et Suffolcius, severe
Regis familiam coercere
   Quærens, defatigatur.

Proceres ædificant,
Episcopi sanctificant,
   Clerus concionatur;
Generosi terras vendunt,
Et, dum rustici contendunt,
   Juridicus lucratur.

Unusquisque sic facessit,
Cor nullius conquiescit,
   Nemo habet satis.
Solus Coriatus sapit,
Nihil perdit quicquid capit,
   Nec stultescit gratis.

XXIX

Incipit Johannes Hoskins.

Cabalistical verses, which by trans-

position of words, syllables, and letters,
make excellent sense, otherwise none,
   In laudem Authoris [Thomas Coryate]

Even as the waues of brainelesse butter'd fish,
With bugle horne writ in the Hebrew tong,
Fuming vp flounders like a chafing-dish,

That lookes asquint vpon a three-mans song:
Or as your equinoctial pasti-crust
Proiecting out a purple chariot wheele,
Doth squeaze the spheares, and intimate the dust;
The dust which force of argument doth feele:
Euen so this Author, this Gymnosophist,
Whom no delight of trauels toyle dismayes,
Shall sympathize (thinke Reader what you list)
Crown'd with a quinsill tipt with marble prayse.

Encomiologicall Antipasticks cō-

> *sisting of Epitrits, the fourth in the first*
> *syzugie, which the vulgar call Phaleuciac*
> *hendecasyllabes; trimeters Catalecticks, with*
> *Antipastic Asclepiads, trimeters Acatalectics*
> *consisting of two dactylicall comma's of some*
> *learned named choriambicks, both together di-*
> *coli distrophi, rythmicall and hyperrythmicall,*
> *amphibologicall, dedicated vnto the vndeclin-*
> *able memorie of the antarkisticall Coryat, the*
> *only true trauelling Porcupen of England.*

Admired *Coriat*, who like a Porcupen,
Dost shew prodigious thinges to thy countri-men.
As that beast when he kils doth vse his owne darts,
So do thy pretty quils make holes in our harts.
That beast liues of other company destitute,
So wentest thou alone euery way absolute.
That beast creepeth a foote, *nec absque pennis*,
So didst thou trot a journey hence to Venice.
Liue long foe to thy foe, fierce as a Porcupen.
Liue long friend to thy friend, kind as a Porcupen.
Hencefoorth adde to thy crest an armed *Histrix*,
Since thy cariage hath resembled his tricks.

The same in Latine.

Se iaculo, sese pharetræ, sese vtitur arcu,
> *In reliquas Histrix dum parat arma feras.*

Se comite ad Venetam tendens Coriatius vrbem,
   Se duce, se curru, se fuit vsus equo.
Et decantat iter se nunc authore stupendum,
   Nec minus à reditu se quoque teste sapit.
Ergo non immeritò peregrinans dicitur Histrix.
   Et laudes à se, non aliundè capit.

No more but so, I heard the crie,
And like an old hound in came I
To make it fuller, though I find
My mouth decayes much in this kind.
The cry was this, they cride by millions,
Messengers, Curriers, and Postillions,
Now out alas we are vndone
To heare [of] *Coryats* paire of sho'ne;
There is no newes we are more sory at,
Then this strange newes of *Rawbone Coryat.*
Who like an Vnicorne went to Venice,
And drinking neither Sacke nor Rhenish,
Home in one paire of shoes did trample,
A fearefull and a strange example,
But what's the news of learned people
In Pauls church-yard and neere Pauls steeple?
Hang vp his shoes on top of Powles
Tyed to his name in parchment rowles,
That may be read most legibly
In Tuttle fields and Finsbury.
Fame is but wind, thence wind may blow it
So farre that all the world may know it:
From *Mexico,* and from *Peru*
To China and to Cambalu:
If the wind serue, it may haue lucke
To passe by South to the bird *Rucke,*
Greater then the Stymphalides
That hid the Sunne from *Hercules.*
And if Fames wings chance not to freeze,
It may passe north nītie degrees,
Beyond *Meta incognita,*
Where though there be no holiday,

Nor Christian people for to tell it,
Horrible Beares and Whales may smell it.
Thence may it on the Northern seas,
On foote walke to the Antipodes,
Whose feet against our feet do pace
To keepe the center in his place.
But when those fellowes that do wonder
As we at them, how we go vnder
From clime to clime and tongue to tongue,
Throughout their Hemispheare along,
Haue tost these words as bals at tennis,
Tom Coryate went on foote from Venice,
This trauelling fame, this walking sound
Must needs come home in comming round,
So that we shall cry out vpon him,
His fame in trauell hath outgone him,
When all haue talked, and time hath tri'd him,
Yet *Coryate* will be *semper idem.*

Scilicet haud animum cœli mutatio mutat,
      Et patriam fugiens se quoque nemo fugit.
Thersites Phrygiis Thersites perstat in oris,
      Nec Plato in *Ægypto desinit esse Plato.*
Nec Thomas Tomyris *visis remigrabit ab Indis,*
      Nec Cordatus erit qui Coriatus erat:
When all haue talked, and time hath tri'd him,
      Yet *Coryate* will be *semper idem.*
            Explicit Ioannes Hoskins.

XXX

Ad chutum & sharpum

Chute meæ infœlix consors et *Acute* ruinæ
      quem mihi comunis iunxit vtrunque dolor
Quæ vestra est pietas! inclūsi carcere versus
      scribitis; heu mestos exigitisque meos.
Non bene Pegasiæ subeunt ergastula musæ
      non bene Castaliæ carceris antra diræ

Suppeditant colles et amœnæ carmina silvæ
  Et quæ Tyrrheis arva rigantur aquis
Pectore dimanant vacuo curisque soluto
  Et sunt tranquillæ carmina mentes opus
Nos vigil exanimat custos et ahenea turris
  iustaque sollicitos Cæsaris ira tenet
Prosa decet potius nostros oratio luctus
  tristis et ad nullam vox modulanda liram
vestra tamen vicit melior sententia, doque
  vinctas, dum recolo crimina nostra, manus
verba modis mihi vincta placent, infausta dederunt
  captivos nobis verba soluta pedes.

XXXI

To his Son Benedict Hoskins

Sweet Benedict whilst thou art younge,
And know'st not yet the vse of Toung,
Keepe it in thral whilst thou art free:
Imprison it or it will thee.

Dum Puer es, vanæ nescisq*ue* incomoda Linguæ
Vincula da Linguæ, vel Tibi Lingua dabit.

XXXII

JACOBO MAGNÆ BRITANNIÆ REGI MAXIMO, CLEMENTISSIMO.

Jam mihi bis centum fluxere in carcere noctes,
  Quælibet at lachrymis nox madefacta meis:
Bis centum rutilante dies candore notati,
  Sed mihi (væ misero) quælibet atra dies.
Nulla fatigatis venia exorata querelis,
  Nec penitus fracto corde petita datur.
Non me amissa movet (minui quam crimine) fama,
  Non me causidici lucra negata fori;
Non movet injusti vindex sibi creditor æris,
  Inque meo quamvis debitor ære tenax;

Non qui justa negat mihi vectigalia, nullo
  Captivos retinens jure colonus agros;
Non qui armenta meis ipsa insultantia vinclis,
  In mea prædator prædia liber agit;
Non nati tristes, non flens sine conjuge conjux,
  Non nimis exiguæ magna ruina domus;
Vnum hoc infausto lapsis ex ore loquelis,
  Me tibi, meque Deo displicuisse dolet.
Omnia perpeterer placato teque Deoque,
  Et mihi paupertas libera grata foret.
Et piget, et doleo, sed quod doleoque pigetque,
  Non sinis (heu) tanta lenius esse mora.
Vt lugere meum est, ita luctu nolle moueri,
  Est nimis a genio res aliena tuo.
Parce, Britannorum mitissime, maxime Regum,
  Anglorum minimo subditus oro minor.
Parce, nec vlterius nostrum aversare dolorem:
  Ille dolet frustra qui sine fine dolet.
Si mihi sit linguæ pœna hæc diuturna procacis,
  Solus apud superos Tantalus alter ero.
Stat miser, et labris poma illudentia perdit,
  Vsque recedentes vsque secutus aquas:
Sic me libertas inhiantem vana relinquit,
  Et magis, vt magis est visa propinqua, fugit.
Est libertatem Jani dare sueta calendis
  Mancipiis olim Roma benigna suis:
Tu melior quovis Romano Cæsare Cæsar,
  Captivum placida me quoque mitte manu.
Sic tibi sæpe novus semper fælicior annus
  Tempora præteritis prosperiora ferat:
Sic tua se longe hinc in cœlum porrigat ætas,
  Tot numerans annos, quot mea vincla dies.

                    Britannorum

                      Minimus,

                      Miserrimus,

                              J. Hoskyns.

XXXIII

The same in English

An hundred nights twice told are come & gone
vnwashed with teares, of all those nights not one
As many dayes adornd with glorious light
But vnto me (poore wretch) as blacke as night
No pardon comes though my complaints are tired
And though my hart yts last hath neere expired
Losse of my place and creditt (wch in part
by this offence is lost) greiues not my hart
Whose vniust money iustly is his foe
That he doeth mine detaine breeds not my woe
That those wch haue no right & pay no rent
doe vse my lands tis not my discontent
Nor y^t my pastures entertaine the theife
Whose stollen cattell glory in my greife
My wife & childrens teares moue not at all
Nor moues my litle famylies great fall
That these my lipps wch I may say weere madd
Haue God & thee displeased that makes me sadd
Had I but kept you two vppon my side
Then might my mouth haue bynne X times as wide
And my estate though poore yet being free
Had brought contentment bringing Liberty
I greiue and sorrow but tis not the way
to lessen greife with such a long delay
As ti's [*sic*] my part in sorrow to lament
So from thy nature neuer to relent
pardon thy meanest subiect then this thing
O thou great Brittaines great & glorious king
pardon & doe not with our griefe contend
In vaine he greiues whose greife doeth know no end
If for my wordes my woe must last for euer
with Tantalus in paine I shall perseuer.
The more his lipps the apple striues to stay
by so much more they Swim & glide away
when after freedome greedyly I gape

Then most of all it hastens to escape
Those w^{eh} as slaues & prisoners did liue
At New yeares tide the Romanes did forgiue
O Greater then the greatest Romane Prince
fforgiue thy prisoner this his great offence
So many happy yeares to the succeed
stryuing therin each other to exceed
Long maist thou liue as many yeares to tell
As I haue nombred dayes within this cell. /
                           (or rather hell)
Thou who dislikest & makest mouthes at mine
if thou darest write, Ile doe as much for thine. /

XXXIV

A Dreame.

Me thought I walked in a dreame
betwixt a caues mouth & a streame
vpon whose banckes sate full of ruth,
three as they seemd, but foure in truth.

ffor drawing nere I did behold
a Widowe fourscore winters old,
a wife wth childe, a little Sonne
but foure yeares old, all four vndone

Out of the caues mouth cutt in stone
a Prisoner lookes, whom they did moane,
he smild (they sigh'd) then smote his brest,
as if he meant, god knowes the rest.

The widow cry'd, looking to heaven
Oh Phoebus I thought I had seaven
like Niobe doe now contest
lend this thy light this sonne my best.

Taught for to speake & liue in light
now bound to silence & to night
why is he close vp in this caue
not basely bredd, nor borne a slaue.

Alas this caue hath tane away
my staffe, & all his brothers stay:
Let that be least, that my gray haires
goe to the graue (alas) wth teares.

I greiue for thee Daughter, q^th she,
thee, & that boy, that babe vnborne
yours though not his, yet others three
he loued as his, but now forlorne.

Tis not the rule of sacred hest
to kill the old one in the nest;
as good be killed as from them hidd,
they die wth greife (o^r god forbidd.)

True quoth the boy, for Tom my page
did finde a birds nest, & we tried,
& put the old one in a cage,
then my poor birds, poore birds they died.

My father nere was soe vnkinde
Who lett him then to speake his mynde,
to speake to me & not to kisse,
oh Mother, say, who can doe this?

Then q^th the Wife, tis Caesar's will,
Caesar can hate, Caesar can kill.
the worst is tolld, the best is hidd:
kings know not all, oh would they did.

He Caesars title then proclaymed
vndoubtedly, when others aymed
at broken hope of doubtfull state:
soe true a man what king can hate.

Caesar, in person & in purse,
he serued when better men did worse.
he sware men vnto Caesar's lawes
by thousands, when false hearts did pause.

He frawd & violence did wthstand,
& helpt the poore wth tongue & hand:
but for the cause he now lies here
the cuntry knowes his soule is cleare.

Why is he now silent & sadd
Whose words make [me] & many gladd;
well could he loue, ill could he fayne,
it was his losse, it is my gaine.

If Kings are men, If kings haue wiues,
& know ones death may cost two liues,
then were it noe vnkinglie part
to saue two liues in me, poore heart.

What if my husband once hath err'd?
men more to blame are more preferrd;
he that offends not doth not liue,
he errd but once, once king forgiue.

Caesar to thee I will report,
long be thy life, thy wrath but short:
this prayer good successe may take,
if all doe pray for whom he spake.

With that they wept, the waters swelld,
the sunne grew darke, the darke caues yelld,
it brake my sleepe, I did awake,
& thought it was my heart that brake.

Thus I my wofull dreame declare,
hoping that no such psons are;
I hope none are, but if there be
god help them pray, pray god wth me. /

XXXV

Mr Hoskins wrott in the windowe
    when he came out of the Tower—

Sic luo, sic merui; sed quod meruique luoque
    Tu pœna & meritis ablue Christe tuis.

XXXVI

Ad has reliquias illustrissimi amicissimique
Richardi Martini, Recordatoris
Londinens., qui fato concessit
ulᵗº Octob. 1618

Tu liber æternæ complectens verba salutis,
    Pignus amicitiæ mœstitiæque liber,
Fac me Martini memorem dum vivo sepulti,
    Fac memorem mortis, fac memoremque Dei.

SALVE LECTOR.

Martinus jacet hic; si nescis, cætera quære.
    Interea tumuli sis memor ipse tui.

VALE JURISCONSULTE.

Accedat totum precibus, quodcumque recedit
    Litibus, æternum sic tibi tempus erit.

XXXVII

Ad D. Joannem Audœnum
de libro

Qvo minus edatur, nihil impedit; aut ego carmen
    Non sapio, aut ætas, si sapit, ista leget.
Ingenij tu rere tui tantum esse periculum:
    Judicij tamen est alea jacta mei.
                Joann. Hoskins J. Consultus

De 3. horum epigrammatum editone
Ad Autorem.

Hic Liber est Mūdus; movet & sine fine movetur:
    Ipse licet taceas, Bibliopola probat.
Nam tua perpetuum exercent epigrammata prelū,
    Ponè fatigatis ter repetita typis.
                Joan. Hoskins J. C.

XXXVIII

In eundem Audœnum

Non expers salis ambulator audi
Hanc propter iacet Oënus columnã.
Ne calces epigrammatũ Poetam
Nam Vindex epigrãma calcat orbem.

XXXIX

Sʳ Fra: Bacon. L: Verulam. Vicount Sᵗ Albons.

Lord Verulam is very lame, the gout of go-out feeling;
  Who (therfor,) beggs the crutch of state, with falling
      sicknes wheeling.
Disease, displeasd greeves sore, that state by hidden fate
      shold perish:
  Vnhappy, whom no hope can cure, nor high protection
      cherish.
Yet can I not but marvel much, at this, in common reason,
  that bacon shold neglected be, when it is most in season.
Perhaps the game of Buck, (now come,) hath vilified the
      Bore,
  or els his Crescents are in waine, that he can hunt no more.
Be it what t'will, the relatiues, their antecedents moving,
  decline to case accusatiue, the dative too much loving.
The red-rose-house lamenteth much that this so fatal day
  shold bring the fall of leafe in March, before the spring
      in May.
Sᵗ Albans much condole the losse of the great vicounts
      charter,
  that suffering for his conscience sake, is turn'd Franciscan
      Martyr.
His men look sad, and are sore grieu'd, so suddenly to see
  the hogshead that so late was broach'd, to run so neare the
      lee.

XL

Mr. Hoskins one a dull Lawyer

As a louse as we cracke, hath a list one his backe
    As a badge of his breeding:
Euen soe hath this clowne, a list one his gowne,
    No badge of his readinge.

Mr. Hoskins one Mr Permenter at the
    Chancerye in London

Mr Permentor stands at ye Cent^{er}
    of the chancerye barre
He rumbles, & tumbles, & mumbles, & grumbles
    Like a man of Warre.

As at a banaquett some meates haue sweet, some soure tast,
    Hoskins reply
Euen so y^r dubelet is too short in the wast.

XLI

Sir Henry Wotton, and *Serjeant*
Hoskins, *riding on the way.*

Ho. Noble, lovely, vertuous Creature,
    Purposely so fram'd by nature
        To enthrall your servants wits.

Wo. Time must now unite our hearts:
    Not for any my deserts,
        But because (me thinks) it fits.

Ho. Dearest treasure of my thought,
    And yet wert thou to be bought
        With my life, thou wert not dear.

Wo. Secret comfort of my mind,
    Doubt no longer to be kind
        But be so, and so appear.

Ho. Give me love for love again,
　　Let our loves be clear and plain,
　　　Heaven is fairest, when 'tis clearest.

Wo. Lest in clouds, and in differring,
　　We resemble Seamen erring,
　　　Farthest off, when we are nearest.

Ho. Thus with Numbers interchanged,
　　Wotton's Muse and mine have ranged,
　　　Verse and Journey both are spent.

Wo. And if Hoskins chance to say,
　　That we well have spent the day,
　　　I, for my part, am content.

XLII

[Epitaphs
on
Benedicta Hoskyns and John Bourne]

Hic Benedicta jacet, de qua maledicere nemo
　　Cui genus aut virtus vel pia lingua potest:
Bournii et Hoskinii conjux et prolis utrique
　　Mater erat, Moyli filia, serva Dei.

Nobilis innocuos transegit Bournius annos
　　Multa legens, callens plurima, pauca loquens.
juridicus causis neque se ditavit agendis
　　Non in habendo locans sed moriendo lucrum.

XLIII

[Verses at Morehampton]

Gratus ades quisquis descendis, amicus et hospes:
　　Non decet hos humiles mensa superba Lares.

Stat cœlum, fateor, Copernice; terra movetur;
　　Et mutant dominos tecta rotata suos.

Hac quicunque orat supplex exoret in æde,
  Nec pereant servis irrita vota tuis.

Est casa, sunt colles, lateres, vivaria, lymphæ,
  Pascua, sylva, Ceres: si placet, adde preces.

Pascitur et pascit locus hic, ornatur et ornat:
  Istud opus nondum lapsus amaret Adam.

XLIV

On a young Gentlewoman

Nature in this small volume was about
To perfect what in woman was left out:
Yet carefull least a piece so well begun,
Should want preservatives when she had done:
Ere she could finish what she undertook,
Threw dust upon it, and shut up the book.

XLV

Hoskins conualescens ad Giffordū medicinæ
Doctorem et suum.

Docte Jacoborū decimas Gifforde meorum
  Accipe fiscali præmia pensa manu
Si renuis, pereunte perit cum iudice merces
  Non licet ingratos esse, perire licet.
Hos tibi, Tu, ne finge datos, sed crede solutos
  Qui tuus est, quod det, nil habet ille suum.
Me fecit Deus, infectum medicina refecit.
  Sum quod viuo Dei, quod valeo Medici
Sic qui soluendo non est, in vincula cedi[t] [MS. torn]
  Et pars est æris debitor ipse sui.

XLVI

Epitaph

On Sr Walter Pye, Attorney of the Wardes,
    dying on Christmas Day, in the morning.

If Any aske, who here doth lye,
Say, tis the Deuills Christmas Pye.
Death was the Cooke, the Ouen, the Vrne,
No Ward for this, The Pye doth burne,
Yett serue it in, Diuers did wishe,
The Deuill, long since, had had this Dishe.

XLVII

Vpon the birth of the
Prince

Cum Rex Paulinas accessit gratus ad aras,
    Emicuit medio lucida stella die.
Dic, diuina mihi tractans ænigmata, Præco;
    Hæc Oriens nobis quid sibi stella velit?
Magnus ab occiduo Princeps modò nascitur orbe:
    Crasque, sub Ecclipsiũ regna Orientis erunt.

While at the Altar of St Pauls ye King
    Approached with a gratefull offering;
At noone a starre appeard. Tell me Deuine,
That preached'st riddles, why it did then shine?
    To the Western world a Prince was newly borne,
And th' East to morrow in Ecclipse will mourne.

XLVIII

Undecies senos exegi strenuus annos
    Jam veniet nullo mors inopina die.
Quæ dixi, scripsi, gessive, negotia, lusus,
    Obruat æterno pax taciturna sinu.

Sin quid iure petunt homines, respondeat Hæres,
  Dissipet ut cineres nulla querela meos.
Quodque Deo decoctor iniquus debeo, solve

Quæso Fidejussor $\begin{Bmatrix} \text{sanguine} \\ \text{nomine} \end{Bmatrix}$ Christe $\begin{Bmatrix} \text{tuo,} \\ \text{meo.} \end{Bmatrix}$

Englished

Years sixty six, I have with vigour Past,
But Death, my Daily Thought, is come at last;
My sayings, writings, Deeds, of trifeling Play,
Lett endless Silence, in her Bosom lay:
Be my wrong Dealings, by my Heir redres't,
That no complaint, my Ashes may molest:
And what's to God, from a vile spendthrift, due,

To Christ, for Payment $\begin{Bmatrix} \text{with his Blood,} \\ \text{in my name,} \end{Bmatrix}$ I sue.

APPENDIX A

NOTES ON CHAPTER I

1. The spelling *Hoskyns* rather than *Hoskins* is adopted in this book, since the former is that which he invariably used in his signature and is the one retained by the family he founded, now headed by the Reverend Canon Sir Edwyn Clement Hoskyns, thirteenth Baronet, President, Fellow, Dean of the Chapel, and Librarian of Corpus Christi College, Cambridge. For John Hoskyns' consistent spelling of his name over a long period of time see his letters in Chapter VII, above. The signature to his will of 1619 and the four signatures in the margins of its folios, as well as that to his will of 1627, read *Hoskyns*. Since his will preserved in Somerset House is a transcript, we cannot know how the original was signed. His signature is *Hoskyns* in all his legal papers which I have seen in the Public Record Office. *E.g.*, see that in *State Papers, Domestic, Charles I*, Vol. 122, no. 130.

2. Besides Aubrey's and Anthony à Wood's accounts of Hoskyns, other biographical items, based chiefly upon these two; several printed examples of his work; and certain references have, of course, kept alive Hoskyns' name. In Camden's *Remaines* (1605 and the later editions) a few of Hoskyns' verses are preserved, and some of his lines appear in the various editions of *Reliquiae Wottonianae*. J. Hannah (*The Courtly Poets from Raleigh to Montrose*, London, 1870, pp. 88-9 and 121-22) prints several specimens of his verse. Several others are printed in Grosart's edition of the *Dr. Farmer Chetham Manuscript . . . a Commonplace Book in the Chetham Library* (Volumes 89 and 90 in the *Publications of the Chetham Society*, Manchester, 1873).

Maurice Castelain (*Ben Jonson, L'Homme et Son Oeuvre*, Paris, 1907, pp. 28 and 42) mentions Hoskyns as '*un homme de loi à la fois très instruit et très bon vivant dont l'amitié fut peut-être utile à Jonson.*'

The *D. N. B.* gives a rather inaccurate account of his life, and the *Cambridge History of English Literature* (1919) mentions him three times (IV, 59, 209, and 265).

Sir Herbert Grierson, besides his reference in the *Cambridge History*, refers to or quotes from Hoskyns in the following books: *The Poems of John Donne* (Oxford, 1912, I, 428-29, and II, 102-3, cl-clii, lvii, and cix-x) ; *Metaphysical Lyrics & Poems of the Seventeenth Century* (Oxford, 1921, pp. 23-4 and 221-22) ; and *The Poems of John Donne* (Oxford, 1929, pp. xxv-vi, xxxiv, and 387-88). For further discussion of Sir Herbert Grierson's contributions toward a study of Hoskyns see comments on No. XXIV in notes on Chapter X, below.

Charles Mills Gayley (*Beaumont, the Dramatist*, New York, 1914, pp. 146-49) mentions Hoskyns as a possible friend of Beaumont's and as a member of the Mermaid group and develops that conjecture further in *Shakespeare and the Founders of Liberty in America* (New York, 1917, pp. 25, 28, 38, 90, and 161).

Malcolm W. Wallace (*The Life of Sir Philip Sidney*, Cambridge, 1915, pp. 234-35 and 327) calls attention to and quotes from *Direccōns For Speech and Style* in *MS. Harl. 4604*, pointing out its connection with Sidney. R. W. Zandvoort (*Sidney's Arcadia, A Comparison of the Two Versions*, Amsterdam, 1929, pp. 180-82 and 200) quotes from the *Direccōns* at slightly greater length. Miss Mona Wilson (*Sir Philip Sidney*, Oxford, 1932, pp. 157, 319, and 304-5) mentions Hoskyns and summarizes briefly the *Direccōns*, and Marcus S. Goldman (*Sir Philip Sidney and the Arcadia*, reprinted from *Illinois Studies in Language and Literature*, Vol. 17, Nos. 1-2, 1934) reveals a desire to see the *Direccōns* in print.

Professors Herford and Simpson (*Ben Jonson, The Man and His Work*, Oxford, 1925, I, 3, n. and 164) suggest that Hoskyns may have been the friend by whom Jonson was 'put to school.' The details of Hoskyns' life, however, make it clear that he is by no means a candidate for this particular honour. Only about seven years older than Jonson and entering school somewhat late, Hoskyns was in no position to aid Jonson financially or in any important way at Westminster. Their acquaintanceship undoubtedly developed later. Professors Herford and Simpson once erroneously refer to Hoskyns as *Sir John* (*op. cit.*, I, 164). He was never knighted, though his grandson bore that name and title. They suggest very plausibly that Hoskyns may have been one of the friends Jonson had in mind when he wrote his dedication for *Every Man out of his Humour* (1616).

In a letter to the 'Literary Supplement' of the London *Times* (No. 1,474, 1 May 1930) I pointed out Ben Jonson's indebtedness to Hoskyns' *Direccōns For Speech and Style* for a portion of his *Discoveries*. 'H. H. C.' commented further in the *T. L. S.* (No. 1,475, 8 May 1930). In 1935 Professor Hoyt H. Hudson's edition of the modernised text, *Directions for Speech and Style by John Hoskins*, was published by the Princeton University Press and was reviewed in the *T. L. S.* (No. 1,795, 27 June 1936) and in *Notes and Queries* (Vol. 171, No. 17, p. 305, 24 October 1936). In the *T. L. S.* (No. 1,809, 3 October 1936) Mr. Bernard M. Wagner called attention to a hitherto unnoticed manuscript of the *Directions* (*MS. Ash. Mus. d. 1*, in the Bodleian).

A reviewer of *The Oxford Book of Seventeenth Century Verse*, writing in the *T. L. S.* (No. 1,709, 1 November 1934), regrets, as does Mr. John Sparrow (*Review of English Studies*, Vol. XII, No. 45, January 1936, p. 89), that one or two poems by Hoskyns are not included in that anthology.

Professor Hardin Craig (*The Enchanted Glass*, New York, 1936, pp. 170-71 and 228) mentions Hoskyns.

These items constitute the chief references to Hoskyns as a literary figure. Thus his life has hitherto been subjected to little investigation beyond that made by Aubrey in his sketch based upon valuable family records and traditions. Aside from Hudson's edition of the *Directions*, Hoskyns' writings have remained largely in manuscript, in part unknown, and are in the present book collected for the first time.

3. Besides the more notable expressions and traditions of contemporary regard for Hoskyns, which are noted at various points throughout this book, the esteem in which he was held during the seventeenth century is reflected elsewhere:

John Heath, a fellow of New College, dedicated an epigram (II, 32) to Hoskyns in *Two Centuries of Epigrammes*, London, 1610.

Richard Zouche in *The Dove*, first printed in 1613, may be referring to Hoskyns when he remarks (see the reprint by Richard Walker, Oxford, 1839, p. 50): 'There is, who hath vndertaken to illustrate by places of the *Arcadia*, all the points of the Art of speaking: I will adde . . . he is rude that cannot discerne, or exceeding austere that scornes to observe therein, worthie behauiour and carriage in both priuate and common businesse . . . .'

Hoyt H. Hudson (*op. cit.*, p. xxviii, n. 31) quotes a tribute to Hoskyns from *The Four Ages of England: of the Iron Age* (1648).

John Prince (1643-1723) in his *Danmonii Orientales Illustres: or The Worthies of Devon*, the dedication for the first edition of which he dated 1697, describes Selden, Ben Jonson, and Hoskyns as the 'greatest wits' of their age. See second edition of *The Worthies of Devon*, London, 1810, p. 577.

4. *Direccōns For Speech and Style.* See Chapter IX, above.

5. Pp. 122-24 in *Discoveries*, 1640-41.

6. Blount's borrowings in his *Academie of Eloquence* (London, 1654, *etc.*) were first noted by Hoyt H. Hudson (*op. cit.*, pp. xxx-xxxvii).

7. In *The Mysterie of Rhetorique unvail'd, Wherein* . . . *The Tropes and Figures are severally derived from the Greek into English, together with lively Definitions and Variety Of* . . . *Examples, Pertinent to each of them apart. Conducing* . . . *to the right understanding of the Sense of the Letter of the Scripture* . . . . *Eminently delightful and profitable for young Scholars* . . . . *By John Smith, Gent.* . . . *London, Printed by E. Cotes for George Eversden* . . . *in Pauls-Church-yard, 1657.*

In the copy of the first edition in the British Museum, the 7 in the date has been crossed out in an early hand and a 6 written in. His address to the reader the author dates from his 'Chamber in Mountague Close Southwark March 27, 1656.' This text reached its ninth edition in 1709, its tenth in 1721, and was abridged by '*J. H.*, Teacher of Geography,' in 1739. Thus it had considerable influence as a text throughout the seventeenth century and well into the eighteenth. Hudson (*op. cit.*, xxxvii-viii) notes Smith's indebtedness and suggests that he probably borrowed from Blount rather than from Hoskyns directly.

8. For these hitherto unpublished letters see Chapter VII, above.

9. *'Brief Lives'* by *John Aubrey*, edited by Andrew Clark, two volumes, Oxford, 1898, I, 417.

10. See Anthony à Wood, *Athenae Oxonienses*, edited by Philip Bliss, five volumes in four, London, 1813-20, II, col. 626. There is perhaps no authority for Wood's statement. He seems to have misunderstood Aubrey's remark on Hoskyns' excellent and trained memory (Aubrey, *op. cit.*, I, 421). It is worth noting that Aubrey's manuscript account of Hoskyns is more 'fairly' written, as Clark points out, than most of his other biographies and shows numerous instances of revision and correction. Aubrey's friendship with Hoskyns' grandson, Sir John Hoskyns, and with Sir John's father, Sir Benedict, only son of John Hoskyns, should be recalled in appraising the trustworthiness of this particular biography of Aubrey's.

11. Aubrey, *op. cit.*, I, 418.

In *Curiosities of Literature* (1st series, New York, 1835, pp. 320 ff.) I. D'Israeli claims to have found a manuscript record of sums paid to Hoskyns and others for revision of Ralegh's *History*. But his reference to *MS. Lansdowne 741*, f. 57, which he says is usually mistaken for a boy's ciphering book, does not reveal information regarding contributions to Ralegh's *History*. Hoskyns' reputation as a master of prose technique and his acquaintanceship with Ralegh lend support, however, to the tradition that he may have revised and 'polished' *The History of the World*.

The autobiography Aubrey mentions seems to have been lost.

12. Here and elsewhere, unless otherwise indicated, dates are given in new style.

13. See Chapter IV, above.

14. *The Winning of the Initiative by the House of Commons*, London, 1924, pp. 47-51.

15. See p. 145, above. Though Hoskyns devised this sentence to illustrate the figure of accumulation, it doubtless reflects prevalent thought.

16. Notestein, *op. cit.*, p. 39, note 5.

17. Hoskyns' phrase in *Direccõns For Speech and Style*. See p. 141, above.

18. In *Direccõns*. See p. 117, above.

19. See Hoskyns' statement, p. 145, above.

20. 'Absence heare my protestation' (No. XXIV in Chapter X, above). Reasons for assigning the poem to Hoskyns are discussed in the notes for that chapter.

21. Admitted a scholar of Winchester in 1577. See Thomas F. Kirby, *Winchester Scholars*, London, 1888, p. 148.

22. Admitted a scholar of Winchester in 1581. See Kirby, *op. cit.*, p. 150. Bastard published his epigrams to obtain money, but by 1618 was in prison for debt, where he died that year. See Thomas Corser, *Collectanea Anglo-Poetica*, Part II, *Publications of the Chetham Society*, Manchester, 1861, pp. 209 ff. In *Chrestoleros* (1598), reprinted by the Spenser Society in 1888, pp. 154-55 and 177, occur the following epigrams attributed, apparently erroneously, to Hoskyns in *MS. Chetham 8012*, pp. 158 and 157:

> And was not death a lusty strugler
> in overthcominge James the Jugler
> His lyfe so little truth did use
> that here he lies: it is noe newes.

> Johannis Sande
> Who would liue in others breath?
> Fame deceiues the dead mans trust.
> Since our names are chang'de in death,
> Sand I was, and now am dust.

23. Kirby, *op. cit.*, p. 149. Davies, afterwards knighted, wrote *Orchestra, Nosce Teipsum, etc.*

24. Izaak Walton, *The Compleat Angler / the Lives of Donne / Wotton Hooker Herbert & Sanderson*, edited by Geoffrey Keynes, London, 1929, p. 283.

25. See Logan Pearsall Smith, *The Life and Letters of Henry Wotton*, two volumes, London, 1912, I, 4.

26. *Register of the University of Oxford*, Volume II, Part II, edited by Andrew Clark, Oxford, 1887, p. 135.

Although the Oxford *Register* specifies Donne's age as eleven, F. P. Wilson in 'Notes on the Early Life of John Donne' in the *Review of English Studies*, Vol. 3, No. 11, July 1927, shows that Donne was at least twelve when he matriculated.

27. Clark, *Register*, II, ii, 138.

28. *Ibid.*, II, ii, 141.

29. *Ibid.*, II, ii, 126.

30. *Ibid.*, II, ii, 156.

31. Epigram 96, Book I, *Epigrammatum Joannis Ovven Cambro-Britanni, etc.*, Lipsiae, 1620.

>   On Sig. A₃ of the same volume occurs this epigram:
>   Ad Jo. Hoskins J. C.
>   Poëtam ingeniosissimum de
>   suo Libro
>   Hic liber est Mūdus: homines sunt, Hoskine, versus
>   Invenies paucos hîc, ut in orbe, bonos.

This was translated by Robert Hayman, *Certaine Epigrams . . . of . . . John Owen*, 1628.

A third epigram (Sig. H₉ *v.*) is addressed to Hoskyns:

>   Epigram 152.   Ad amicum suum, D. Joan.
>   Hoskins Juriscons.
>   Claudit amicitiam Numerus plerumque Dualis;
>   Vix in Pluralem multiplicatur amor.

32. See J. Bruce Williamson, *The History of the Temple, London*, London, 1924, pp. 119-26; 176-77; and 189. See also Stow, *op. cit.*, pp. 66-7.

33. Sir William Dugdale, *Origines Juridiciales*, London, 1671, pp. 90-91.

34. For some time before 1614 the Reader, or learned lecturer on law for a given period, and for that time the highest dignitary of the society, was privileged to admit without fine whomever he pleased. But on 28 October 1614 the Parliament of the Middle Temple recorded this decision: 'Readers shall be allowed but one admittance during their reading, and if they exceed, they shall pay the usual fine, except in case of noblemen, knights, or men of great worth, whom Readers shall have full power to admit.' See Charles Henry Hopwood, K. C., *Middle Temple Records*, four volumes, London, 1904-1905, II, 585.

By 7 November 1614, however, the four Inns decreed that 'because the institution of these Societies was ordained chiefly for the profession of the law, and secondarily, for the education of the nobility and gentry, and in no sort for lodging or abode of country gentry, which would disparage them and turn them from *hospicia* to *diversoria*, no knights or gentlemen, foreigners or discontinuers, shall be allowed to lodge or be in commons except they be allowed Utter Barristers.'

35. Hopwood, *op. cit.*, I, 98.

36. *Ibid.*, I, 330 and 338.

37. *Ibid.*, I, 204.

38. Under oath at his trial in 1603 Ralegh declared that he had never read a word of law before his imprisonment in the Tower. See Thomas B. Howell, *State Trials*, London, 1816, II, 16.

39. Hopwood, *op. cit.*, I, 285-86.

40. *Ibid.*, I, 335.

---

41. *Ibid.*, II, 552.

42. Quoted from *MS. Harl. 5353* by C. F. Tucker Brooke, *Shakespeare of Stratford*, New Haven, 1926, p. 108.

43. E. K. Chambers, *The Elizabethan Stage*, four volumes, Oxford, 1923, III, 260-62.

44. *The Comedies and Tragedies of George Chapman, Now First Collected* [edited by R. H. Shepherd], three volumes, London, 1873, III, 91-3. This volume gives a reprint of the lawyers' masque, pp. 87-122, from which my quoted descriptions are taken. The masque was licensed at the Stationers' Register on 27 February 1613.

45. The Middle Templars had admitted Inigo Jones on 21 February 1612. See Hopwood, *op. cit.*, II, 561.

46. See Chambers, *op. cit.*, III, 262.

47. It was no doubt Hoskyns' younger brother John who contributed one of the 286 poems in *Epithalamia* (Oxford, 1613) presented by Oxford University to the King, the Queen, and the bridal pair. The poem is signed *Joh. Hoskins LL. Bacc. Nov. Coll. Soc.* The elder Hoskyns would not have been described as *LL. Bacc.*

48. Chambers (*op. cit.*, III, 262) quotes a letter of a young lawyer who remarks regarding this masque: 'It is a duty for ye honour of our Inn, and unto which I could not refuse to contribute with any credit.'

49. This was a 'showe at all parts so nouell, conceitfull and glorious, as hath not in this land, (to the proper vse and obiect it had porpos'd) been euer before beheld. Nor did those honorable Inns of Court, at any time in this kinde, such acceptable seruice to the sacred Maiesty of this kingdome, nor were return'd by many degrees, with so thrice gratious, and royall entertainment and honor.' See *George Chapman's Works*, ed. cit., III, 94-5.
A suggestion that the favour the Inns gained on this occasion was diminished by royal irritation is recorded by Thomas Birch, *The Court and Times of James the First* (two volumes, London, 1848, II, 359-60), referred to by A. Wigfall Green in his *The Inns of Court and English Drama* (New Haven, 1931, pp. 93-4).

50. See Chambers, *op. cit.*, I, 170.

51. *Ibid.*, I, 169, n. 2. See also Hudson, *op. cit.*, p. 109, n. 2.

52. *Le Prince d'Amour, or the Prince of Love, with a Collection Of Several Ingenious Poems and Songs. By the Wits of the Age*, London, 1660, pp. 37-40.

53. Hudson (*op. cit.*, pp. 108 and 113) has seen the speech in *MS. HM 1338*, in the Huntington Library, subscribed *John Hoskins*. In the British Museum *MS. Add. 25,303*, ff. 184. b-185, the speech is signed *Jo: Hos. his Tuffa*. Hoskyns more than once quotes from the speech in *Direccōns*.

54. *MS. Malone 16*, ff. 74. b-75. a. See Chapter VIII, above.

55. Chambers (*op. cit.*, I, 169, n.) conjectures that Prince Martino was played by Richard Martin. John Prince (*Danmonii Orientales Illustres: or, The Worthies of Devon,* London, second edition, 1810, p. 577) had already stated that 'Martin had been Prince de la More of the Middle Temple in the time of Christmas.' Prince's statement is confirmed by his quotation (*ibid.*) from Hugh Holland's eulogy of Martin: *Princeps Amorum, Principium nec non Amor: Legumque,'* etc. See also Aubrey *op. cit.*, II, 49.

56. *E.g.*, he was known to John Davies of Hereford, who was an associate of many literary men more important than himself. In The *Scourge of Folly* (London, 1610, p. 223) Davies printed this epigram:

To my beloued M^r. Iohn
Hoskins.

Iohn of all *Iohns,* if I should Stile thee so
>   Thou might'st except against it; sith it points
But at some Sott. Then, art thou such a one? No.
Thy witt (good *Iohn's*) too nimble in the Ioynts
>   *To stand for such: but, for witt, thou maist bee*
Iohn *of all* Iohns; *at least, so held of mee.*

Hudson (*op. cit.*, p. xii, n. 7) mentions Davies' commendatory lines in *Wits Bedlam* (1617), the apparently unique copy of which I have not seen.

57. No. XLI, in Chapter X, above.

58. No. XXVIII, in Chapter X, above.

59. Cranfield, in 1621, was a competitor for the place of Lord Keeper of the Great Seal. Hacket (*Scrinia Reserata: A Memorial Offer'd to the Great Deservings of John Williams, etc.*, two parts, London, 1693, Part I, pp. 51 and 105) describes Cranfield as a man 'Married in the kindred that brought Dignity to their Husbands; a man of no vulgar head-piece, yet scarce sprinkled with the Latin Tongue.' He held the post of Master of the Wards and was created Earl of Middlesex in 1621, after he had failed of becoming Lord Keeper.

60. See Notestein, *op. cit.*, pp. 30-31.

61. So described on the title-page of the first edition of the lawyers' masque by Chapman, referred to in note 44, above.

62. Ben Jonson dedicated *Poetaster* to Martin in the 1616 folio. Moreover, John Davies, though he soon broke a cudgel over Martin's head, dedicated *Orchestra* to him in 1596.

63. See *D. N. B.*, XII, 259-61.

64. The title-page reads as follows: *Thomas Coriate/ Traueller for the English VVits: Greeting. From the Court of the Great Mogvl Resi/dent at the Towne of Asmere, in / Easterne India. /* Printed by W. Iaggard, and Henry Featherston. / 1616.

65. Sir Edward had died by October 1614; but Coryate, with meagre news from London, was, of course, unaware of the fact. See *Calendar of State Papers Domestic, 1611-1618,* London, 1858, p. 256.

66. Here he styles Hoskyns 'M. Equinoctiall Pasticrust of the middle Temple.' Elsewhere he refers to Hoskyns by name as well as by this fantastic title.

67. See *Journals of the House of Commons,* Reprinted, London, 1803, I, 447, *etc.* The *Journals* are henceforth referred to as *C.J.*

68. Izaak Walton, *op. cit.,* p. 223.

69. *L.W.* was no doubt Laurence Whitaker, secretary to Sir Edward Philips, and mentioned elsewhere in Coryate's book.

70. *Thomas Coriate / Traueller for the English VVits,* p. 32. I have not identified *M. Protoplast.*

71. See No. XXVIII, in Chapter X, above.

72. Donne's foreign travel from November 1611 to September 1612 would, of course, have prevented his regular presence at these meetings.

73. Author of *Pvrchas his Pilgrimage,* London, 1613.

74. It is interesting to observe that Hoskyns appears to have associated with both Jonson and Wotton. The supposed original of Sir Politic Would-Be does not appear, however, to have attended the *Convivia Philosophica.* Of course, Wotton was in Italy during part of this period.

75. In Ben Jonson's *Leges Conviviales* the nature of the meetings of the literary wits is suggested.

76. Aubrey, *op. cit.,* I, 418.

77. It is barely possible that Hoskyns may have been connected with the Herberts. Joseph Bradney, genealogist, of Tal-y-Coed, North Monmouth, Wales, in a letter of November 1929, wrote as follows to the Reverend Sir Edwyn Clement Hoskyns, Bart.: 'By your shield of arms you would appear to have been a branch of the great Herbert family, your crest being a variant of Herbert.' Since in sixteenth-century England family connections were perhaps rather persistently maintained, the Herberts, if such kinship existed, may have accorded Hoskyns some hospitality.

78. See *Poems written by the Rt. Hon. William, Earl of Pembroke, . . . many of which are answered by way of repartee, by Sᵣ Benjamin Ruddier, Knight . . .,* London, 1660.

Rudyerd was a student at Oxford during part of Hoskyns' period there. For their associations in the Temple see Hopwood (*op. cit.,* I, 355; 368; and 378). See Aubrey (*op. cit.,* I, 418) for the account of their duel and subsequent reconciliation.

79. George Puttenham, *The Arte of English Poesie. Contriued into three Bookes: The first of Poets and Poesie, the second of Proportion, the third of Ornament.* London, 1589, p. 49.

80. See J. William Hebel's edition of *Poly-Olbion*, in Vol. IV of his *Tercentenary Edition of Michael Drayton*, Oxford, Basil Blackwell, 1933, p. v.*

81. Michael Drayton, *ed. cit.*, III, 231.

82. In a letter to Sir Henry Goodyere. See E. K. Chambers, *Poems of John Donne*, two volumes, London, 1896, I, xxxvii.

83. See his poem, No. XLVIII, in Chapter X, above, for his statement of indifference to fame.

NOTES ON CHAPTER II

1. This information is furnished in a letter to me by Sir James Du Boulay, late Bursar of Winchester College, from the original entry in the College Register, where Hoskyns is described in the record for 15 December 1579 as 'being of the age of 13 on the previous 1st March.'

2. Hopwood, *Middle Temple Records*, I, 333.

3. See *MS. Add. 35,280*, f. 192. b, which contains a pedigree of the Hoskyns family drawn up from wills at Hereford by C. J. Robinson in preparation for his proposed but unpublished second edition of *A History of the Mansions and Manors of Herefordshire*, the first edition of which came out in 1873.

4. *MS. Add. 35,280*, f. 192. b, contains a reference to this will.

5. *The Paston Letters*, edited by James Gairdner, Westminster, 1901, I, ccxliii-cclv.

6. *E.g.*, by Anthony à Wood (*op. cit.*, II, 510). John the younger (1579-1631) was the sixth son of John and Margery and was educated at Winchester (Kirby, *op. cit.*, p. 155) and at New College (Aubrey, *op. cit.*, I, 424), where he became D. C. L. in 1613. By 1618 he had married Frances Bourne, step-daughter of his brother John the elder. Letters in Chapter VII, above, refer to his being made prebendary of the cathedral of Hereford and master of the hospital of St. Oswald's near Worcester. The *D. N. B.* points out that he became chaplain to James I and rector of Ledbury, Herefordshire. He was the author of *Sermons preached at Paul's Cross*, London, 1615. His brother frequently refers to him as 'Dᴿ Hoskyns.'

7. William Rees Williams, *The History of the Great Sessions in Wales, 1542-1830*. Brecknock, 1899, p. 173.

8. Aubrey, *op. cit.*, I, 416.

9. *E.g.*, C. J. Robinson, *op. cit.*, p. 131. Also Burke's *Peerage*.

10. *Members of Parliament . . . the names of every member returned to serve in each Parliament . . . up to the present Time . . . Ordered, by the House of Commons, to be Printed* 1 March 1878, Part I, 1878, pp. 418 and 438. See also W. R. Williams (*op. cit.*, p. 167).

11. Aubrey, *op. cit.*, I, 417.   Aubrey had the information from Hoskyns' son Benedict.

Original records for this period are not extant.

12. *E.g.*, in *D. N. B.*, XXVII, 397.

13. Kirby, *op. cit.*, p. x.   I am indebted to this work for several facts in this chapter relating to conditions at Winchester toward the close of the sixteenth century.   See particularly his pp. viii-xv.

14. Clark, *Register of the University of Oxford*, II, iii, 148.

15. Sir James Du Boulay, late Bursar of the College, after an examination of the records wrote to me as follows on 28 January 1930: 'In the old register of scholars those admitted as Founder's Kin are distinctly so characterised . . . . There is no such mention in the case of John Hoskyns, and I think that this is clear evidence that, whether he could trace any connection with the Founder or not, he was not admitted as Founder's kin.'

16. Isaac Walton's description of Winchester, in his life of Wotton, *ed. cit.*, p. 283.

17. Kirby, *op. cit.*, p. xi.

18. *Ibid.*, p. xv.

19. Aubrey (*op. cit.*, I, 417) says: 'There were many pretty stories of him when a schooleboy, which I have forgott.'   He did, however, remember the anecdote of how Hoskyns had prodigiously memorized, at a single reading, another boy's exercise, and after repeating it as his own, had allowed the schoolmaster, in the ensuing misunderstanding, to whip his erstwhile benefactor for supposedly stealing an exercise which he could not himself repeat.

20. See No. I in Chapter X, above.

21. Aubrey, *op. cit.*, I, 417.   See the illustration opposite p. 168, above.

22. See the article by Herbert Chitty, Esq., Keeper of the College Archives, in *The Wykehamist*, No. 652, p. 12, Winchester, 4 November 1924.   The present Trusty Servant was last painted in 1809 by William Cave.

23. Clark, *Register*, II, ii, 141.

24. *Ibid.*, II, ii, 141.

25. Aubrey, *op. cit.*, I, 424.

26. *Ibid.*

27. Clark, *Register*, II, iii, 148.

28. The 'determination' comprised certain exercises that had to be performed before the degree B.A. was complete.   'Without determination the degree of B.A. was incomplete and *ipso facto* lapsed.'—*Ibid.*, II, iii, 3.

29. *Ibid.*, II, iii, 148.

30. At this point consideration for chronology makes it necessary to note that in 1590 a John Hoskyns was involved with Oswald and

John the younger in a suit for tithes, brought by Thomas Jones. See *Acts of the Privy Council, New Series, 1590-1591*, London, 1900, XX, 60-61; 117-18; and 353. Since his brother, John the younger, was only nine at this time, the suit may, however, have been directed against Serjeant Hoskyns' brother Oswald and their father and their father's brother, John.

31. John Evelyn so describes the *terrae filius* under the date of 10 July 1669 in his *Diary* (edited by William Bray, London, 1890, p. 341).

32. *N. E. D.*

33. Thomas Blount, *Glossographia*, London, 1656. Quoted in *N. E. D.* under *terrae filius*.

34. See John Evelyn, *op. cit.*, p. 340.

35. *Ibid.*, p. 341.

36. So Evelyn (*ibid.*) characterizes a speech which he heard in 1669.

37. Aubrey, *op. cit.*, I, 424, n. 2.

38. Aubrey, *op. cit.*, I, 417.

39. See *The Particular Description of the County of Somerset Drawn up by Thomas Gerard of Trent, 1633*, edited by E. H. Bates, and published as Vol. 15, the *Publications of the Somerset Record Society*, London, 1900, p. 203. If Ilchester reached this stage of ruin by 1633, it had been, doubtless, in almost the same state of decay in 1592.

40. Aubrey (*op. cit.*, I, 417) says that he had seen this work. One of the early published Greek lexicons was the Greek-Latin work by Simon Grynaeus, *Lexicon Graecvm*, Ioan VValder, Basileae, 1539. Grynaeus, a German theologian, was a friend of Melanchthon, Luther, and Erasmus, professor of Greek at Heidelberg, and in 1529 professor of theology at Basle. In 1534 he re-organized the University of Tübingen. Other early lexicons were the *Dictionarivm Graecvm* of A. P. Manuzio, published at Venice at the Aldine Press in 1524, and the *Thesaurus Graecae Linguae* of Henri Estienne, published at Geneva in 1572.

NOTES ON CHAPTER III

1. So described by Thomas Gerard, *op. cit.*, p. 203.
2. Hopwood, *op. cit.*, I, 333.
3. Spenser, *Prothalamion*, lines 132-33.
4. Aubrey, *op. cit.*, I, 417.

At Sizergh Castle, preserved with Hoskyns' letters, is a handsome chamois glove embroidered in blue silk and ornamented with small gold discs applied in elaborate design. Tradition in the family has it that the glove was the Serjeant's; and, if tradition is correct, it gives evidence of his fastidious taste.

It would be easy to imagine, however, that at the first, contrary to Aubrey's statement, Hoskyns may have been unable to wear the clothes his tastes dictated. In *MS. Add. 22,603* (f. 11), a commonplace book of the seventeenth century, occur some lines which, for their allusion to Shakespeare and for the picture they give of a young wit of Hoskyns' sort entering upon the study of law in London, seem worth noting. Entitled 'A Poeticall Revenge' they are presumably written by a young university wit learned in Latin but a mere initiate in law. Because of his threadbare cloak he is scorned by one of the satin-clad young gallants from an Inn of Court,—the sort 'that is rauish'd with a Cocke-pit play.' In revenge the young scholar flings several curses at him, one of which is the hope that the gallant's father may 'take him' in his study 'at Shakespeares Plays instead of the Ld Cooke.'

5. The epigrammatist, later attorney-general for Ireland, and a former schoolmate of Hoskyns'. See also n. 23 for Chapter I, above.

6. Kirton was from Somerset. See Hopwood, *op. cit.*, I, 279-80.

7. *Ibid.*, I, 351.

8. *Ibid.*, I, 355, 368, 380, 382, 383-84, 396, 420; II, 444, 571, 638-39.

9. *Ibid.*, I, 396.

10. *Ibid.*, I, 382.

11. Thomas Carew was bound with Nathaniel Clattworthy and George Carew. See Hopwood, *op. cit.*, II, 552-53. Upon admission, Benjamin Rudyerd was bound with his father. *Ibid.*, I, 312.

12. See pages 10-11, above, and Chapter VIII, above.

13. *E.g.*, Hopwood, *op. cit.*, I, 382-83.

14. *Ibid.*, I, 403.

15. *I.e.*, a senior barrister. See J. Bruce Williamson, *op. cit.*, pp. 107-108.

16. Sir Francis Bacon's *Learned Reading . . . upon the Statute of uses . . . Grayes Inne* (London, 1642) is an example of this type of instruction.

17. Williamson, *op. cit.*, p. 176. The 'cupboard' (*ibid.*, p. 118) was a square table at which the Reader stood.

18. See also Evelyn, *op. cit.*, pp. 336 and 343.

19. From the MS. of Robert Brerewood as quoted by Arthur Robert Ingpen, K. C., in *The Middle Temple Bench Book*, London, 1912, p. 27.

20. *I.e.*, those admitted to practice in certain courts after a residence, in Hoskyns' time, of seven years in the Temple. See Williamson, *op. cit.*, pp. 116 and 189.

21. To indicate the proportion thus absent, one may note that Robert Brerewood in his MS., preserved in the Middle Temple Library, gives a total list of 189 Utter Barristers of the Middle Temple in 1638. See Ingpen, *op. cit.*, p. 45.

22. Hopwood, *op. cit.*, I, 408, 413, 416, 422, 426.

23. Arthur J. Jewers, *The Registers of the Abbey Church of SS. Peter and Paul, Bath,* two volumes, London, 1900-1901, I, 205.

24. *MS. Add. 24,491,* ff. 202-204. These are Joseph Hunter's MS. notes for the biographies of English poets.

Anthony à Wood (*op. cit.*, II, 625) says that Benedicta was the daughter of Robert Moyle of Buckwell. Robert was the son of John Moyle, according to Edward Hasted, *The History and Topographical Survey of the County of Kent,* four volumes, Canterbury, 1778-1799, III, 172. Sir Hungerford Hoskyns, in a letter to Thomas Streatfield, topographer and genealogist of Kent, says (*MS. Add. 33,929,* f. 286) that she was the daughter of Robert Moyle, but Sir Hungerford's letter contains several inaccuracies. However, she may have been the daughter of Robert.

25. Hopwood, *op. cit.*, I, 312. Bourne is there described as the son of Francis Bourne of Witlington, Somersetshire. He was admitted to the Middle Temple in 1590, coming there from New Inn.

26. Jewers, *op. cit.*, II, 338.

27. Woodhall 30, Somerset House. The will was proved 9 May 1601. See Arthur L. Humphreys, *Somersetshire Parishes,* two volumes, London, 1906, II, 668. See also Frederick Brown, *Abstracts of Somersetshire Wills . . .* (First Series, London, 1887, p. 29). The will is also indexed under the year 1601 on p. 53 of the *Index of Wills Proved in the Prerogative Court of Canterbury, 1584-1604* (Vol. IV, edited by Edward Alexander Fry, London, 1901).

28. Jewers, *op. cit.*, II, 338.

29. Mentioned in his father's will as Robert. He was perhaps *John Robert,* since he was admitted to the Middle Temple as *John Bourne.* See Hopwood, *op. cit.*, II, 571. Francis Bourne bequeathed to this son thirty pounds a year for his maintenance.

30. Mentioned in her father's will as *ffraunces.* To her Francis Bourne bequeathed one hundred pounds, his executors to have 'the disposing of yt for her good and maintenance.' See also n. 6 for Chapter II, above.

31. Jewers, *op. cit.*, I, 13.

32. Joseph Hunter (*MS. Add. 24,491,* ff. 202-204) gives her age as fifty at the time of her death in 1625.

33. It is to be noted that Hoskyns did not depend upon his wife's fortune to gain admission to the Temple as has been stated erroneously in the *D. N. B.* and by H. W. Woolrych (*Lives of Eminent Serjeants-at-Law of the English Bar,* two volumes, London, 1869, I, 245).

34. See her letters to her husband in Chapter V, above, and his to her in Chapter VII, above.

NOTES ON CHAPTER IV

1.   *Members of Parliament . . . the Names of every Member returned to serve in each Parliament . . . up to the present Time . . . . Ordered, by the House of Commons, to be Printed* 1 March 1878, Part I, p. 443.

2.   Samuel R. Gardiner's *History of England from the Accession of James I to the Outbreak of the Civil War* (ten volumes, London, 1883) and J. R. Tanner's *Constitutional Documents of the Reign of James I, A.D. 1603-1625, with an historical commentary* (Cambridge, at the University Press, 1930) are among the invaluable aids in forming a conception of governmental problems and activities of this period.

3.   *E.g.*, the imposition on currants rose from eighteen pence to five shillings, sixpence.   See *The Parliamentary Diary of Robert Bowyer, 1606-1607*, edited by David Harris Willson, University of Minnesota Press, Minneapolis and London, 1931, p. 105.   The frequent references to this edition throughout this chapter indicate its value in a study of this Parliament or its members.   In 1930 Professor Wallace Notestein first called my attention to Bowyer's diary and kindly lent me his transcript of it from *MS. Harl. 4945.*

4.   Bowyer, *op. cit.*, pp. 109-10.

5.   See notes on his speech on free trade (*C. J.*, I, 987).   Wherever possible Hoskyns' views are reported in his own language as recorded by his contemporaries.   Often he affected his hearers as much by his colourful language as by the sheer substance of his speeches; and though the full significance of his argument occasionally has proved evanescent in the hasty notes, the pungent flavour of his rhetoric remains in many phrases which the note-takers found irresistible.

6.   *C. J.*, I, 427.

7.   *C. J.*, I, 293.

8.   Bowyer, *op. cit.*, p. 7.

9.   *C. J.*, I, 285.

10.   *C. J.*, I, 957.

11.   *C. J.*, I, 374.

12.   *C. J.*, I, 446.

13.   Bowyer, *op. cit.*, p. 58.

14.   *Ibid.*, p. 59.

15.   *C. J.*, I, 954.

16.   *C. J.*, I, 995.

17.   *C. J.*, I, 998.

18.   *C. J.*, I, 416.

19.   *C. J.*, I, 372.

20.   *C. J.*, I, 310.

21.   *C. J.*, I, 419.

22.   *C. J.*, I, 304.

23. *C. J.*, I, 413.
24. *C. J.*, I, 416 and 997.
25. *C. J.*, I, 960.
26. *C. J.*, I, 347.
27. *C. J.*, I, 291 and 296-97.
28. *C. J.*, I, 399 and 410.
29. *C. J.*, I, 365.
30. *C. J.*, I, 285.
31. *C. J.*, I, 340.
32. *E.g.*, see *C. J.*, I, 368, 394, 397, 960.
33. *C. J.*, I, 420.
34. Bowyer, *op. cit.*, p. 49.
35. See also *C. J.*, I, 284.

36. *E.g.*, on 31 March 1606, Hoskyns was added to the committee to consider Chepstow Bridge (*C. J.*, I, 291). On 11 April the bill was again brought in 'wholy made new, and twice so long as before.' See Bowyer, *op. cit.*, p. 117.

37. *C. J.*, I, 441: 'Lawyers of the House to be put in Writing, and to be noted, if they be absent.' *Ibid.*, I, 403: 'all lawyers absent to be sent for.' *Ibid.*, I, 412: 'No Lawyer, nor other, to depart without publicke leave in the House. The Deficients of Lawyers, if they come not before this Day Sennight, to be sent for by Warrant.' *Ibid.*: 'That the Lawyers, Serjeants, and others may be sent for:—A Collection of them.'

38. *MS. Harl. 4945*, f. 207.
39. *C. J.*, I, 949.
40. *C. J.*, I, 1003.
41. Bowyer, *op. cit.*, p. 237.
42. *Ibid.*, p. 226.
43. *C. J.*, I, 427.
44. *C. J.*, I, 300.
45. *C. J.*, I, 399.

46. Professor Wallace Notestein (*op. cit.*, p. 32) points out that grievances during the period of 1603 to 1621 received new emphasis in the House and that 'in Subcommittees those members gained position who could uncover abuses; in the Committee of the Whole House, those who could there state most cogently the case against the Government.' He adds that in the session of 1610 'one can see the lines clearly drawn; Sandys, Fuller, Hoskins, and others are stating the case against the Government and Privy Councillors are rushing to the defence.'

47. *I.e.*, Robert Bowyer, Keeper of Records in the Tower and author of the diary referred to above.

48. *C. J.*, I, 957.

49. On 26 March 1606, he was mentioned as a member of the committee for privileges. See *C. J.*, I, 290.

50. *C. J.*, I, 412.

51. Bowyer, *op. cit.*, p. 77.

52. *Ibid.*, p. 133.

53. See *Calendar of State Papers Domestic, 1598-1601*, p. 537, and *Calendar of State Papers, Domestic, 1603-1610*, p. 331. I am indebted to David Harris Willson (p. 133 of his edition of Bowyer) for the first of these references.

54. *I.e.*, Sir Edward Dyer. Although any criticism of Dyer is implied rather than direct, it seems doubtful that he could have been wholly unaware of his agent's methods. A mild defence of the Commissioners was offered by several members of Parliament after Hoskyns' attack (Bowyer, *op. cit.*, p. 147). For details concerning other relations of Dyer and Tipper during the ten years (1588-1593 and 1601-1606) that they held warrants to seek for concealed lands, see Ralph M. Sargent's *At the Court of Queen Elizabeth. The Life and Lyrics of Sir Edward Dyer* (Oxford University Press, London and New York, 1935, pp. 133-40).

55. Bowyer, *op. cit.*, pp. 106-107.

56. *I.e.*, *barratry*, 'the offence of habitually moving or maintaining law-suits.'—*N. E. D.*

57. 'The action of wrongfully aiding and abetting litigation.'—*N. E. D.*

58. Bowyer, *op. cit.*, pp. 132-33.

59. *Ibid.*, p. 61.

60. *Ibid.*, p. 65.

61. *Ibid.*, p. 66.

62. *Ibid.*, p. 43.

63. *C. J.*, I, 266.

64. Bowyer, *op. cit.*, pp. 77-8.

65. *C. J.*, I, 289.

66. *C. J.*, I, 995.

67. S. R. Gardiner, *Parliamentary Debates in 1610*. Printed for the Camden Society, Westminster, 1862, pp. 9-10.

68. *Ibid.*, pp. 130-31.

69. *Ibid.*, pp. 144-45.

70. *C. J.*, I, 447 and 450.

71. Gardiner, *Parliamentary Debates in 1610*, pp. 75-7.

72. *Ibid.*

73. *Twelfth Report of the Historical Manuscripts Commission*, Appendix, Part IV, v. 1, p. 425. (The MSS. of the Duke of Rutland) London, 1888. On the same page Thomas Screven, reporting the proceedings in Parliament from 13 November 1610 until it was prorogued, remarks: 'Divers free speakers why *rebus sixtantibus* we should not give as Lukenors, Fuller, Wentworth, and Hoskinges, the i sent for by the Lord Tresorer.'

NOTES ON CHAPTER V

1. *C. J.*, I, 455.

2. *Members of Parliament*, 1878, Part III, p. xxxviii.

3. The notes on James's speech are derived from a transcript of it in *MS. Harl. 280*, f. 145.

4. *E.g.*, Sir John Holles wrote on 28 April: 'I came hither some few days before Easter as a bear to the stake, unwilling to have been of the House at this time, conjecturing this would begin where the other Parliament left. Neither was I deceived.' See *Reports of the Historical MSS. Commission, The MSS. of the Duke of Portland*, London, 1923, IX, 27.

5. *C. J.*, I, 467.

6. It is interesting to note that Hoskyns represented the majority of his shire in his reluctance to vote for large subsidies. Herefordshire did not contribute one penny to the royal funds from 1614 to 1617. See J. R. Green, *A Short History of the English People*, New York, 1886, p. 478.

7. *C. J.*, I, 482.

8. *C. J.*, I, 506.

9. *State Papers, Domestic, James I*, Vol. 40, no. 60, f. 139. b, and the *Calendar of State Papers, Domestic, Addenda, 1580-1625*, London, 1872, p. 541.

10. *State Papers, Domestic, James I*, Vol. 40, no. 60, f. 138.

11. *The Portland MSS.*, catalogued by the Historical MSS. Commission, London, 1923, IX, 134. A report of the Parliament written by Sir John Holles furnishes the passage quoted here.

12. *Ibid.*

13. Winwood, on 16 June 1614, wrote to Carleton that he had never seen so much faction and passion or so little reverence for a King. 'The break-neck,' he added, 'was some seditious speeches, which made the King impatient, and it was whispered to him that they would have his life and that of his favourites before they had done, on which he dissolved them.' See *Calendar of State Papers, Domestic, 1611-1618*, p. 237.

14. See p. 32, above.

15. The revolt of the Sicilians against the government of Charles I of Anjou, in 1282.

16. This is Sir John Holles' report of Hoskyns' speech (*Portland MSS.*, IX, 138), the exact nature of which seems not to have been preserved. See also Aubrey, *op. cit.*, I, 421.

17. *Acts of the Privy Council of England, 1613-1614*, London, 1921, p. 456. The entire warrant is not printed. I have assumed it was similar in phraseology to the one which is printed on p. 456.

18. *Ibid.*, pp. 459-60. I have here assumed that the letter regarding Hoskyns followed exactly the form of the one printed on p. 459 of the *Acts*.

19. But released 29 June 1614, *ibid.*, p. 476.

20. Released 10 July 1614, *ibid.*, p. 490.

21. Chute, a native of Kent, had been holding the post of carver in the royal household. He was discharged from the Tower on 2 October 1614 (*Acts of Privy Council*, p. 576).

22. *Acts of the Privy Council of England, 1613-1614*, pp. 459-60.

23. Sharpe was of King's College, Cambridge. He had served as Chaplain to the Earl of Essex and later to Henry, Prince of Wales. Afterwards he was rector at Malpas in Cheshire. In 1614 he was minister of Piverton in Devon and Archdeacon of Berks. See Bishop Kennett's MS. notes in *MS. Lansdowne 984*, ff. 92-3.

24. Former ambassador to Spain. He was the son of Sir Thomas Cornwallis.

25. See Sir Henry Wotton, *Reliquiae Wottonianae*, London, 1672, pp. 434-35, and also *Acts of the Privy Council of England, 1613-1614*, p. 465.

26. Quoted from *MS. Malone 19*, p. 95. Also found with variations in *MS. Rawl. Poet. 26*, f. 2. a; and in Chamberlain's letter to Isaac Wake, 22 October 1614, in *State Papers, Domestic, James I*, Vol. 78, no. 29, p. 2, preserved in the Public Record Office; and in *Portland MSS.*, IX, 165.

27. The quotations are from a transcript of Cornwallis' letter in *MS. Harl. 1221*, ff. 96. b-99. a. The original letter is preserved in the Public Record Office in *State Papers, Domestic, James I*, Vol. 77, no. 42.

28. Cornwallis further stated that Sharpe had affirmed that he, Cornwallis, had promised to give Hoskyns £20 'in regard of his loss of his practise in the term.' This Cornwallis denied. See *MS. Harl. 1221*, f. 98. b.

29. *Op. cit.*, II, 247.

30. For evidence that the Earl of Somerset, at least, spoke against Hoskyns when he was expected to speak for him see Hoskyns' Letter IX in Chapter VII, above.

31. *Calendar of State Papers, Domestic, 1611-1618*, London, 1858, p. 239.

32. *E.g.* (*Calendar of State Papers, Domestic, 1611-1618*, London, 1858, p. 289), Chamberlain confused Serjeant Hoskyns with the latter's brother Dr. Hoskyns, when he said, 'Sir Charles Cornwallis, and Drs. Sharpe and Hoskyns, released from the Tower.'

33. Sir Henry Wotton wrote to Sir Edmund Bacon, as follows: 'The second [*i.e.*, Hoskyns] is in for more wit [*than Chute*], and for licentiousness baptized freedom: For I have noted in our House, that a false or faint Patriot did cover himself with the shadow of equal moderation; and on the other side, irreverent discourse was called honest liberty.'—See *Reliquiae Wottonianae*, third edition, London, 1672, p. 432.

34. *C. J.*, I, 425. He seems on the same occasion to have added an epigrammatic remark on 'The Freehold, the Conscience, the Life of Men.'

35. Chute was released in October 1614. See *Calendar of State Papers, Domestic, 1611-1618*, p. 256.

36. Wotton, *op. cit.*, p. 438.

37. From the original letters in the possession of the Reverend Sir Edwyn Clement Hoskyns, Bart., of Corpus Christi College, Cambridge.

38. Later Benedicta presented a poem by Hoskyns to the king, but to no avail. See No. XXXIV in Chapter X, above. Her husband seems to have composed the lines. See notes on the poem, below.

39. A manor in Herefordshire, leased by Hoskyns. There are references to "Tittely" and "Tittley" in *MS. Harl. 6726*, ff. 243-44. This MS. is a collection of notes on Herefordshire, prepared about 1655.

40. This may refer to some comment on her presentation of a rimed petition to James I. On 23 February 1615 Chamberlain wrote: 'Hoskins and his compeeres are still in the towre and no speech of theyre releasing, though Hoskins wife that is a poetesse hath ben a longe suitor, and presented the King wth a petition in rime which I here send you.' *State Papers, Domestic, James I*, Vol. 38, no. 80, catalogued in *Calendar of State Papers Domestic, 1611-1618*, p. 275. The verses are not enclosed nor is there evidence as to the exact date upon which they were sent to the King.

41. MS. seems to read *if*.

42. *Acts of the Privy Council of England, 1613-1614*, pp. 548-49. This letter is the first one relating to Hoskyns after his committal to the Tower on 8 June.

43. John, the younger, was a clergyman. See n. 6 in Chapter II, above. Oswald was a member of the Merchant Taylors' Company and in 1609 had adventured five shillings towards 'the honorable plantacōn in Virginia.' See Alexander Brown, *The Genesis of the United States*, 2 volumes, New York, 1891, I, 304-5. In 1611, as Hudson (*op. cit.*, p. x) observes, John Hoskyns, the subject of this study, had adventured £37. 10s. See Brown, *op. cit.*, I, 467.

44. See No. XXXII in Chapter X, above.

45. *Acts of the Privy Council of England, 1615-1616*, London, 1925, p. 46.

46. See Letter VII in Chapter VII, above.

47. *Acts of the Privy Council of England, 1615-1616*, pp. 191-92.

48. *Ibid.*, pp. 193-94.

49. *Ibid.*, p. 299.

50. *Ibid.*, pp. 413-14. Sharpe was granted liberty on 22 February 1616 to 'repaire to anie of his ecclesiasticall charges within this kingdome.'

51. *Ibid.*, p. 274. [Quotations from the *Acts of the Privy Council* and the *Calendars of State Papers* (obtainable from H. M. Stationery Office Sales Office, Adastral House, Kingsway, London, W. C. 2) are made with permission of the Controller of H. M. Stationery Office.]

NOTES ON CHAPTER VI

1. *State Papers, Domestic*, Vol. 90, no. 53, in the Public Record Office, and *Calendar of State Papers, Domestic, 1611-1618*, p. 432. Chamberlain adds that the 'L. Chancellor begins fayre and softly to resigne some of his offices, as the lieutenancie of Buckinghamshire to the L. Villers.' Thus Hoskyns seems to have been allied with those who were yielding before Buckingham's increasing power. By 1621, however, Buckingham was aiding Hoskyns. See p. 51, above.

2. The case is not reported in Howell's *State Trials*. In the Star Chamber the Lord Keeper or Lord Chancellor presided. Hence Hoskyns' reference to Bacon's cordiality in June 1617 (in Letter X in Chapter VII, above) indicates that he escaped the fines and ignominies of the Star Chamber.

3. See Letter IX in Chapter VII, above. This seems to be the only reference that has come to light regarding Somerset's connection with Hoskyns' imprisonment. In various commonplace books appear bitter lines on Somerset's disgrace. May Hoskyns have composed some of them? *Cf.* these from *MS. Chetham 8011*, p. 38:

> Though some ar set in highest place
> Yet some are set in great disgrace
> Though some ar set in mighty power
> Yet some are set within the Tower.

4. See Letter XXI in Chapter VII, above.

5. See Richard Johnson, late Town Clerk [of Hereford], *The Ancient Customs of the City of Hereford*, second edition, London, 1882, p. 181.

6. George Lord Carew wrote to Sir Thomas Roe in 1615: 'Dr. Sharpe and Mr. Hoskins, sett free from prison, and will no more burne there fingers with Parliament business.'—*Calendar of State Papers, Domestic, 1611-1618*, p. 344.

7. *Fourth Report of the Royal Commission on Historical Manuscripts*, Part I, Reports and Appendix, London, 1874, p. 315.

8. Hopwood, *op. cit.*, II, 634.

9. *Ibid.*, II, 638.

10. *Ibid.*, II, 641, and Ingpen, *op. cit.*, p. 70.

11. From the original letter in the collection of Henry Hornyold-Strickland, Esq., at Sizergh, Kendal, Westmorland.

12. For the extravagance of these feasts, see p. 21, above.

13. Ingpen, *op. cit.*, p. 199.

14. Hopwood, *op. cit.*, II, 646.

15. *Ibid.*, II, 653.

16. *Ibid.*, II, 660.

17. *MS. Harl. 6726*, f. 239.

18. *Ibid.*, and also Letter XXIII in Chapter VII, above.

19. 'Englishmen . . . termed it the *Gilden Vale* . . . for the golden, wealthy and pleasant fertility thereof. For, the hils that compasse it in . . . are clad with woods; under the woods lie corne fields on either hand, and under those fields most gay and gallant medowes.'— William Camden, *Britain, or a Chorographicall Description of . . . England, etc.*, London, 1637, p. 617.

20. See also Letters XXIII and XXIV in Chapter VII, above.

21. William, Lord Compton, Earl of Northampton. He is addressed as the Lord President of the Warders of Wales in a letter of 10 July 1621 in *State Papers, Domestic, James I*, Vol. 122, no. 11, preserved in the Public Record Office.

22. Sir Lionel Cranfield, who was a guest at the Mitre. See n. 59 for Chapter I, above.

23. His appointment is recorded on p. 344 of the *Grant Book, State Papers, Domestic, James I*, Vol. 141, in the Public Record Office, as follows: '3 July A Grant to John Hoskins Esq[r] of the Office of one of the Justices in the Countyes of Carmarthen Pembrocke, and Cardigan—during pleasure.' The grant is listed under the heading 'De Anno decimo nono Jacobi.'

24. The yearly salary towards the close of Elizabeth's reign was fifty pounds with an additional thirty pounds 'for diet.' See f. 1 of *The Present State of the Courts of your Ma[ts] Counsell established in the Principalitie and Marches of Wales*, a parchment MS. carefully prepared for Queen Elizabeth by Henry, second Earl of Pembroke, Lord President in the Marches of Wales, and preserved in the Library of Trinity College, Cambridge, as *Western MS. R. 7. 8*. Also see W. R. Williams, *op. cit.*, p. 17.

25. Morehampton, the farm Hoskyns bought and made his home from this time until his death, is situated in the Golden Valley, Herefordshire, northeast of Abbey Dore. When I visited the farm in the summer of 1933, Mr. John Watkins, who now lives there and who has known the estate all his life, pointed out the place where the seventeenth-century house stood. The hall, he said, was twenty by fourteen yards in size and contained three windows. He explained that he knew the size of the hall because the outlines of its foundation stood out clearly one hot dry summer. An old stone cottage still stands to the northwest of the present farmhouse. The remains of a moat may still be seen. Morehampton Park Farm is now a piece of five hundred acres but seems originally to have contained 505 acres.

26. Benedicta Hoskyns' son by her former marriage. He was admitted to the Middle Temple 4 November 1613, where he shared his stepfather's chambers. See Hopwood, *op. cit.*, II, 571.

27. 'The Judges and Serjeants when they ride Circuits, are to wear a Serjeants Coat of good Broad Cloath with sleeves, and faced with Velvet . . . . And they are to have a Sumpter, and right to ride with six men at the least.'—Dugdale, *op. cit.*, p. 102.

28. See also Letter III in Chapter VII, above.

29. See Letter XXIV in Chapter VII, above.

30. W. R. Williams, *op. cit.*, p. 25.

31. *Ibid.*, p. 159.

32. Stow, *op. cit.*, p. 67.

33. Sir William Dugdale, *Chronica Series*, p. 107, quoted from Patent Rolls and printed as part of *Origines Juridiciales*.

34. Hacket, *op. cit.*, Part I, p. 110.

35. *Ibid.* Chamberlain, who mentioned fifteen as the number appointed, wrote thus: 'I have not known so great a call for number; though, for other abilities, they are thought to come short of many, or most that went before them. Sir George Croke, Sir Heneage Finch the recorder, Thomas Crew, Davenport, and Hoskins are the prime men; the rest . . . being of little note or name.' See Thomas Birch, *op. cit.*, II, 424.

36. Dugdale, *op. cit.*, p. 137.

37. Birch, *op. cit.*, II, 424-25.

38. It was 'an ancient and uninterrupted Custom and Usage of Serjeants on their Call to that Degree to present the Treasurer and each of the Masters of the Bench with a Ring.'—Ingpen, *op. cit.*, p. 92.

In his will of 23 June 1627 (in the possession of the Reverend Canon Sir Edwyn C. Hoskyns, Bart.) Hoskyns bequeaths his eleven serjeant's rings to the warden and the ten fellows of New College.

On the subject of rings Dugdale (*op. cit.*, p. 112) says that each serjeant gave rings of gold 'to the value of forty pounds sterling at the least . . . . For every such Serjeant, at the day of his creation, useth to give unto every Prince, Duke, and Archbishop being present at that solemnity; and to the Lord Chancellor and Lord Treasurer of England, a Ring of the value of xxvi s. 8 d. And to every Earl and Bishop being . . . present, and also to the Lord Privy Seal; to both the Lords Chief Justices, and to the Lord Chief Baron of the King's Exchequer, a Ring of the value of xx s.' Rings of appropriate value were given to lesser clerks.

39. *Cf.* Dugdale, *op. cit.*, pp. 111-12, and p. 135. One such feast cost £258. 14s. 11d. It was customary to serve 'spiced bredde, comfeits and oder godely conceyts with ypocras.'—*Ibid.*, p. 114.

This particular feast was 'honoured with the presence of the French, Venetian, and States' ambassadors; with all the council and great men about this town.' See Chamberlain's letter to Carleton, Birch, *op. cit.*, II, 424-25.

40. *I.e.*, their liveries. Dugdale (*op. cit.*, p. 112) says: 'They give . . . Liveries of Cloth in one Suit or Colour, in great aboundance;

not only to their Houshold meany, but also to their other friends and acquaintance; which during the time of the solemnities attend upon them.'

41. Hacket, *op. cit.*, Part I, 111-13.

42. Chamberlain to Carleton. See Birch, *op. cit.*, II, 424.

43. Hoskyns, being already a Justice, probably wore a cloak closed upon the right shoulder, without the hood. The description of their traditional vesture is derived from Dugdale, *op. cit.*, p. 99.

44. See the Serjeants' oath referred to by Woolrych, *op. cit.*, I, p. xxvii.

45. From *Chancery Bills and Answers, Charles I*, Bundle H 30/37, in the Public Record Office.

Another example of his affairs in the courts may be observed in an account of how he managed a case in which he was himself sued 'for not paving of the King's highway in the County of *Middlesex* in *S. Johns street, ante tenementa sua.*' But 'in the Indictment it was not shewed, How he came chargeable to pay the same; nor was it shewed that he was seised of any house there, nor that he dwelt there, nor was it averred that he had any Tenement there. The opinion of the Court was, that the Indictment was incertain; for it might be that his Lessee dwelt in the house, and so the Lessee ought to have repaired it, and also mended the high-way. And for these Incertainties the Indictment was quashed.' See John Godbolt, *Reports of Certain Cases, Arising In the severall Courts of Record at Westminster; In the raignes of Q. Elizabeth, K. James and the late King Charles. With the Resolutions of the Judges . . . Collected by very good Hands, and lately Reviewed . . . by the late learned Justice Godbolt. And now Published by W: Hughes*, London, 1653.

Something of Hoskyns' manner in court may be gathered from the following anecdote 'Of Serjeant Hoskins' (*MS. Sloane 1757, f. 1 d*), for the reference to which I am indebted to R. E. Bennett: 'Master Hoskins Serjeant at Law, being of Councell in Chancery for the Lady Townsend, relict of Sir Horatio, that stood in Contempt upon Proces, The Serjeant having pleaded long, and well for his Clyent, The Lord Chancellor Elsmeere asking him But Mr Serjeant What can you say in discharge or excuse of the Contempt? I hope (said the Serjeant) your Lordship will consider, how easy a matter 'twas for a Lady that in her youth, had been of great account, if in age she chanc'd to fall into Contempt. The Lord Chancellor, smyling at the Seriants conceit, past by the Contempt.'

(The reference to Ellsmere places the incident before 1617 and therefore before Hoskyns had become a serjeant-at-law.)

46. See Stow, *op. cit.*, p. 67.

47. In *MS. Harl. 6395*, f. 53 (No. 336), a reference I owe to R. E. Bennett, may be found this anecdote revealing the Serjeants' conversation in lightest vein: 'Hoskins used to call Serieant Hecham his

Ape, because of his writhen Face, and meering [*sic*] hooke; and one day the Lawyers being merry together, one askt his Brother Hecham when he would marry? neuer sayes he, I had rather leade Apes in Hell: nay faith says Hoskins, if it comes to that once, I am sure thou wilt pose all the Diuells in Hell, for there will be such gaping and enquiring which is the Man which is the Ape; and they can neuer distinguish, unlesse thou goest thither in thy Sergeants Robes.'

48. Hopwood, *op. cit.*, II, 681.

49. *Ibid.*, II, 723.

50. *Ibid.*

51. *Ibid.*, II, 727.

52. Dugdale (*op. cit.*, p. 331) reproduces Serjeant Hoskyns' coat of arms as it appeared in one of the windows in the dining hall at Serjeants' Inn in 1664. Letter XXX in Chapter VII, above, indicates that in June 1629 Hoskyns was still residing in the Middle Temple.

53. For the Latin verses at Morehampton, see No. XLIII in Chapter X, above.

54. Benedict and Benedicta. The latter married John Markey, the son of William Markey and Sybil Kyrle. In Rudhall Chapel at Ross, Herefordshire, the inscription on John Markey's tomb reads as follows: '*Johannes Markey de Alton Court arm liberalis et urbanus uxorem duxit Benedictam filiam unicam illustrissimi Johannis Hoskins S. L.*,' etc. See William Henry Cooke, *Collections towards the History and Antiquities of the County of Hereford. In Continuation of Duncomb's History*, London, 1882, III, 113 and 127. For an account of Benedict, later created baronet, see Burke's *Peerage*.

55. Morehampton remained in the possession of Hoskyns' descendants until 1828 when Sir Hungerford Hoskyns sold it to a Mr. Hamp of Hereford. In 1870 it was purchased from the latter's representatives by William Laslett, M.P. for Worcester. See Charles J. Robinson, *op. cit.*, p. 2.

56. *MS. Add. 24,491*, ff. 202. b-204. c.

57. See No. XLII in Chapter X, above.

58. See n. 38, above.

59. Information furnished by the Rev. A. L. Browne, Esq., Rector of Great Rissington. Mr. Browne wrote on 6 January 1930: 'The marriage entry in question is somewhat faded. It does not indicate the source of the licence, which may have been issued from the Prerogative Court of Canterbury or from the Court of the diocese of Gloucester. The name of the officiating clerk is not given either; presumably he would be Dr. Whittington, the rector at the time. No particulars are given of the age, *etc.*, of the contracting parties.'

60. W. P. W. Phillimore and Thomas M. Blagg. *Gloucestershire Parish Registers. Marriages*, London, 1914, XVII, 62. Phillimore records the bride's name as 'Mrs. Habett Barrett Harding.' Joseph Hunter, *MS. Add. 24,491*, f. 203, wrote: 'I suppose he [*i.e.*, Hoskyns]

must be the person who appears in a pedigree of Riseley of Chitwood in Bucks as the 3rd husb. of habet d. of Will. R., esq., whose second husband was Devereux Barret.' It is therefore possible that *Isabel* should read *Habet*. Mr. Browne remarked that the name looks more like *Isabel*, but may be *Habet*.

61. Letters XXVI and XXVII in Chapter VII, above.

62. She is not mentioned in Hoskyns' last will. See n. 83, below.

63. *Members of Parliament*, 1878, Part I, p. 475.

64. See *C. J.*, I, 879; 880; 889; 895; 903; 913.

65. Wallace Notestein and Frances H. Relf, *Commons Debates for 1629*, Research Publications of the University of Minnesota, Minneapolis, 1921, p. 14.

66. One of the 'Sireniacal' gentlemen. See Chapter I, above.

67. Notestein and Relf, *op. cit.*, p. 16.

68. *Ibid.*, p. 64.

69. *Ibid.*

70. *Ibid.*, pp. 74-5.

71. *Ibid.*, pp. 75-6.

72. *Ibid.*, p. 211.

73. *Ibid.*, p. 220.

74. *Ibid.*, p. 119.

75. *Ibid.*, p. 120.

76. For the report of the Committee of Religion containing the declaration of their position, see Notestein and Relf, *op. cit.*, pp. 23 and 117-18.

77. *Ibid.*, p. 102.

78. *Ibid.*

79. *C. J.*, I, 932.

80. I have found no further information on this point, though the town was not Hereford.

81. An account of this episode is found in Notestein and Relf, *op. cit.*, pp. 103-106.

82. See Aubrey, *op. cit.*, I, 422.

83. His last will, preserved in Somerset House (127 Lee), follows: 'I do giue to my sonne All my landes rents & rev^{er}cõns whatsoever and wheresoever to him and his heires forever, I give him alsoe all my leases plate houshol stuffe and goodes and chattles whatsoever and I praie God blisse him and I thanke God for him, I give my daughter nothing but what it shall please him to bestowe vpon her when hee is able nor anie thing then vnles her husband & shee sufficiently release and convey vnto him all their estate and title in all the landes that I purchased in her name, When it shall please god that my sonne shall haue discharged all my debtes which I hope in god hee will doe, and I praie Godes speciall assistance in itt then I intreate him to remember my purpose in my last will before this towardes my cosen John

Hoskins my cosen Richard Hoskin's children John Borne and my servantes and to doe somewhat therein In what measure hee thinkes fitt and shalbe able for the burthen that lyes vpon vs nowe is greate, I doe revoke all former Willes and of this I make my sonne Bennett my sole executo^r In witnes whereof I subscribe my name and putt my seale the last day of January 1635. J. Hoskins.'

84. John Hacket, *op. cit.*, Part I, 1.

NOTES ON CHAPTER VII

The letters and papers in Chapter VII were transcribed from the original manuscripts by their present owner, Henry Hornyold-Strickland, Esq., of Sizergh, Kendal, Westmorland, who graciously permitted me to compare the originals with his careful transcripts. In the letter of 6 June 1629 are three words which neither of us could make out. In almost every other case, I think, the reading is clear. The initial *p*, for *per*, *par*, *pro*, *etc.*, has not been expanded, and my intention has been to give as exact an impression of the manuscripts as possible.

The manuscripts are now preserved in the muniment room of Sizergh Castle, Kendal, Westmorland. To the gracious generosity of both Mr. Hornyold-Strickland and his aunt, Miss W. B. de La Chere, I am indebted for the privilege of using them. Miss de La Chere inherited them from her uncle, the late Viscount Llandaff, a descendant of Elizabeth Bourne, Hoskyns' stepdaughter, and her husband, William Hoskyns of Bernithen Court, the son and heir of John Hoskyns' brother Oswald.

In this collection of thirty-seven letters and papers, twenty-nine are by John Hoskyns to Benedicta, his wife, or to Elizabeth Bourne, his stepdaughter. His instructions to his clerk, William Taylor, may be looked upon as a letter, disclosing vividly and delightfully conditions of domestic life of the period. Hoskyns' will is printed for the light it throws upon his possessions, his way of living, and his family connections. Of the remaining six letters we have already seen (in Chapter VI, above) one by his brother, Dr. John Hoskyns, reporting the Reader's Feast at the Middle Temple, and that of William Taylor, announcing to Benedicta her husband's appointment as a judge in Wales. Of the other letters in the collection two are by Dr. Hoskyns to Benedicta; one is by Thomas Coningsby to Hoskyns; and one is by a suitor of Elizabeth Bourne's. These four miscellaneous letters are printed at the close of this section of notes.

Most of Hoskyns' letters are in his own hand, although that of 16 February 1625/6 was obviously dictated to a clerk, Hoskyns merely adding the closing phrase and signature. Likewise the will of 1618/9 is in the hand of someone else.

Frank (or Frances), John, and Bess are Hoskyns' stepchildren. *Ben* refers sometimes to his wife, sometimes to his son Benedict; *Dic* or *Dicke*, to his daughter Benedicta.

Notes on the individual letters follow:

I

The prose of this letter retains something of the rich pattern of the Arcadian school of Sidney and yet introduces the type of imagery which we have come to associate with the 'metaphysical' poetry of the seventeenth century. In true Arcadian vein Hoskyns writes of 'the only fuell to mayntain the passions of loue, the only wynd that would [have] fild the sayles of those thoughts, wch might loose themselues in an Ocean of sighs, teares, throbs, & tempests that poore lovers endure.' But with a touch of 'metaphysical' imagery he declares, 'Now I am but a shadow devided from myne own lyfe and essence.'

This letter may be compared with Hoskyns' poetic treatment of the theme of absence in No. XXIV in Chapter X, above.

Widmarsh streete] Widemarsh Street is still an important thoroughfare in Hereford, containing several seventeenth-century houses.

six weeks] Hoskyns and Benedicta had been married on the preceding 1 August. He has doubtless been at the Middle Temple since the beginning of Michaelmas term.

II

This letter was written sometime after the birth in 1609 of his son Benedict referred to in the last sentence as *Ben.*

Mr. Pembrug] Probably Anthony Pembridge, who was returned to Parliament on 29 October 1605 for the city of Hereford.

My brother John] The divine, who took the degree D.C.L. at Oxford in 1613. See also n. 6 for Chapter II, above.

Dr. Lake] Arthur Lake (1569-1626), a brother of Sir Thomas Lake, at one time secretary of state. Dr. Lake was educated at Winchester and at New College where he received the degree D.D. on 16 May 1605. In 1608 he was made dean of Worcester Cathedral; in 1613, a warden of New College; in 1616, vice-chancellor of Oxford; and in 1616, bishop of Bath and Wells. It is probable that at the time this letter was written, John Hoskyns the younger was soliciting Lake's aid in securing a benefice. In 1614 John Hoskyns the younger was made master of St. Oswald's near Worcester, perhaps with Lake's recommendation.

my brother . . . cloake] His brother Oswald, a woolen draper in London.

Mr. Wallwyn]   A family of Wallwyns lived at Brockebery, Heref., in 1587. See Hopwood, *op. cit.*, I, 289.

my lord]   Doubtless Robert Bennet, Bishop of Hereford, and god-father to Hoskyns' son, Benedict.

III

In a later hand this paper is headed 'Instructions By Serjeant Hoskyns For The Regulation Of The Conduct Of His Clerk Mr W. Taylor.' In what is apparently Taylor's own hand is this heading: 'A note to instruct me in my vocation.'

Although in the original manuscripts this note to Taylor is the twenty-seventh item, I have placed it third, since it was probably written before 1611, for Taylor is instructed to teach the child Frances to write and Bess (born in 1601) to read.

Litleton]   Sir Thomas Littleton (1402-1481). The first edition of Littleton's *Tenures* seems to have been the Norman-French (*Tenores nouelli*) of 1481. Many editions followed in Norman-French and in English. Sir Edward Coke published commentaries on Littleton in 1628, *etc.*, and William West was an earlier editor.

West presedents]   William West (fl. 1568-1594), besides his numerous editions of *Les Tenures du monsieur Littleton* (1581, *etc.*), wrote *Symbolæographia. The art, description or image of instruments* (1590). Numerous later editions and augmentations of the work appeared. The edition of 1610 is entitled *The first (second) part of Simboleography . . . . Newly augmented with divers presidents touching Marchant affaires.* Later editions are described as augmented 'with divers new Presidents.'

To some edition of West's *Symbolæographia* Hoskyns no doubt refers as *West presedents*. West was of the Inner Temple.

booke of entries]   In 1566 was published William Rastell's *A Colleccion of entrees, of declaracions, barres, replicacions, reioinders, issues, verdits, etc.* Other editions followed. It is probably to Rastell's work that Hoskyns refers.

In 1614 was printed Sir Edward Coke's *A Book of Entries containing perfect and approved Presidents of Courts, Declarations, Informations; &c.* Hoskyns' note to Taylor seems, however, to have been written before Coke's work was printed.

fitter to be forgiven]   Apparently William Taylor had a weakness for 'riotous living.' See his letter quoted on p. 51, above.

IV

Mrs. Richard]   I have not identified her.

Jorney]   Now obsolete. The *N. E. D.* lists uses of the word in *c* 1305, 1400, and 1422, and quotes Blount's definition in his *Glossographia* (1656).

my lord president] Ralph Lord Eure, Lord President of the Marches of Wales.

matter put to frends] The meaning is clear enough, but I find no mention of the phrase in the *N. E. D.*

umbles] 'The edible inward parts of an animal, usually of a deer.'—*N. E. D.*

Mr. Delahay] John and Morgan Delahay are mentioned in the next letter.

I turnd my back . . . lett[r]] Here and elsewhere Hoskyns gives details that are as delightful as those in Pepys.

V

Dydley] An estate in the parish of St. Devereux, Herefordshire.

Colipep] *I.e., Colipeper's.* There were various persons of that name in the Middle Temple at this period.

Churchehill & Bemwell lands] Estates at Churchill and Banwell in Somersetshire.

Mr. Clarke] The Clarkes seem to have been friends in Herefordshire. See also Letter VI, above. One of them seems to have been Hoskyns' clerk. See p. 51, above.

Dover Court] Probably Dover Court in Essex.

Bernithen] An estate in the parish of Llangarren, Herefordshire.

fine] Here probably a contract or agreement. See *N. E. D.*, meaning II. 6. c. Or the meaning may be (*ibid.*, meaning III. 7. a.) a 'fee . . . paid by the tenant . . . to the landlord.'

my lord Bishop] Robert Bennet, Bishop of Hereford is doubtless meant.

Garway] In Herefordshire.

my 2 Bens] Benedicta and their son Benedict.

y[r] *2 girles*] Benedicta's daughters, Frances and Elizabeth Bourne.

John Boorne] Benedicta's son. Though he was not admitted to the Middle Temple until October 1613, he was probably receiving preliminary training in London in 1611.

4 . . . in the morning] Aubrey says that Hoskyns rose regularly at four.

VI

See also Benedicta's letters to her husband while he was in the Tower, printed in Chapter V, above.

in straw] The first recorded use in the *N. E. D.* is that in Fuller's *Worthies*, 1661, where the quotation shows that the phrase was then a proverbial one, the meaning, of course, *in childbed*.

VII

See Chapter V, above, for the background for this letter. Hoskyns, still a prisoner in the Tower, was not released until three months after the writing of this letter.

antipathy] A fairly early use of the word. The first recorded in the *N. E. D.* is one of 1601.

y^r Doctor the late . . . example of suictors] A reference to Dr. John Hoskyns' seeking a suitable post in the Church upon resignation of his fellowship in New College in 1613.

M^r of an hospitall] Dr. Hoskyns had just received the mastership of the charitable institution of St. Oswald's near Worcester.

2: March 1614] *I.e.*, 1615, new style.

VIII

my lord Chaũcelor] Sir Thomas Egerton.

my lord Chyefe Justice] Sir Edward Coke, chief justice of the King's Bench.

IX

Sr Thomas Overbery] Sir Thomas Overbury was imprisoned in the Tower in the spring of 1613 through the influence of Robert Carr, later Earl of Somerset, whose secretary Overbury had been, and of Henry Howard, Earl of Northampton. Both men feared that Overbury would attempt to cut off the possibility of the marriage of Somerset with Frances Howard, Countess of Essex. The pretext for Overbury's imprisonment seems to have been his refusal on 26 April 1613 of the Russian embassage. His commitment followed immediately. By 20 July he was extremely weak and ill. On 13 September 1613 he died in the Tower under strange and not wholly explained circumstances, but supposedly poisoned by Richard Weston, his keeper, at the instigation of Frances Howard, Countess of Essex, and Mistress Anne Turner, her accomplice, and perhaps with the knowledge of the Earl of Northampton and of Somerset. Northampton died before the trial took place. Frances Howard, by that time the Countess of Somerset, and Somerset himself were both convicted of the murder, though they were pardoned to the extent of escaping the death penalty.

the Lieuetenãt] Sir Gervase Helwys (1561-1615) was appointed Lieutenant of the Tower on 6 May 1613 through the influence of Northampton. He was tried on 16 November 1615, charged with abetting Weston in the poisoning. It would seem that he knew something of what was going on but remained silent and condoned the criminal acts.

As we see by the next letter, Helwys, for some undetermined cause, owed Hoskyns fifty pounds. It is not likely that Hoskyns collected the sum before Helwys' execution on 20 November 1615.

Mrs Kempe] Elizabeth Kempe is referred to several times as Hoskyns' sister. However, the passage regarding her here suggests that she was more closely connected with Benedicta than with Hoskyns himself. I think that likely she was Benedicta's sister rather than his.

Weston] Richard Weston, who had formerly been in the employ of an apothecary, was under-keeper to Sir Gervase Helwys of the Tower at the time of Overbury's death. Weston was hanged at Tyburn for his confession of guilt. For an account of his trial see Howell, *op. cit.*, II, 911-30.

Sr John Swyñerton] Sir John Swynerton was returned to Parliament for East Grinstead Burough, Sussex, on 8 February 1604. He is mentioned in *Acts of the Privy Council, 1613-1614*, pp. 372-73.

Sr John Wentworth . . . Sr John Hollis] In Howell (*op. cit.*, p. 930) we learn that Sir John Holles and Sir John Wentworth, 'out of friendship to the earl of Somerset, rode to Tyburn, and urged Weston to deny all that he before confessed: but Weston . . . resisted their temptations, sealing . . . the truth of his confessions with his last gasp; and sir John Hollis, sir John Wentworth, together with Mr. Lumsden . . . were afterwards prosecuted in the Star-Chamber, for traducing . . . justice.'

Holles was fined one thousand pounds for questioning Weston at Tyburn. See *MS. Add. 12,511*, p. 109, for an account of the proceedings in the Star-chamber against Holles and others.

Sir John Lidcot had a warrant to visit Overbury in the Tower on 20 July 1613. For Lidcot's testimony at the trial see Howell, *op. cit.*, II, 986.

Sr Tho Vavasor] Knight Marshall of the Household for life from 31 November 1612. See *Calendar of State Papers, Domestic, 1611-1618*, pp. 159 and 326.

Mrs Turnor] Anne Turner, the reputed innovator of the saffroned ruffs of the period, was an associate of Frances Howard, Lady Essex, in supposed plans to poison Overbury. Mrs. Turner was tried on 7 November 1615 and was condemned and hanged at Tyburn for her part in the alleged poisoning. See Howell, *op. cit.*, pp. 930-35.

the Countesse] I have not identified her.

Burtons poole] In Herefordshire.

make some certayn perch] The *N. E. D.* defines the substantive *perch* (III. 5. a) as 'a measure of length, especially for land palings, walls, *etc.*; in Standard Measure equal to 5 1/2 yards.' The phrase Hoskyns uses apparently means to take a definite measurement.

of the ringe hedge] According to the *N. E. D.*, the same as a ring-fence: 'A fence completely enclosing an estate, farm, or piece of ground.' No example of the use of *ring-hedge* is recorded in the *N. E. D.* and the earliest for *ring-fence* is one in 1769.

In John Speed's maps of Herefordshire one may see the ring-hedge drawn around Morehampton Farm.

My Lord Chauncelor and *. . . lord Cooke*] Egerton and Sir Edward Coke.

Mr of the Rolls] Sir Julius Caesar.

the Chaũcery] I find no reference to Hoskyns in *Lists and Indexes*.

No. XXIV. Index of Chancery Proceedings (Series II.) Preserved in the Public Record Office. Vol. II. 1579-1621, London, 1908.

the Earl of somerset] This is the only reference I have come upon connecting Somerset with Hoskyns' imprisonment. See Chapter VI, above.

Thomas] Hoskyns' brother, apparently general overseer of Hoskyns' estates.

stank] A dam. Now dialectal and technical. The *N. E. D.* lists uses from 1604 to 1883.

quicksett] To plant with slips of the white-thorn. The quickset hedges may have been so-called in contrast to those of holly, of slower growth.

X

my lord keeper] Sir Francis Bacon, who succeeded Sir Thomas Egerton, Lord Ellsmere, upon the latter's death in March 1617.

Trelewisdee] I have not identified this estate unless it be that of Trelough in the parish of St. Devereux, Herefordshire.

your grand-child] Perhaps the child of Frances Bourne and Dr. John Hoskyns. From the letters it is evident that their marriage took place after 1613 and before May 1618. See Letter XVIII, Chapter VII, above.

XI

This letter doubtless gives a not entirely fair statement as to why Benedicta so carefully garnered her husband's letters.

XII

Lord Compton] William Lord Compton, afterward first Earl of Northampton, of the Compton line, was appointed Lord President of the Marches of Wales on 24 November 1617.

David] I have not identified him. It is unlikely that he was Hoskyns' son, since Benedict upon his admission to the Middle Temple in 1620 was described as his father's only son. If David had been a son of Hoskyns, he would apparently have been born after Benedicta, born during her father's imprisonment. In that case, David would not have been old enough to learn to read in 1617.

XIII

Secretary Winwood] Sir Ralph Winwood, secretary of state, died on 27 October 1617.

my lord byshop] Doubtless Robert Bennet, bishop of Hereford, who died on 25 October 1617.

Sr James scudamore] Scudamore had accompanied the Earl of Essex to Cadiz and had sat for the county of Hereford in the first Jacobean Parliament. Hoskyns seems not to share Spenser's admiration for 'the gentle Scudamour,' whom Blandamour hated

> 'Both for his worth, that all men did adore,
> And eke because his loue he wonne by right.'

Indeed, Spenser immortalised the Scudamore name in Books III and IV of *The Faerie Qveene*. For other praise of Sir James and his father see the quotation from Higford's *Instructions* printed in *The Works of Edmund Spenser, A Variorum Edition*, edited by Greenlaw, Osgood, and Padelford, II, 223-24.

The Scudamores lived at Holme-Lacy on the Wye, Herefordshire. Sir James died in 1619.

my brothers cause] Probably some concern of Dr. John Hoskyns'. Seven years later he was engaged in a dispute regarding ecclesiastical government, concerning which Secretary Conway wrote to the Archbishop of Canterbury: 'Dr. Hoskins has lost his labour in coming to Court . . . . He is a good man and has a good cause, and is much missed in his country.' See *Calendar of State Papers, Domestic, 1623-1625*, p. 387.

Mr Harbyn] Apparently a friend from Herefordshire. See Letter XV in Chapter VII, above.

Sr Robert Oxenbrugge] Sir Robert Oxenbridge, probably the man referred to here, was returned to Parliament on 8 December 1620 for Whitchurch Borough, Southampton, and twice later.

Sr Guy Palmes] Palmes was returned to Parliament for Rutland County on 15 January 1624. I have found no details of his life or relations with Hoskyns.

the hospital] The hospital of St. Oswald's in Worcestershire, where Dr. Hoskyns was master.

band] Probably in the archaic sense of agreement, or promise, binding on him who makes it. The *N. E. D.* gives examples of its use from 1441 to 1814. It may mean security given; a deed legally executed. The *N. E. D.* cites uses with the latter meaning from 1521 to 1818.

XIV

ashenkeys] The fruit of the ash tree. The *N. E. D.* quotes from Turner, *Herbal*, II, 6: 'They are called in Englishe ashe Keyes, because they hangh in bunches after the maner of Keyes.'

new lord president] William Lord Compton.

XV

6th Feb^r 1617] *I.e.*, 1618, new style.

Doctor Gifford] See No. XLV in Chapter X, above. Gifford, a leading physician of the day, was one of those making a report on the condition of Henry Prince of Wales at the time of his death. See Howell, *op. cit.*, II, 1002.

Gale] Gall.

He . . . pension] Probably his brother Thomas.

XVI

Tom] I have not identified him.

Charles] Charles was the seventh son of John and Margery Hoskyns, and the youngest brother of Hoskyns the writer. He was educated at Winchester and at New College, where he was admitted a fellow in 1606, took his B.A. on 13 April 1608, and died in 1609. One of his Oxford friends, John Heath, also a fellow of New College, wrote of Charles as follows (*Two Centuries of Epigrammes*, London, 1610, Epigram II, 71) :

> *In memoriam Charoli Hoskins nov. Coll. quondam*
> *Socij, & sui familiaris de functi.*
> That thou wer't witty, if I tell thy name,
> I know there's none will contradict the same.
> Oh had thy body answer'd to thy minde,
> Thou would'st (or els affection makes me blinde)
> Haue beene one of the mirrours of our dayes,
> Borne both thine owne, and countreyes name to raise.
> Pitty it was (but that it was Gods will)
> That so diuine a wit did dwell so ill.

In *MS. King's 12A. LXIV*, ff. 44-5, are some lines by Charles Hoskyns addressed to Christian IV, along with some fifty other folios of verse, all done by members of the University of Oxford. (I am indebted to Mr. R. E. Bennett for this reference.)   Another Latin poem by Charles is preserved in the Bodleian (*Funebria, Wood, 460*) in *Encomion Rodolphi VVarcoppi ornatissimi . . . qui . . . extinctus est . . . Aug. 1605 . . . . Oxoniæ, Apud Iosephum Barnesium,* 1605.

Aubrey says that Charles Hoskyns 'killed himself with hard study.'

Oswald] Oswald's will (30 Meade) was proved in 1618. See *The Index Library. Prerogative Court of Canterbury Wills, 1605-19. Issued by The British Record Society,* XLIII, 1912, T. M. Blagg, General Editor.

Oswald was buried on 29 April 1618 at St. Augustines, London. See Robinson, *op. cit.*, p. 133.

See also n. 43 for Chapter V, above.

XVII

shop & wares] The shop and goods of his brother Oswald.

barre me my fees] Apparently the citizens of Hereford were unwilling to pay him for his parliamentary services. 'Members of the House of Commons were formerly remunerated for their services by assessments made on the citizens . . . . An entry appears in the Corporation Minute Book [of Hereford], 1618, when it was ordered . . . "That the common council . . . shall assess their wards with a double tax for satisfying John Hoskyns, Esquire, late of Parliament . . . of ninety-two pounds, allowed him by the king's writ . . . for his parliamentary expenses for nine hundred and odd days, after the rate of two shillings per diem." ' Quoted from Richard Johnson, *op. cit.*, p. 181.

Lord Chaũcelour] Sir Francis Bacon.

XVIII

Ledbury] Dr. John Hoskyns was by this time rector of Ledbury, where he died in 1631.

XIX

rother beasts] Now obsolete or dialectal for oxen or horned cattle.

my sister] Possibly his sister-in-law, the widow of his brother Oswald, who was buried in the preceding April. Oswald's daughter Frances is mentioned in Letter 46 in the family papers of Mr. Henry Hornyold-Strickland. Hoskyns' reference to his sister's former residence in London and his prayer for the 'fatherlesse' strengthen the conjecture that Oswald's widow may be the person referred to.

XX

My last will] He made at least two others: in 1627 and in 1635/6. For his last will see n. 83 for Chapter VI, above.

Fraunces Hoskyns my daughter in law] I.e., his stepdaughter. The same term appears elsewhere in the letters, and was commonly used in this sense in the seventeenth and eighteenth centuries.

John Dunne] I have not been able to identify John Dunne. Could this be a reference to the poet? In Letter XIV, above, Hoskyns refers to David Doñe, presumably a neighbour; and it is likely that the John Dunne referred to here is a Herefordshire man and not the poet. In his will of 1627 Hoskyns speaks of the four closes which he had of John Doñe, at Bernithen, Herefordshire.

bason] Basin.

(24 March) *1618*] I.e., 1619, new style.

XXI

3. Feb. 1620] I.e., 1621, new style.

kersey] A kind of coarse narrow cloth, woven from long wool and usually ribbed. The *N. E. D.* cites uses of the word from 1390 to 1834.

germashes] Not in the *N. E. D.* Could the word be connected with the Scotch dialectal *gernis* or *jerniss*, 'the state of being soaked in rain or water'?

It is obvious that some sort of protection against inclement weather is Hoskyns' meaning.

Wright (*The English Dialect Dictionary*) defines *jarness* as 'a marshy place, or any place so wet as to resemble a marsh.'

pantofles] Slippers. 'In common English use from *c* 1570 to *c* 1650-60; after that chiefly an alien or historical word.'—*N. E. D.*

aqua caelestis] The *N. E. D.* does not describe this particular water, nor record the word.

Rosa solis water] 'A cordial or liqueur originally made from or flavoured with the juice of the plant sundew.'—*N. E. D.*

Sir Walter Pye] Hoskyns' neighbour, of the Mynde, Herefordshire. See also No. XLVI in Chapter X, above.

my comittment] *I.e.*, to the Tower. See Chapters V and VI, above.

undertakers] Those 'who in the reigns of Jas. I, Chas. I, and Chas. II undertook to influence, the action of Parliament, esp. with regard to the voting of supplies.'—*N. E. D.*

XXII

Tilt boat] 'A large rowing boat having a tilt or awning formerly used on the Thames, esp. as a passenger boat between London and Gravesend.'—*N. E. D.*

XXIII

Mr *Parry*] Stephen Parry, from whom Hoskyns was purchasing Morehampton.

commissiō for pressing mayds to Virginia] In October 1618 one Owen Evans, Messenger of the Chamber, was pretending to possess such a commission. He 'frightened away forty from one parish, who have fled to such obscure places that their parents cannot find them.' He acknowledged the receipt of ten shillings for exempting the parish of Ottery from his commission for pressing 'maidens for the Bermudas and Virginia.' See *Calendar of State Papers, Domestic, 1611-1618*, p. 586.

Chamberlain (in Birch, *op. cit.*, II, 108-109) tells of one Robinson who was hanged for various offences, one of which was compelling rich yeomen's daughters to compound to escape being 'pressed to Virginia.'

XXIV

Prebendary Williams] Hoskyns was mistaken, for John Williams, prebendary of the Cathedral of Hereford and later made Archbishop of York, succeeded Bacon as Lord Keeper of the Great Seal on 10 July 1621.

Arkston] In the parish of Kingston, Herefordshire.

Meres Court] This may be a reference to Moor Court or Murcutt, a manor within the manor of Pembridge, Herefordshire. See Robinson, *op. cit.*, p. 226.

XXV

My cosen Will] Actually his nephew, William Hoskyns, son of Oswald. *Cousin* is here used in the general sense of *kinsman*. Apparently a hasty and unfortunate marriage by William was being annulled. Further reference to the matter is made in Letter XXIX, in Chapter VII, above.

Wills sisters] Margaret and Magdalen. See John and George F. Matthews, *Abstracts of Probate Acts in the Prerogative Court of Centerbury*, London, 1902, I, 30. Reference to Magdalen is made again in Letter XXXI, above, and they are doubtless among the 'gentlewomen' referred to in Letter XXIX, in Chapter VII, above.

my daughter Megg: Bourne] Apparently the wife of Hoskyns' stepson John Bourne. See abstract of Margaret Bourne's will proved in 1630, in which she refers to her 'brother Dr Hoskins' (*Abstract of Somersetshire Wills . . . Frederick Brown, First Series*, Privately Printed, 1887, p. 29). Since Dr. John Hoskyns had married Frances Bourne, John Bourne's sister, this appellation would be appropriate.

pke] Park.

Sÿsses] The assizes.

Glouc] Gloucester.

Mr Jefferies letter] MS. reads 'Mr Jefferies lre.'

the valley] The Golden Valley, Herefordshire, in which Morehampton is situated.

Lewis] I have not identified him.

ffebruary. 1625] *I.e.*, 1626, new style.

XXVI

In the MS. collection this letter follows No. XXVII. To me, however, it seems to have been written before XXVII; therefore I have changed the order.

St Thomas eve] *I.e.*, 20 December.

to walke with our Claret] The *N. E. D.* lists similar instances of *walk*, in this now obsolete use, from 1555 to 1691.

XXVII

mother-in-law] *I.e.*, stepmother.

XXVIII

Geue Will. Hoskyns good counsell] Elizabeth later married Will Hoskyns, and this may be a hint of her stepfather's approval of such a match.

XXIX

suiet in the Arches] A suit in 'the ecclesiastical court of appeal for the province of Canterbury, formerly held at the church of St. Mary-le-Bow (or "of the Arches"), so named from the arches that supported its steeple.'—*N. E. D.*

fynding of the office] Probably the returning of the verdict. See *N. E. D.* (*office, sb.,* 7).

Jony Boornes wardship] Doubtless 'Jony Boorne' was the son of John and Margaret Bourne. John Bourne, Hoskyns' stepson, had died sometime between October 1624 and May 1627 (Hopwood, *op. cit.*, II, 695 and 721): Margaret Bourne in her will proved in 1630 (*Abstract of Somersetshire Wills . . . Frederick Brown, First Series,* p. 29) refers to her son John.

XXX

these bee dd.] *I.e.,* 'These be delivered.'

four of Morehampton house at London] Benedict and his cousin Will Hoskyns were both at the Middle Temple. See Hopwood, *op. cit.*, II, 747. Who the other two were I have not been able to determine. Apparently Oswald's children made Morehampton their home after their father's death in 1618. See references to Will's sisters in Letters XXV and XXXI in Chapter VII, above.

. . . .] Three undeciphered words in MS.

tyffany] The *N. E. D.* defines *tiffany* as a 'kind of thin transparent silk; also a transparent gauze muslin, cobweb lawn.'

XXXI

my brother] Doubtless Oswald, the woolen draper.

Magdulen] His niece, the daughter of his brother Oswald. See notes for Letter XXV, above.

heartiful] The *N. E. D.* does not give this form.

––––––––––

The following four letters add in their own way to the picture of seventeenth-century life which those of John Hoskyns the elder have already furnished. The first is from John Hoskyns the younger just after he had received the degree D.C.L. at Oxford in 1613. It is addressed to his sister-in-law, Benedicta:

Good Sister,

God in heaven grant y^u health. Before I tooke a foolish degree I could visit y^u easily and alone, but nowe I have made myselfe vnfitt for such a duty except I had both horse & mã. I pray y^u

thĩke not y^t I love y^u the lesse because I com not to y^u. Whẽ
I am furnished y^u shall have enough of my cõpanie, & vntill thẽ
& for ever my prayers. I desire my brother should vpõ his
first arrival make som meanes to deale with Clemẽt about my
prebend, for there is noe reason I should still pay for others
fruites & enioy noe profitt, these first entrãces into spiritual liviḡs
if they be noe more thẽ first entrãces will soone vndoe a man:
my brother cõsiders not y^t I have paid tenths & fees for y^e
former prebend, whereas (except he had accepted the rent) I
might have stood vppõ ye forfeiture of Mr. Sebornes lease as
Dr. Best & Dr. Kerry would have donn. I write not this to make
eyther of those doctors my rules, for I followe none but Christ
in all thĩgs, but I was overseere in y^t prebend, I would not be
soe in this.

If it please my brother soe to cõclude y^t I may be sent for in y^e
visitation-weeke (know [?] he must send me horse and mã or
else I cã hardly com) I may be installed otherwise I must
keepe Trinity tearme in Oxford and thẽ there may be som danger
of ye coõodities of this yeare for ye prebẽd if not of ye prebend
it selfe. Whẽ I keepe horses I shall have lesse vse thẽ he, & soe
may somtymes steed hĩ. I shall much desire y^{ur} presence at
Oxford at ye Act, if y^u cã brĩge y^{ur} sicke body thither I trust
it shall not be [*sicker* crossed out] more sicke at y^{ur} returne.
I must entertayne som, there is none livĩge whõ I would more
willĩgly entertaine thẽ y^u, I will provide a conveniẽt place for
y^u If y^u can com: but of this whẽ I see y^u next. Meanewhile
god keepe y^u.

I am god helpe me

> A Doctor wthout mẽ or horses, a purchaser wthout money,
> and a Vicar without meanes of hospitality, but god will
> provide and I must not overshoote myselfe in vnnecessary
> provisiõ at ye first.
>> Once more ye Lord preserve y^u for ever
>>> y^{ur} brother in love and
>>>> good affectiõ ever
>>>>> J. Hoskyns.

May 10, 1613./
If y^{ur} maid will make me sõ good bãds
and y^u lay out ye money, I will
reckõ wth y^u like an honest
brother.

The second letter is from Sir Thomas Coningsby to John Hoskyns
the elder, inviting him to a conference at what Camden called his

'passing faire house' at Hampton Court on the Lugg River in Herefordshire:

To the wor^ll [*i.e., worshipfull*] & well esteemed John Hoskyns
   esquire give this at his house in Hereford.
Well esteemed Mr. John Hoskins
   In my affaires at the Assises you were one of them in list of my direction to Tho. Eaton to be entreated to employ the skill of your profession, untill we heard that you were not returned from London; and since he informes me that you cominge home but soddenlie, would not (I thancke you) of your own accord stand to looke on where I had matter of interest & reputation; and nowe beinge by the good successe of them at leisure to thinke of other things amongst the rest there occurred a further consideration to perfect (if God will) my pious intentions in your neighborhood there.   And for that purpose doe desire conference with you, and an houres examination of particulars.   And doe hereby invite you to kepe the second Saboath of August here with me. And that you wilbe pleased soe to direct your journey as that you may be here on the Saturday night by fower of the Clocke that we may have leisure to consult & over-reade and afterwards to sett down & perfect that (yf yt please God) wch is yet imperfect, untill when I leave you to your other good occasions, and ever rest

your very loveng Freand
Tho. Conyngesbye

If you will bringe
Mrs. Hoskins to take the
aire of our gardens   Hampton Courte
I will bid her welcome.   30 July 1618.

   At the time Dr. John Hoskyns wrote the following letter to Benedicta, she had become his mother-in-law through his marriage with Frances Bourne.   The 'ould Lord Treasurer' to whom he refers is Thomas Howard, first Earl of Suffolk, who was Lord Treasurer from 11 July 1614 to 19 July 1619.   In the autumn of 1618 he was accused of defrauding the King of £240,000 in jewels and of several other shocking irregularities in the treasury.   His wife, the former Catherine Knevet, thought largely to blame for her husband's crimes, was herself charged with extorting money, chiefly through the agency of Sir John Bingley, the remembrancer of the exchequer.   At the conclusion of their trial in the Star Chamber the Earl and Countess were fined £30,000 and sentenced to the Tower.   However, they were soon released and their fines greatly reduced.   See the *D. N. B.*

It is interesting to note that here again Hoskyns and Bacon were legal opponents, for Bacon bitterly attacked the three persons on trial, whereas this letter tells us that Hoskyns defended Bingley. It is also interesting to observe that Hoskyns' son Benedict later married Anne, the daughter of Sir John Bingley.

To his very lovinge Mother
    M^ris Benedicta Hoskyns at Hereford
        these

                                    Novr 23. 1619.

Good Mother
    It is not amisse that W. Hoskyns is returned, he should have ben sent and delivered in another manner. I knowe noe newes but that the ould Lord Treasurer & Sir John Bingly this day com to be censured in the starre chāber, where my brother spake of late for Sir John Bingly with greate applause and to good purpose for himselfe for his client and for the comon wealth. I thĩke M^ris Harbyn will com downe with me for want of better company; I pray God keepe us all that we be not stollen away by worldly mē or worldly meanes from him. Good mother I had tyme only to salute y^u thus shortly and wish y^u all happines in ye Lord, remayninge at y^ur service y^ur dutifull lovinge sonn
                               J. Hoskyns.

The fourth letter presents a suitor of Elizabeth Bourne's:

To the fayre handes of my most esteemed
    M^ris Elizabeth Burne
att Morhampton in the County of Hereford.
Right worthy M^ris
    Compliments are tegious, only I must appologise for my neglect wch was that I heard not of the Assises in Hereford untill the Saturday before. And because urgent occasions for the instant required speedy dispatch, I was enforced to omytt a duty of greater consequence, but because I am only to be censured by your sweete self I hope I am halfe pardoned, for what remaynes punish me att my next meetinge wch shalbe with all expedition, in the meane time & alwayes I wilbe yor faythfull servant & thinke myself sufficiently graced to be obliged thereunto, & thus not doubting of yor favourable acceptance I will ever remayne if not yo^rs not myne owne nor any others.
                               Jo. Bowen.

Roblingston
xv^th of Aprill 1628.

NOTES ON CHAPTER VIII

1. See pp. 10-11, above.
2. For identification of Martino as Richard Martin see n. 55, Chapter I, above. Professor Hudson (*op. cit.*, p. 110) points out that the orator was Charles Best, who was to be in 1602 a contributor to Davison's *Poetical Rhapsody*.
3. Hoskyns' phrases from *Direccōns*.
4. The performance was popular enough to give its name at least to the revels in Middle Temple in 1635. See Hopwood, *op. cit.*, II, 880. The second performance may have been a revival of the one considered in this chapter.
5. *Le Prince d'Amour*, p. 61.
6. *Ibid.*
7. Wilson had quoted an extreme example of the aureate language with sufficient introduction to render it virtually a parody. See G. H. Mair, *Wilson's Arte of Rhetorique*, Oxford, 1909, p. 162, quoted by John M. Berdan, *Early Tudor Poetry*, New York, 1920, p. 142. Hoskyns' references to *milhors, horse mil, drink ere y^u go, etc.*, are borrowed from Wilson, p. 203.
8. The text of the speech printed in Chapter VIII is found in *MS. Malone 16*, ff. 74. b-75. a.

Below is a collation of it with that printed in *Le Prince d'Amour* (1660, pp. 37-40) and reprinted by Professor Hudson (*op. cit.*, pp. 110-13). Asterisks in the text itself call attention to these variants. It will be seen that the Malone manuscript is nearer to *MS. Add. 23,303* than to the printed text of *Le Prince d'Amour*. The manuscripts have the same heading, with its reference to Ralegh.

In the following collation the readings from *MS. Malone 16* are given first:

but alas]   For alas!
purgited]   pasted
Tropical]   Topical
course]   concise
no Reader]   not a Reader
frend ffogassa]   servant *Reniger Fogassa*
dost it]   dost ill
much good]   then much good
if wet snuff]   if well, then snuffe
in self]   it self
the regal state]   his Royal Seat
to ffollow]   and to follow
the stones]   stones
to exclame]   or to exclaim
Titus Situs]   Silas Titus
estates]   States

momental inclinatiōs] momentary inclinations

Mathematicall] Anarchical

not Tobacco w^t made me address] not Tabacco. What was the cause of the Aventine revolt, and seditious deprecation for a Tribune? it is apparent it was not Tabacco. What moved me to address

it reconciles not] nor reconcileth

no cities] no new Cities

it mends] nor mends

yet ye one or ye other] yet the one, the other

merie conceited Heraclytas] merry-conceited Poet *Heraclitus*

haue ever an historical consideratiō] shall have ever an Historical compensation

vnto my words] to my words

find note] find none

Beast] Best

this is] this,

deme wits] demerits

by y^r Herald frō on of an ancient house of the famous Calphurnius Beastia] by your Herald that he is descended from an Ancient house of the *Romans*, even from *Calphurnius Bestia,*

generatiō] the generation

til this praesent beast] to this present beast

I therefore in al humility] therefore in all humility I

that might] that he might

of his stalle] of the Stable

of beggars] of the Beggars

pro eloquentia] *foris Eloquentiae*

y^{er} may sit] that he may sit

oratorously] oratoriously

into y^r apprehensions] unto your apprehension

NOTES ON CHAPTER IX

Introduction

1. Aubrey, *op. cit.*, I, 418.

2. See pp. 122-24 of *Timber: or, Discoveries; Made Vpon Men and Matter: As They have flow'd out of his daily Readings; or had their refluxe to his peculiar Notion of the Times. By Ben: Jonson, London, Printed M. DC. XLI.*

The *Discoveries* with the title-page just given was printed for the first time in the second volume of the so-called 1640 folio.

3. Hopwood, *op. cit.*, I, 379.

4. *E.g.*, Felix E. Schelling, *Timber or Discoveries*, Boston, 1892, p. xvii; Gifford, *The Works of Ben Jonson*, VII, 150; Maurice Castelain, *Ben Jonson, Discoveries*, Paris, no date (but licensed to be

printed in 1906), p. xi; and Herford and Simpson, *Ben Jonson, The Man and His Work*, Oxford, 1925, II, 439-40. Herford and Simpson, without dating the *Discoveries* definitely, incline to the opinion that the material was collected and composed after Jonson's fire in 1623.

5. *E.g.*, W. W. Greg, *Ben Jonson's Sad Shepherd with Kaldron's Continuation*, published as Number 11 in *Materialien zur Kunde des alteren Englischen Dramas*, Louvain, 1905, pp. iv-v; Frank Marcham, 'Thomas Walkley and the Ben Jonson "Works" of 1640,' in *The Library*, XI, 225-29, September 1930; and W. W. Greg, 'Thomas Walkley and the Ben Jonson "Works" of 1640,' *ibid.*, pp. 461-65, March 1931.

6. Castelain (*op. cit.*, pp. 107-109) prints the parallel passage from Bacon's *Advancement of Learning*. The passage influenced by Bacon immediately precedes that borrowed from Hoskyns.

7. Hudson, *op. cit.*, p. xxviii.

8. See reference to Lipsius' notes in Janus Gruterus' *Notæ in Martialis Epigrammata*, a book listed as in Jonson's library by Herford and Simpson, *op. cit.*, I, 266.

9. Charles Algernon Swinburne, *A Study of Ben Jonson*, New York, 1889, p. 177.

10. *Ibid.*

11. Schelling, *op. cit.*, p. xix. Professor Charles Read Baskerville (*English Elements in Jonson's Early Comedy*, No. 178 in *Bulletin of The University of Texas Humanistic Series*, No. 12, 8 April 1911, p. 22, n.) refers to Jonson's admiration for Castiglione's *The Courtier* and Cicero's *De Oratore*. This admiration was doubtless felt by Jonson, but the expression of it referred to is Hoskyns'.

12. Schelling, *op. cit.*, p. xxiv.

13. Castelain, *op. cit.*, p. xix. His section 125 begins with the phrase 'In writing there is to be regarded.'

14. *Ibid.*, pp. xix-xxiv.

15. Hopwood, *op. cit.*, I, 396.

16. The only other reference to a D. Manwaring that I have seen is one in *MS. Ashmole 47*, ff. 85. b-88. b, where there are verses 'Vppon Mrs Sarah Manwaring' by D. Manwaring and two others. These verses are followed by lines dated 'Aprill 1631.'

17. See *Letters of the Lady Brilliana Harley*, edited by Thomas Taylor Lewis for the Camden Society, London, 1854, p. 6.

18. For an account of Hugh Sanford and his revisions of the *Arcadia* see Frances A. Yates, *John Florio*, Cambridge, 1934, pp. 192-209.

19. Castelain, *op. cit.*, pp. 110-16.

20. Hudson, *op. cit.*, pp. 54-6.

21. *Ibid.*, pp. xxiii and 62.

22. *Ibid.*, pp. xxiii-xxiv and 74.

23. See *Avdomari Talæi Rhetorica & P. Rami Prælictionibus observata*, Francofurti, 1584.

24. *The Arcadian Rhetorike: Or Praecepts of Rhetorike made plaine by examples, Greek, Latin, English, Italian, French, Spanish, out of Homers Ilias . . . Sir Philip Sydnei's Arcadia, . . . Torquato Tassoes Goffredo, . . . By Abraham Fraunce At London Printed by Thomas Orwin 1588.*

The broad field from which Fraunce chose his illustrations is suggested by the title-page. It is interesting to observe that Fraunce's treatment of metre (Sigg. C₁-C₄, *verso*) and of elaborate stanza forms preceded Puttenham's by a short period.

Since the whole of Sig. B is wanting in the unique copy of the *Arcadian Rhetorike*, we cannot be sure of Fraunce's procedure; but in the extant portion he scatters his quotations over a wide field and illustrates from poetry more frequently than from prose.

In the second part, Fraunce treats of the tone of voice to be used and the gestures to be employed on various occasions. For example, 'in desiring' one is to use a 'smoothing and submisse voice' (Sig.I₆). The suitable employment of such gestures as the rolling of the eyes, the movement of the lips, *etc.*, he illustrates from the actions of Sidney's characters in the *Arcadia*. In doing so he furnishes an early and naïve analysis of characterization in fiction not unlike Hoskyns' own, though more detailed. Regarding oratory Fraunce says (Sig.K₂): 'The casting out of the right arme is as it were an arming of the speach.' Again (Sig. K₄, *verso*): 'For the feet; it is vndecent to stand waggling now on one foote, now on another.'

Fraunce's *The Lawiers Logike*, London, 1588, is interesting for its analyses of logic but apparently has no direct hearing upon Hoskyns' method in his treatise in a related field.

25. William Fulwood, *The Enimie of Idleness: Teaching the maner and stile how to indite, compose, and write, all sorts of Epistles and Letters*, London, 1568.

26. George Puttenham, *The Arte of English Poesie*, London, 1589.

27. Raphe Leuer, *The Art of Reason, rightly termed Witcraft*, London, 1573.

28. In *Sir Philip Sidney as a Literary Craftsman*, Cambridge, Massachusetts, 1935, pp. 5, 21, 110-93, *etc.*

On p. 23 Mr. Myrick fails to note that Jonson's phrase, 'a diligent kind of negligence,' is a modification of a phrase of Hoskyns' in *Direccōns*.

29. Quoted from *Albions England: . . . . First penned and published by VVilliam VVarner: and now reuised*, London, 1597, p. 49.

30. Quoted from *The VVhole VVorkes of Samvel Daniel . . . in Poetrie*, London, 1623, p. 123.

Notes on the Text of *Direccōns For Speech and Style*

Figures in bold type refer to pagination in this book.

115   *Arcadia the first edition*] *The Covntesse of Pembrokes Arcadia, written by Sir Philippe Sidnei. London   Printed for William Ponsonbie. Anno Domini, 1590.*

Hoskyns' references to this edition may be found in Oskar H. Sommer's reprint: *'The Countess of Pembroke's Arcadia'* . . . *The original Quarto Edition (1590) in Photographic Facsimile*, London, Kegan Paul, Trench, Trübner and Co., Ltd., 1891.

For Hoskyns' references as found in Albert Feuillerat's reprint of the 1590 edition (*The Complete Works of Sir Philip Sidney*, Cambridge, 1912, Vol. I) see table of references at the conclusion of the notes for this chapter. His edition is referred to as 'F' in these notes.

116   *To the forwardnes of many virtuous hopes . . .*] Professor Hoyt H. Hudson (*Directions for Speech and Style*, pp. 54-6) shows the influence of Pierre de la Primaudaye's *L'Académie Françoise* upon Hoskyns' opening remarks upon the relation between clear understanding and lucid expression. Pierre de la Primaudaye's book was translated by T. B[owes] as *The French Academie* in 1586. A second edition, also translated by 'T. B.' was printed in London in 1589 and a third in 1594, to the last of which was added *The Second Part of the French Academie*. From the second and third editions, the only ones I have seen, I quote below the passages which show important parallels with Hoskyns' remarks. Professor Hudson quotes all these except the last three, which to me seem likewise to have influenced Hoskyns' phrasing:

'In writings of the learned we finde mention made of a double speech or reason: the one internall, or of the minde, called the divine guide: the other vttered in speech, which is the messenger of the conceits and thoughts of man.'—pp. 119-20, edition of 1589.

'And so wee say, that there are two kindes of speech in man, one internall and of the minde, the other externall, which is pronounced, and is the messenger of the internall, that speaketh in the heart. Therefore that which is framed in voyce, pronounced in speech, and brought into vse, is as a riuer sent from the thought with the voyce, as from his fountaine. For before the thought can vtter any outward speech by meanes of the voyce, first the minde must receiue the images of things presented vnto it by the corporall senses . . . . For if a man be dull witted, or haue his fantasie and imagination troubled, and his memory slow and heauy, he shall haue much adoe to speake that which he thinketh and conceiueth in mind . . . . For he onely is to bee accompted eloquent, who can conceiue well in his spirite and minde that

which he ought to speake, and then is able to expresse it well,
both by apt wordes, and by sentences that are well tied and knit
together . . . . For the glorie, maiestie, and vertue of the Father
is alwaies hid from vs, but only so farre foorth as it sheweth it
selfe ingraued in his sonne and in his word, as the image of the
minde appeareth imprinted and ingrauen in the speach that is
vttered . . . . Rhetorike maketh it [*i.e.*, speech] not onely as it
were a picture well set foorth with faire and liuely colours of all
sortes, but also adorned and enriched. . . . Wherefore as there
is a great difference to looke vpon these two pictures, so is there
of speech in respectes of the eares, as it is propounded eyther
more plainely and simply, or more decked and garnished. . . .
For seeing God would haue the tongue to be the messenger, and
as it were the Interpreter of the spirite and minde, and of all
the thoughts thereof . . . .'—*The Second Part of the French
Academie*, 1594, pp. 88, 89, 90, 100, 101.

Cicero] See *Brutus, de claris oratoribus*, vi, 23.

7   *Jo: Hoskins*] In *MS. Harl. 850* the name is blotted out.

8   *there is to be regarded . . . Invencõn & the fashion*] Maurice
Castelain has pointed out the similarities between this section by
Hoskyns and the *Epistolica Institutio*, by Lipsius. I quote the most
important parallel passages. I have used the *Iusti Lipsi Opera*, two
volumes, Lvgdvni, 1613, I, 379 ff. *Caput II: Haec definitio Epistolae.
Ex quâ partes praecipuas eius duas facio; Materiam et sermonem . . . .*
before it come] *before the other come*, in *MS. Harl. 850*, f. 3.

    The first is Brevity] Lipsius, *Caput VII: De Sermone. Quae de
eo dicenda; et primum de Breuitate. . . . De Habitu igitur sermonis
epistolici, praecipio vt quinque ista serues; Breuitatem, Perspicuitatem,
Simplicitatem, Venustatem, Decentiam. Prima illa, prima mihi
sermonis virtus est: adeoque epistolae propria, vt, si longior, (cum
Demetrio sentio) Libri iam nomen assumat, Epistolae amittat.*

9   *yf to yor Superio^r. . . . .*] Lipsius, *Caput VII: si Seria Epistola
aut Sapiens: diffundi paulo magis velim, et rei per se graui addi
verborum aliquod pondus. Si Familiaris, contrahi . . . . A Qualitate,
a captu. Ab illâ: vt si ad Ignotos aut Magnates scribitur; vberior &
floridior paullo epistola sit . . . . Aliter si ad amicos aut aequales. . . .
Qui fiet igitur Sermo breuis? obseruatione triplici: Rerum, Composi-
tionis, Verborum . . . .*

    places] *p^refaces*, in *MS. Harl. 850*, f. 3, in *Discoveries*, and in
MS. Ash. Mus. d. 1.

    Quintilian] Cf. Quintilian, *Institutio Oratoria*, IV, ii, 41.

0   *affeccõn*] *affectation* in *MS. Harl. 850*, f. 3. b.

    As Ladies . . . their Attyre] Lipsius, *Caput IX: Tertiam virtutem
posui Simplicitatem: . . . Quod feminas ornare dicitur, non ornari:
hoc epistolam.* Mr. Hoyt H. Hudson has also called my attention
to the following parallel in Cicero's *Orator, cap.* xxiii: *Nam ut*

mulieres esse dicuntur nonnullae inornatae, quas id ipsum deceat, sic haec subtilis oratio etiam incompta delectat; fit enim quiddam in utroque, quo sit venustius, sed non ut appareat. Cf. also F. 75, 104, and 376.

121　*Apprehensivenes*] The first recorded use of the word in the *N. E. D.* is in 1639, although its use there is by Hoskyns' contemporary, Sir Henry Wotton, whose work was published after his death.

Complem^ts] the first recorded use of *complements* was in 1419. See the *N. E. D.* Hoskyns doubtless means *compliments*, the first use of which recorded in the *N. E. D.* was in 1578. See *complement*, substantive, meaning 9.

Spirrit] *Spirit* as a noun was in very early use. Its first use as a verb as recorded in the *N. E. D.* was in 1599.

accomodate] *Accommodate* was used in 1525. See *N. E. D.* But see also Hudson, *op. cit.*, p. 60.

pithy sayings] Lipsius, *Caput* X: *Primum, vt Adagia Allusionesque ad dicta aut facta vetera, versiculos aut argutas sententias utriusque linguae interdum immisceas, secundum, vt iocis salibusque opportune condias; quos animam et vitam epistolae esse non fugiam dicere.*

Courtier] *I.e.*, Castiglione's *Libro del Cortegiano*, translated by Thomas Hoby in 1561 as *The Courtyer*.

respect] Lipsius, *Caput* X: *Quod fiet aspectu duplici: Personae & Rei. Personae dupliciter; si tuam respicis, & eius ad quem scribis.*

Angel Day deals with much the same property in his *The English Secretorie, Or Methode of Writing of Epistles and Letters*, London, 1607, Part I, pp. 2-4. The first edition came out in 1586, a copy of which I have not seen.

include the rest] *conclude the rest, because it includes the rest*, in *MS. Harl. 850*, f. 3. b.

God: Nature] *Good nature* in *MS. Harl. 850*, f. 3. b.

will serue Yo^w.] Lipsius, *Caput* X: *Nec verba hic perdam: quia scio Iudicij totam hanc rem esse: quod a Deo & a Naturâ pete, non ab Arte.*

sights] *sighs*, in *MS. Harl. 850*, f. 5, and in F. 491.

hungry . . . bloud] F. 444.

122　*Her Nature (defence,)*] *her natural Defence*, in Smith (*op. cit.*, ed. of 1706, p. 53). Cf. F. 470.

goodly Audience of sheepe] Cf. Wilson, *op. cit.*, p. 166.

shoulders] See F. 151-52. *Souldiers*, in *MS. Harl. 850*, f. 5.

123　*seething pot of iniquity*] F. 429.

ingenious Acts] Thus in MS. for *Arts*.

naturall] Expanded from *nrall* (with *tt* superscript) in MS.

skye . . . Sorrow] F. 369.

124　*the Earle is gone into Ireland*] A reference to the Earl of Essex and his expedition to Ireland in 1599.

5   *to kill him*] F. 209.

   being sister . . . fortune] F. 182.

6   *wch loved*] *Why* in *Arcadia*, F. 484.

7   *Prince*] *Princess* in *Arcadia*, F. 259.

   gods] *Goddesse* in *Arcadia*, F. 259.

   weight] *I.e., wight*

   Rhetoricke] *Cf.* Hoskyns' fustian speech quoted in Chapter VIII, above.

   overthrowe . . . overthrowe] F. 155.

8   *either not striving . . . striue*] F. 278.

   to conquerrers] An error for *she conqueres*. Folio 9 should read 279 (F. 404).

   shewed such furie . . . furie] F. 418.

9   *M^r. P.*] Professor Hudson identifies 'Mr. P.' as Thomas Playfere (1561?-1609) and cites Playfere's *A Most Excellent and Heavenly Sermon*, 1595. See also *The Meane in Mourning*, 1597; *etc.* As further example of Playfere's excessive use of antimetabole, these lines may be quoted from *The Pathway to Perfection. A Sermon preached at Saint Maries Spittle in London on Wednesday in Easter weeke, 1593.* London, 1611, p. 124:

> 'Therefore we that do not die vnder the law, but liue vnder grace, must not be like the law, but like the Gospell. . . . Perfectly vnperfect when they beginne: vnperfectly perfect when they end. . . . Because indeed hee that remembers his vertues, hath no vertues to remember.'

   mill-horse] See Wilson, *op. cit.*, p. 203.

   rymes . . . ratling rowes] Quoted from the fifteenth sonnet of Sidney's *Astrophel and Stella*. See also his *Apologie for Poetrie* (ed. by Evelyn S. Shuckburgh, Cambridge, 1928, p. 57), where Sidney refers to this device as 'the method of a Dictionary.'

   L Lloid] Professor Hudson (*op. cit.*, p. 69) identifies him as Lodowick Lloyd, Sergeant-at-Arms usder Queen Elizabeth and King James, and finds the quotation given by Hoskyns in Lloyd's 'An Epitaph vpon the death of Syr Edward Saunders,' reprinted in Hyder E. Rollins' edition of *The Paradyse of Daintie Devises*, pp. 101-105.

30   *199. b*] Abraham Fraunce uses the same illustration from the *Arcadia*. See *The Arcadian Rhetorike*, London, 1588, Sig. D₅ *v*.

   whist] Thus in MS. for *whilst*.

   Doctor Mathew] *I.e.*, Tobie or Tobias Matthew (1546-1628), who became archbishop of York. He was a Herefordshire man.

   tuff taffata Orato^{rs}.] See Chapter VIII, above.

   prosper] A word, apparently *continew*, has been replaced in the MS. by *prosper*.

31   *force of virtue*] At this point in the MS. the phrase *that their exiles were ho.^{blye} entertayned* has been crossed out to appear below in its proper place. This in itself is evidence of transcription from

some now unknown copy of the treatise. The MS. is not in Hoskyns's hand.

132   *Amphiorames*] Hudson, following Blount, corrects the reading to *Amphiaraus.*

133   *Thuagoras*] A mistake for *Evagoras.*

Vastus] An error for *Vascus.*

Quilon] A seaport in west-central Travancore state, South Madras, India. Mr. Hudson reads *Quiloa* and identifies it as the modern Kilwa Kisiwane on the southeastern coast of Africa north of Mozambique. To me, however, the reading seems definitely *Quilon.*

Moramba] Probably, as Mr. Hudson suggests, Mozambique is intended.

134   *of the Arches*] See n. for Letter XXIX, Chapter VII, above.

135   *lawyer . . . bastinadoe*] A reference, apparently, to John Davies' attack on Richard Martin in Middle Temple Hall, on 9 February 1598. See Hopwood, *op. cit.,* I, 379.

136   *You shall haue . . . examples*] MS. reads *your*, etc.

Bacon . . . first colonie] Hudson (p. 76) shows that this is an error for *Bacon in his fifth colour,* a reference to Bacon's 'Of the Coulers of good and euill a fragment,' published with the *Essayes* in 1597. Hoskyns' quotation is from f. F₄.

A faint trace of scorn may be detected in Hoskyns' remark that Bacon took the idea 'out of the Rhetoritians.' See Professor Hudson's remarks (*op. cit.,* pp. 58 and 92) on Hoskyns' attitude toward Bacon's sententious style. Their lack of accord on political matters has been pointed out in Chapter IV, above.

J:Ds poeme of dauncing] Sir John Davies' *Orchestra,* 1596.

appelleth] Apparelleth.

137   *playd the secret*] To me this phrase has, from my first reading of it, meant *were coyly incommunicative.* Thus the passage would mean: 'If she were scornful, he would conform his speech and action in that soberness to her humour, as might beguile her passion by way of false confederacy; if she walk't or were coyly incommunicative, [he would] praise her face, her eyes,' *etc.*

Though I find no authority for *secret* in this use in the *N. E. D.,* such an interpretation seems plausible and obviates the necessity for emendation.

Professor Hudson (p. 23) reads the passage: 'If she walked or played, the secret [was to] praise her face, her eyes,' *etc.* He quotes Blount's reading: 'if she walked or played, the secret praise of her face, . . . was the application of most conceipts, whatever gave the ground of them.' See collation with *MS. Ash. Mus. d. 1,* below.

invert] Invent in *MS. Ash. Mus. d. 1.*

138   *subdued my witt*] Smith reads 'subdued my *will.*'

139   *an English*] 'An English sentence to be rendered into a foreign language.'—*N. E. D.,* meaning 3 of the substantive.

Paragnomies] Like Professor Hudson, I fail to find the word in any dictionary. He suggests (p. 77) that it may mean striking or humourous similes.

40 *stores*] Hudson (pp. 26 and 77) emends to *scores* and records Blount's reading as *scorns*. To me, emendation seems unnecessary if one interprets *stores* as *holds*, or *keeps in reserve*. I regard *come* and *make* as parallel verbs, though Mr. Hudson inserts the sign of the infinitive before *make*. Cf. *MS. Ash. Mus. d. 1.*

speech of D. H.] Hudson suggests that this may be a reference to a speech about Sir Christopher Hatton's tomb, an extravagantly costly one.

41 *that Bisp. . . . that built 2 absolute colledges*] Hoskyns is referring to William of Wykeham, who founded Winchester College and New College, Oxford, the two colleges in which Hoskyns himself was educated.

fee] Thus also in *MS. Ash. Mus. d. 1.*

42 *egregious*] *N. E. D.*: '2. remarkable in a good sense, *obs.*'

43 *The first . . . as Hyperbole*] *MS. Ash. Mus. d. 1* correctly reads *is* for *as*.

enquirie making . . . inquirie] F. 63.

frontiers of possibilitie] The word in the MS. was originally *impossibilitie*, but the first two letters have been blotted out, intentionally I think. For a thing to be barely possible it may be said to be in the frontiers of possibility. *MS. Ash. Mus. d. 1* and *Harl. 4604* agree.

Professor Hudson prefers the reading *impossibility*. Smith (*op. cit.*, p. 46) reads *Impossibility*, suggesting that he may have had access to another source besides Blount, since the latter reads *possibility*.

accusacōns] Hudson, like Blount, emends to *occasions*, the reading in *Arcadia*, F. 33-4.

wordes & blowes . . . thunder] F. 456.

a certaine quantitie] Hudson (p. 29) adopts Blount's reading of *no* for *a*.

I pswaded . . . nay sues to be taken] F. 405.

44 *yet a while . . . armed man*] Hudson (p. 81) points out that this quotation is from the 'Geneva Bible,' 1583, *Proverbs* xxiv: 33-4.

It is . . . Princes] Cf. *Proverbs* xxii: 29, 'Geneva Bible,' 1583.

Titerinus] Hudson corrects to *Titormus* and points out an allusion to him in Herodotus (VI, cxxvii).

45 *spite, rage . . . . vpon hatred*] F. 456.

47 *warish*] Smith (*op. cit.*, p. 117) reads *froward*. Sidney's meaning seems to be *peevish* or *crabbed*. See *wearish* in the *N. E. D.*, meaning 4.

receiue the flatt style . . . tales] *MS. Ash. Mus. d. 1* reads: 'to recreate the flatt style of Affirmations, from downe-right telling of tales.'

oh Sun . . . pporcōn] F. 145-46.

o! endlesse endeavoᵣˢ . . . . forgetfullnes] I am not in accord with
Professor Hudson in his division of this passage into sentences. He
makes separate questions of *Where?* and *In Europe?* and concludes
the next one after *Accōns.* I prefer the passage thus: 'Where in
Europe, how, canst thou be famous? When Asia & Affricka, that
haue thrice as many people, hear not of thy actions, art not thou then
thrice as obscure as thou art renowned?'
  Smith (*op. cit.*, Sig. P₈, *v.*) quotes the passage.

148   *Daniell*] *I.e.*, Samuel Daniel.
  <*>] A blank space in the MS. and a cross in the margin suggest that the copyist intended to fill in later a synonym or antonym
for *desert.* Hudson (p. 34), following Blount, inserts *crime*, also
found in *MS. Ash. Mus. d. 1.*
  newe built] This seems to me the indubitable reading in the MS.
Mr. Hudson prints *never built.*
  mortall Accons] There is a cross above *mortall*, and another is in
the margin.

149   *not altogeather modest*] *Immodest*; F. 297.
  erroneous] Hudson, following Blount, changes to *ironious.* But
Hoskyns may have intended *erroneous*, since he remarks, 'But these
figures are but counterfeits of amplificacōn.'

150   *witty ignorance*] F. 507.
  Hernies] A cross above the word and another in the margin of
the MS. indicate that the copyist was in doubt as to the reading.
Hudson (p. 37) emends to *terms* and points out that Blount reads
Sturmius. Hoskyns may have intended *Hirmos*, which Smith (*op. cit.*,
p. 141) identifies with Hoskyns' *accumilacōn.* The reading is *termes*
in *MS. Ash. Mus. d. 1.*

151   *Askam*] For Ascham's letter see his *Works*, edited by J. A. Giles,
London, 1864-65, I, 192.
  Sturnius] The scribe's error for *Sturmius.*
  Comparison] Throughout this section Professor Hudson emends
comparison to *compar* and suggests that the copyist probably mistook
the latter word for an abbreviation of *comparison*, which Hoskyns had
already discussed as the first method of amplification. The catchword
on f. 19. b introducing the section is '*Compar:*,' which suggests that
Hoskyns intended to use that term throughout this section rather than
comparison. See also Hudson, *op. cit.*, p. 87.
  Biᵖᵖ of W :] Thomas Bilson, Bishop of Winchester. The following notes from his writings show his inclination to use parison,
'mingled' with agnomination and *similiter cadens*:
    'The places be many, the words plaine: you can not shift them
    vnlesse you will desperately take flesh for spirit, bodie for soule...
    a dumme and dead creature for the liuing and euerlasting sonne
    of God: which were not onely sensible blindnes, but inexcusable

madnes.'—From p. 625, *The True Difference Betweene Christian Svbiection and Vnchristian Rebellion*, London, 1586.

'I wish the learned aduisedlie to consider, and the rest carefully to remember.'—From p. 182, *The Perpetval Government of Christes Chvrch*, 1593.

'So agreeable is this doctrine to the christian faith, and so comfortable to all the godly, that few would refuse it, except such as are waspishly wedded to their owne fancies.'—From p. 166, *The effect of certaine Sermones*, 1599.

52   *a Syndeton*] Thus in MS., but evidently an error of the copyist's for *Asyndeton.*

her witt indeed by youth . . . affeccõn] *Her wit endeared by youth* in Smith (*op. cit.*, p. 158). *MS. Ash. Mus. d. 1* reads: *endeared* and *affliction*, as does F. 333.

plawses] The *N. E. D.* gives *plaw* as an old form of *play*, the substantive. Hence from meanings 1 and 4, allowing for indifferent spelling, we might suppose that Hoskyns meant *free movements* or *varieties.*

Mr. Hudson (p. 90) emends to *phrases* but suggests that the Latin *plausus* may be the word intended. *MS. Ash. Mus. d. 1* reads *pauses.*

inter pretacons] *MS. Ash. Mus. d. 1* reads *interruptions.*

53   *a sentence is a pearle in a discourse*] Cf. Quintilian, VIII, v, 26-34.

Briarcus] An error for *Briareus*, one of the three-hundred-armed, fifty-headed Hecatoncheires of Greek mythology.

these short breathed gent: these Judicious myndes] This is probably another allusion to Bacon and his sententiousness.

Moiosis] I.e., *meiosis.*

It is a foolish wittines . . . thinkes] F. 99.

54   *fearefullnes . . . making Clinias. . .*] F. 432.

course] Cross above the word and in the margin as though the scribe were doubtful of the reading. *MS. Ash. Mus. d. 1* reads *coursed.*

In or pfession . . . straightnes of these maximes] Professor Hudson (p. 92) points out that this is probably a criticism of Sir Francis Bacon's style.

<*>] A blank space follows the cross, and a cross appears in the margin. *MS. Ash. Mus. d. 1* reads *called.*

6   *noted in yor book &c*] Hudson emends *&c* to *pc.*

Arle] I.e., Aristotle.

pnte] I.e., *present.*

7   *Jocus and Ambiguo*] Professor Hudson (p. 97) emends to *jocus ab ambiguo*, the reading in Blount. *MS. Ash. Mus. d. 1* reads *jocus, and ambiguum.*

libtie] I.e., *libertie.*

8   *Thrift . . . yor owne estate*] This sentence is found among other

quotations scribbled on the first folio of the *Dirrecōns* in *MS. Harl. 850.*

Valerius Logique] Professor Hudson identifies Valerius as Cornelius Valerius (1512-1578). He was the author of *Tabulae, quibus totius dialecticae praecepta maxime . . . necessaria breviter . . . exponuntur, etc.,* Antverpiae, 1582, of which there were, apparently, earlier editions.

paphr.] I.e., *paraphrasis.*

Till . . . fortune] F. 193.

160   *Prosopoesis*] Hudson emends rightly, I think, to *prosapodosis* and points out the similarity between this passage and Quintilian, IX, iii, 93-5.

Tyme . . . desires] F. 96.

To say . . . womanish] Hoskyns here is paraphrasing a passage in the *Arcadia* (F. 77) which Fraunce had quoted in his *Arcadian Rhetorike,* Sig. D₂.

161   *it hath . . . incongruity*] F. 467.

seeking to saue him . . . in] F. 392.

162   *plentifull piury*] I.e., *plentiful perjury*; F. 384.

make his sword . . . widdowe] F. 428.

making courtesie . . . mischiefe] F. 362-63.

163   *speech to the needle . . . the silke*] F. 402.

learning] Cross above word and in margin.

delibating] I.e., *deliberating.*

speakinge well] Cross above *well* and another in the margin.

165   *comfortable speeches*] Cross above *speeches* and in the margin.

fustian speech] A reference to his own speech, printed in Chapter VIII, above.

Collation of *Direccōns* in *MS. Harl. 4604* with *Discoveries, 1640-41*:

116   Interpᵉᵉᵗer] the Interpreter

that could] who could

were a right Orator] were the best Writer, or Speaker

tongue were only disgraced by it] tongue onely thereby were disgrac'd

the kinge in a Seale of waxe] a King in his Seal

sealeth itt, as to the king] seal'd it, as to the Prince

whome it resembleth] it representeth

wᶜʰ giue it forth, or] that give it forth as

the thoughts wᶜʰ put it forth, as to the right pporcōn & Coherence] to the disproportion, and incoherence

wrongfully expressed] negligently expressed

Yet cannot his mynde bee thought in tune] Neither can his mind be thought to be in tune

sentences are] sentence is

fancie cleare] Elocution cleare

an honor to a Prince] not a dishonour to a mighty Prince

be defaced?] be disgrac'd?

Careless speech] Negligent speech

personage] person

doth discreditt the oppinion of his reason and iudgment it discredit-teth the truth, force] discrediteth the force

he be thought] he then be thought

whose leasure & whose head] whose leasure and head,

eyes, could yeald] eyes, yeeld

& sharpnes] or sharpnesse

116-17 in his writing . . . . . Hoskins] *Jonson omits everything to* In writing,

118 In writing of letters there is] In writing there is

given yo^w, then] given, then

of all the seu^{er}all occasions of all pticuler mens lives] from the severall occasions of mens particular lives

busines] basenesse

letter] Letters

vnto yo^w., my] to you.) Or, [My

to certify my Love towards yo^w] to testify my love to you,

Or, Haue yo^w] Or, [Sir, have you

to the remembrance] to the remembring

assurance, wch yo^w haue long had in me,] assurance you have long possest in your servant;

oppertunity to make me happie] opportunity, make him happy

wth any imployment yo^w shall assigne me,] with some commands from you?

or such like wordes, wch goe] Or, the like; that goe

(if yor] and that your

nor meere Ceremonyes] or meere Ceremony

earnestnes] earnest:

& the disgestion of the pts] and digesting the parts

is sought out of Circumstances] is had out of two circumstances.

the pson] the Persons

yo^w write] you are to write

of the sentences for mens capacity & delight; yo^w are to weigh] of your Sentence. For mens capacity to weigh,

first wth great delight & attenc͠on] with greatest attention, or leisure

leaue most satisfaccon] leave satisfaction

memoriall & briefe] memoriall, and beliefe

The rules . . . it selfe] *omitted in Jonson*

of the sentences] of Sentences

yo^w must see] you must bee sure

clause doth (as it were) giue the Q:] clause doe give the *Q*.
to the other] one to the other
bee (as it were) spoken before] be bespoken ere
This for Invencõn] So much for *Invention*
2 *fashion* (*in margin*)] Modus. 1 Brevitas. (*in margin*)
it consisteth in 4 things or quallities] it consists in four things,
which are qualities

118-19   letters must not] they must not
119   discourcings] Discourses (your Letters)
amonge learned men & eaven amongst them] to learned . . .
among them
or saving] and saving
are yoᵂ to] you are to
yoʳ sweetest] the sweetest
significant English wordes, that yoᵂ] significant wordes you
mans conceipt] mans apprehension
& to penn it fully] and open their meaning fully
letter, But] your letter. And
pte after this] part following this
yet nowe still] yet now here, and still
must I here remember] I must remember
& sences yoᵂ] cense as senses, you
a a taske to his brayne; yf to] a taske to his braine) venter on a
knot. But if
bound in him to measure .3. further points] bound to measure him
in three farther points:
yoʳ interest in him, his Capacitie] First, your interest in him:
Secondly, his capacity
of yoʳ letters] in your letters
& his] Thirdly, his
& favor] or favor
quicker or fuller] quicker, and fuller
With yoʳ better] with your betters
of yoʳ wit] of wit
wordes; nor to cause] words: not to cause
too plenteously] too riotous
by the matter in] in matter, by
places] Prefaces
penthesis] Parentheses
supfluous & wanton Circuits] superfluous circuit
by the composicõn omitting] In the composition by omitting
both one] both the one
such idle pticularities] and such like idle Particles
By breaking] but braking
longe Journey is made shorter] short journey is made long

baytes] unnecessary baits
of ptes . . . that make] of the partes . . . that makes
rowed apace] rowed a pace
& spake w^th] and speake with
this last] these last
Perspicuity (*in margin*)] Perspicuitas (*in margin*)
next good pptie] next property
is often tymes indangered by the former quallity (Brevity) often-
times] is often times
by affecõn] by affectation
darken the speech] darken speech
light hurts] light hurteth
yor letter] your Letters
like an English statute] like English Statutes
This is obteyned, & their vices] and this is obtain'd. These vices
eschewed] are eschewed
conceiving of yor selfe] concerning your selfe
to light] to the light
That is the reason] For that is the reason
stumblingly] fumblingly (as also in *MS. Harl. 850* and in *MS.
Ash. Mus. d. 1*)
ffor this reason talkatiue] Hence it is, that talkative
reasonable] reasonably
Interogatories] to Intergatories
to the first, second, &c.:] As to the first, first; and to the second,
secondly, &c.
in method & word to vse (as Ladies vse)] in method to use (as
Ladies doe
a kinde of dilligent negligence, & though] a diligent kind of negligence, and their sportive freedom; though
deliu^erie of most weighty & important] delivery of the most
important
though not excesse] though no excesse
variety, & soe] variety: but everso,
sence in hazard] Sense of the first in hazard
as App^rehensivenes] as Accommodation
Complem^ts Spirrit accõmodate &c:] Complement, Spirit, &c.
places, as others: Thereof followeth] place, as others. There
followeth
wch is the very strength] and Quicknesse, which is the strength
penning, made vpp by pithy sayings] penning by pretty Sayings
conceipts, Allusions to some] and Conceits, Allusions, some
Last is respect] The last is; Respect
to include the rest] to conclude the rest, because it doth include all
as another truly sayth is given] as one truly saith, is gotten

Collation Showing Chief Variations between *MS. Harl. 4604* and
MS. Ash. Mus. d. 1:

116   in a gent of the Temple] in a young Gent
       speaking vnskillfully] speaking ill
       if the tongue were only disgraced by it] if the tongue thereby were
only disgraced
       Yet cannot his mynde] His mind cannot
       as great an indignity] as great indignitie
       I terrify and threaten yo^w] I terrifie you, and threaten you
117   in yo^w most willing] in you as willing
       of the Temple] of the Inns of the Court
       nor had become Clyents to any student of her Ma^ts Lawes] *Omitted*
       Jo: Hoskins] *Omitted*
118   for the invencōn that ariseth] Invention ariseth
       given yo^w] given
       all pticular mens lives] all mens particular lives
       letter wth comēndacōns] letter with my commendations
       vnto yo^w] to You
       the other is the Coherence of the sentences for mens capacity]
another is, The Coherence of the sentences. For Mens capacity
       first wth great delight & attencōn] first with greatest attention,
and pleasure:
       The rules of Decency . . . by it selfe] *Omitted*
       This for Invencōn & order] *Omitted*
       Nowe for fashion] ffor fashion
       it consisteth] it consists
119   discourcings] discourses
       places] prefaces
       composicōn omitting coniunctions] Composition in omitting
conjunctions
       pticularities] particles
       I was admytted] was admitted
120   affeccōn] Affectation
       stumblingly] fumblingly
       method & word] method and words
121   Terms of the tyme] termes of the times
       Last is respect] The last is Respect
       include the rest] conclude the rest, because it doeth include the rest
       feyned sights] feigned sighs
       of bloudshed] to bloodshed
       beyond the significacōn] beyond the true signification
       one thinge] one thing invented
122   in a gardin of purpose beholds but one flower] beholds seriously
but one flower in a garden
       of the same matter in another place] Another of the same matter

& in nomber of places . . . in the margent]   *Omitted*
& pportionable]   and that proportionablie
tempting her by force]   attempting her by force
123 ingenious]   ingenuous
pfessions from ingenious Acts to please the learned]   professions to please the learned
& from seuᵉrall Arts to please the learned of all sorts]   of all sorts
yoʷ may assure . . . this note (M) &]   *Omitted*
plant a castle]   Paint a Castle
124 The adiunct . . . for the subject of it, as]   *Omitted*
noe doubt . . . where they are]   *Omitted*
125 & such like . . . familliarly]   *Omitted*
& yoʷ may . . . can nowe meet wᵗʰ]   *Omitted*
the fine convᵉrsants of oʳ tyme]   the five Conversants of the Time
126 goodnes]   goods
The like . . . Clause]   *Omitted*
127 yoʷ haue an example . . . fustian speech . . . Rhetoricke]   *Omitted*
128 dilligence to speake well]   diligence to speake, and write well
execercise]   exercise
as 2. a . . . 205]   *Omitted*
this]   this tricke
Men venter liues . . . venturing]   Men venture lives to conquer, She Conquers lives without ventureing
129 There is a swynish poem . . . Allexander kild]   *Omitted*
130 hee made away]   he made way
not only Lilly]   Not onely with Mʳ Lilly
131 gaine of mens myndes two the]   gaine mens minds to two the
things contrary, equal]   things equall, different, or contrary
132 as in my speech of a widdowe . . . rigging]   *Omitted*
133 to be fauorable vnto yoʷ by reading]   *Omitted*
Quilon]   Quiloa
established to his vse]   established, and fortified to his use
134 defrauding the intent]   wronging the intent
135 we that pfesse lawes]   they that professe lawes
136 of this yoʷ . . . Contentio meet]   *Omitted*
first colonie]   fift Colonie
breake it]   breake youʳ Matter
137 Soe to say . . . want of variety]   *This passage follows* 'Soe you may divide . . . pratling.'
walk't or playd the secret praise]   walked, or sung, or played, he would praise
such dissembled Arte . . . varietye]   cunningly dissembled Art, but never with want of varietie
invert]   invent
division, wᵗʰ vse]   Division which Logicians use
138 but thereof . . . only note that]   *Omitted*

could not be conceipted] could not have been conceaved

Yo^w will be . . . my direction] *Omitted*

139 of this sort yo^w . . . Paragnomies] *Omitted*

140 stores euerie degree] scornes every degree

142 his owne good advantage] his owne good, and advantage

143 wherein I . . . *Arcadia*] *Omitted*

flatt impossibilitie] flatt unpossibilitie

frontiers of possibilitie; accustomed] frontiers of possibilitie, thus, accustomed

accusacõns] ocasions

ingeniously] ingenuously

144 write well] write, and speake well

145 notes of whom] notes of which

146 These .2. figures . . . conceipt] *Omitted*

147 the like . . . of myne] *Omitted*

gent that bestowed . . . throwne] Gent. who bestowing . . . hath throwne

receiue] recreate

to a downer right] from a downe-right

where in Europe . . . famous? when Asia] where? In Europe . . . famous when Asia

148 a great . . .] a great crime

possest of hono^r] possessed, and satisfied with ho^{nor}

149 yor pp hono^r] yor proper humor

severall tymes] severall places

yor *Arcadia*] *Arcadia*

modest] immodest

fantasticall mynded people] fantasticall mind-infected people

150 impatient patient] impatient patience

captivitie . . . captivitie] *Omitted*

admiracõn] admonition

Hernies] termes

151 *Comparison*] Compar

tolerable wth a comparison] tolerable with a Compar

152 Compison] Compar

wch is a Syndeton] *Omitted*

her skull] Her face

lovingnes] *Corrected to* lovelines

witt indeed] witt endeared

affeccon] affliction

plawses, & int^{er}pretacons] pauses, and interruptions

since I was first fellowe of newe Colledge] *Omitted*

153 Briarcus] Briareus

eye sight; There is] eyesight and, is it not a sentence thus uttered, Is not man's experience woman's best eyesight? There is

154 his accõns] his axiomes

from a position to a supposicõn] *Omitted*
course] coursed
& it shall appeare in a sett treatise] the truth is
may sort] may consort
a slender reason to ground] And therefore you are not to ground
in oᴿ profession] In the profession of the law
that* . . . them poesies] who called them posies
56 but pollicy . . . in yoᴿ booke &c] *Omitted*
is discribed] *Omitted*
from 69. to 72] *Omitted*
in conveyance] to further you in conceaveing
where evident & liuely discripcõns are . . . this noate des:] Evident
and lively Descriptions
where the pson is aptly] and the Person aptly
: dc:] *Omitted*
57 relation of each word] reason of relation of each word
Ambiguo] ambiguum
Ambigus] ambiguum
58 this *Virtus . . . consentaneus*] *Omitted*
setting forth] setting forward the suit
better by the howre-glass] knowne to be a morning better by the
houre-glasse
59 write well] write, and speake well
60 in *Arcadia*] *Omitted*
to write well] to speake, and write well
62 These . . . for Illustracõn] *Omitted*
or Prosopopeia] *Omitted*
hast thou to hope for] *Revised as* canst thou hope for
63 speakinge well] speaking, and writeing well
may not yoᵂ . . . worldly cares?] may not I lose you? nay, may
not you lose yoᴿselfe in a labarinth of Worldly care?
64 iust & equall] just and rightfull
matters covertlie] matters
Thus yoᵂ . . . Subiectio] *Omitted*
There is . . . *Arcadia* 112.] *Omitted*
65 And if yoᵂ will reade ouᵉʳ . . . speech] In which speech
yoᵂ shall find] are

Table of References

to Folios of the 1590 Edition of the *Arcadia* and the Corresponding
Pages in the Feuillerat Reprint of 1912, Pages in the Latter Being
Preceded by the Letter *F*:

289. b — error for 189. b — F276
291 — F420
293 — F423
294 — error for 284 — F410
295 — F426
298. a — F430
299 — F432-33
305 — F440-41
309 — F446
313 — F452
313. b — F452
314 — error for 315 — F454
316. a and b — F456
318 — F458
321. a — error for 321. b — F463
321. a — F462 (seeking hono*r*.)
322. b — F464
323. b — F466
327 — F471

331 — F477
332 — F479
334. b — F482
335. a — F483
336. a — F484
337. a — F485
338. b — F487-88
340 — F490
341 — F491
342. b — F493
349 — F502
352. b — F507
356. a — F512
359. a — F516-17
359. b — F517
375 — error for 175 — F255
392. b — error for 192. a — F279
419 — error for 119 — F174
920 — error for 120 — F176

NOTES ON CHAPTER X

In the following notes on Hoskyns' verse the first item represents the source from which the present text is printed. Except in the few instances noted the text is given as found in that source.

Besides the items collected in Chapter X Hoskyns wrote, Aubrey tells us, an anthem in English to be sung at 'Hereford Minster at the assizes'; an excellent poem in Latin in praise of ale; and the Latin epitaph for the tomb of Sir Moyle Finch at Eastwell, Kent. These I have not come upon.

The forty-eight items printed in Chapter X have been arranged in approximately chronological order and represent Hoskyns' versifying from his schooldays at Winchester until his sixty-sixth year.

I

The Gentleman's Magazine, London, February 1812, Vol. 82, Part I, p. 114. The verses were submitted by 'W. E.' of Llywell in Breconshire as 'A Piece of Antiquity Printed on the wall adjoining to the Kitchen of Winchester College.'

Of them Aubrey wrote (*op. cit.*, I, 417): 'The Latin verses in the quadrangle at Winton College at the cocks where the boys wash their hands were of his making, where there is a picture of a good servant, with hind's feet . . . *etc.*'

Andrew Clark (*ibid.*) quotes Aubrey's letter from *MS. Wood F. 39*, f. 142: 'At Winton College is the picture of a servant with asses eares and hind's feet, a lock on mouth, *etc.*, . . . with a hexastique in Latin underneath . . . . It was done by the serjeant when he went to school there.' J. E. Jackson had also called attention to Aubrey's letter (*Notes and Queries*, First Series, VI, 495). Sir Frederick Madden (*Notes and Queries*, First Series, VI, 12-13) points out that in 1535 Gilbert Cousin, secretary to Erasmus, wrote on the subject of painted figures of the trusty servant in his Οικετης, *sive de Officio Famulorum.* Madden quotes Cousin's Latin prose description, from which it would seem that the schoolboy at Winchester derived details for his Latin poem.

Tradition has it that the trusty servant's original doublet and hose were replaced by his present costume when he was repainted in honour of a visit made by George III to Winchester. Mr. Herbert Chitty, Keeper of the Archives at Winchester College, has written a delightful account of the trusty servant (*The Wykehamist*, 4 November 1924, No. 652) and has reproduced the drawing found in Robert Mathew's *De Collegio Wintoniensi*, 1647.

'W. E.' (in the *Gentleman's Magazine*, referred to above) prints a translation, which, I think, is not to be regarded as Hoskyns':

> A trusty Servant's portrait would you see,
> This emblematic figure well survey.
> The Porker's snout, not nice in diet shews.
> The Padlock shut no secret he'll disclose.
> Patient the Ass his Master's wrath will hear,
> Swiftness in errands the Stag's feet declare.
> Loaden his Left-hand, apt to labour, saith.
> The Vest is neatness, open Hand his faith.
> Girt with his Sword, his shield upon his arm,
> Himself and Master he'll protect from harm.

II

MS. Add., 15,227, ff. 48. b-49. a. It is signed 'Hosequinus.' Another copy of the poem is found in *MS. Hatfield 204.43*. In the latter version these lines appear at the beginning:

> Ille ego qui nostis socij sim quantulus adsum
>   Mane sed in somnis Lovaniensis eram.
> Cos mihi carmen erat condendi Lipsius autor
>   Musus ego hunc tali solicitare prece.

This apostrophe is added in the Hatfield MS.:

> Hæc mihi Cos et si non hæc diuturna dedisti
>   Gaudia, campanæ non tua, culpa fuit.

The lines are endorsed 'Mr. Hoskins' verses' and were sent on 1 December 1598 to 'Mr Percivall . . . at the house of . . . Sir Robert Cecill' by a Mr. Warwicke of Winton. R. Percival was a protégé of Sir Robert Cecil's.

The lines furnish an interesting commentary on the study of Lipsius' editions in Winchester College during Hoskyns' period there. For an appraisal of Lipsius by a modern scholar see Morris W. Croll's *'Juste Lipse et le Mouvement Anticicéronien à la Fin du xvie Siècle'* in *Revue du Seizième Siècle*, 1914, II, 200-42.

III

MS. Chetham 8012, p. 157. The epitaph is here assigned to Hoskyns.

MS. Chetham 8012 was edited by Alexander B. Grosart as *The Dr. Farmer Chetham MS. being a Commonplace Book in the Chetham Library, Manchester, temp. Elizabeth, James I, and Charles I.*, Two Parts, Vols. 89 and 90 in the Publications of the Chetham Society, Manchester, 1873. Grosart's edition of this Chetham MS. will henceforth in these notes be referred to as *Grosart Chetham 8012*.

These lines appear in *Grosart Chetham 8012*, II, 182.

IV

MS. Chetham 8012, p. 158. The lines, anonymous here, probably are Hoskyns', since they occur in the midst of a rather long collection assigned to him. See *Grosart Chetham*, II, 185.

V

MS. Aubrey 8, f. 15. b, assigned by Aubrey to Hoskyns. The epitaph also occurs in *MS. Malone 36*, f. 121. a, anonymously.

VI

MS. Add. 30,982, f. 36. b. The verses are anonymous here, but in *MS. Chetham 8012*, p. 157, they are subscribed *Mr Hoskyns*. See *Grosart Chetham 8012*, II, 182. They occur anonymously in *MS. Egerton, 923*, f. 8. b; *MS. Harl. 1107*, f. 10. b; *MS. Rawl. Poet. 172*, f. 15. b; and *MS. Add. 15,227*, f. 15. In John Manningham's diary, *MS. Harl. 5353*, f. 46, the verses are subscribed *B : J :* in ink of a different color. However in *MS. Rawl. D. 1372*, f. 9. a, the verses are headed: 'Of ye bellowsmaker of Oxford, by J : Hoskins'. They appear in Camden's *Remaines* (1605 and later editions) among the epitaphs ascribed to Hoskyns.

VII

MS. Ashmole 38, p. 181. The verses are subscribed *Serj^t Hoskins*. They appear in Camden's *Remaines*, 1637, *etc.*

VIII

MS. Chetham 8012, p. 157.   The epitaph is subscribed *J : Hoskynes.*
See *Grosart Chetham 8012*, II, 181.   Grosart thinks the epitaph may
be on Sir Philip Sidney.   It has no title in the MS.

IX

MS. Chetham 8012, p. 76, with the title: 'Of ye losse of time.   Per
J: Hoskyns.'   See *Grosart Chetham 8012*, I, 84.   The poem was
printed by John Hannah, *The Courtly Poets from Raleigh to Montrose*, London, 1870, p. 122.   Archdeacon Hannah changed *spent* in the
first line to *lent*.

X

MS. Chetham 8012, p. 159.   See *Grosart Chetham 8012*, II, 186.
The verses are also ascribed to Hoskyns in *MS. Malone 19*, p. 95,
and in Camden, 1605, *etc.*

XI

MS. Chetham 8012, p. 158, ascribed to Hoskyns.   See *Grosart
Chetham 8012*, II, 184.

XII

MS. Chetham 8012, p. 158.   The couplet is here ascribed to
Hoskyns.   See *Grosart Chetham 8012*, II, 185.   See also Camden,
1605, *etc.*   It was printed by Hannah, *op. cit.*, p. 122.   It appears
anonymously in *MS. Ashmole 38*, p. 172; *MS. Sloane 1489*, f. 11, and
MS. Add. 15,227, f. 11. b; and, in a variant form, in *MS. Tract Dd.
v. 75*, f. 15. b, in University Library, Cambridge.

XIII

MS. Chetham 8012, p. 158.   The epitaph is here ascribed to Hoskyns.
See also Camden, 1605, *etc.*   It appears anonymously in *MS. Malone
19*, p. 150.

XIV

From the inscription on the north wall of New College Cloisters,
Oxford.   Peter Woodgate was from Kent and matriculated in Queen's
College, Oxford, on 18 March 1586.   The lines are ascribed to
Hoskyns by Aubrey (*op. cit.*, I, 419) and are printed anonymously in
Camden's *Remaines*, 1605, *etc.*   Camden says (p. 54) that this epitaph
was written for Woodgate, who had bequeathed two hundred pounds
to 'one who would not bestowe a plate for his memoriall.'

XV

Peplvs. Illvstrissimi Viri D. Philippi Sidnæi Svpremis Honoribvs Dicatvs, Oxford, 1587, pp. 14-27.

This small quarto of 54 pages is dedicated to Henry Herbert, Earl of Pembroke; and the poems, almost all in Latin, are by New College men in praise of Sir Philip Sidney, whose death they lament. The title, as Madan points out (*Oxford Books*, I, 24), is an allusion to the spurious *Peplus* of Aristotle, a commemoration of the heroes who fell in the siege of Troy.

The lines by Hoskyns are signed *Ioannes Hoschines*.

XVI

MS. Lansdowne 104, ff. 195-98. The lines are here attributed to Hoskyns.

Anne Cecil, eldest daughter of Sir William Cecil, Lord Burghley, was married to Edward Vere, seventeenth Earl of Oxford, in December 1571. She died on 6 June 1588 and was buried in state at Westminster Abbey.

XVII

Oxoniensivm Στεναγμός, Siué, Carmina ab Oxoniensibus conscripta, in obitum illustrissimi Herois, D. Christophori Hattoni Militis, summi totius Angliae, nec non Academiæ Oxoniensis Cancellarii, Oxford, 1592.

Falconer Madan (*Oxford Books*, II, 31-2) describes this rare volume, only one copy of which is known to exist. From that copy in the Lambeth Library these lines, signed *Johannes Hoskins*, are transcribed. Fifty-six persons contributed memorial poems on the death in 1591 of Sir Christopher Hatton, the Lord Chancellor and Chancellor of Oxford University. The volume is dedicated to Lord Buckhurst and seems never to have been publicly issued.

To R. E. Bennett, Esq., I am indebted for the reference to this poem by Hoskyns.

XVIII

VLYSSES REDUX / TRAGOEDIA NOVA / IN AEDE CHRISTI OXONIAE / PUBLICE ACADEMICIS RE- / CITATA, OCTAVO IDVS / FEBRVARII. 1591 / OXONIAE, . . . M. D. LXXXXII.

These commendatory verses, headed 'Iohannes Hoschines,' occur on Signature A₄ *v.* in the only edition of *Ulysses Redux* by William Gager (*fl.* 1580-1619). The volume is an octavo dedicated to the Countess of Pembroke.

To Professor C. F. Tucker Brooke I am indebted for knowledge of these lines by Hoskyns.

XIX

MS. Chetham 8012, p. 157. The verses are here assigned to Hoskyns. See also *Grosart Chetham 8012*, II, 182. The lines appear anonymously in *MS. Add. 10,309*, f. 140 and in *MS. Rawl. Poet. 172*, f. 15. b, and in *MS. Add. 5832*, f. 205.

In *MS. Add. 30,982*, f. 28. a, the verses are headed: 'An Eph. on Dr Fletcher bishop of L: K. C.'

Lambeth MS. 658, f. 193, contains a supplication entitled 'Reasons to moue her Ma:^{ty} in some comiseration towards ye Orphanes of ye late Bisshopp of London.' One reason given is that he 'hath satisfied ye errour of his late marriage wth his vntimely & vnlooked for death wch proceded spetially frõ ye conceipt of her [Elizabeth's] high displeasure.' The letter is dated 2 August 1596.

Richard Fletcher, bishop of Worcester and later of London, died in 1596. He had married the sister of Sir George Gifford and widow of Sir Richard Baker. See the *D. N. B.* Bishop Fletcher was the uncle of Phineas and Giles Fletcher and the father of John Fletcher the dramatist.

XX

MS. Chetham 8012, p. 158. The verses are here assigned to Hoskyns. See *Grosart Chetham 8012*, II, 184. They are printed by Camden, 1605, *etc.*, and they appear anonymously in *MS. Rawl. D. 1372*, f. 9. b, and in *MS. Ashmole 38*, p. 170. Since Henry Herbert, second Earl of Pembroke, instituted the Salisbury race and himself won the bell early in 1600, the lines may refer to him.

XXI

MS. Sloane 1446, f. 28. b. The poem, anonymous here, is subscribed *J. H.* in *MS. Chetham 8012*, p. 77. It also appears anonymously in *MS. Add. 22,603*, ff. 10. b-11. a; *MS. Add. 25,303*, f. 138. b; *MS. Sloane 1792*, ff. 6. b-7; and *MS. Add. 10,309*, f. 91. Sir Herbert Grierson has seen it in a manuscript in Trinity College, Dublin, where it is signed *H.* See Grierson, *The Poems of John Donne*, 1912, II, cix, n.

In *MS. Add. 25,303* an additional stanza appears between the first and second of the text as printed from *MS. Sloane 1446*:

> Yo^u that finde out the easiest wayes
> through eu'ry strongest gate and wall
> that none yor passage spies or stayes
> not Jealousy that watchet [*sic*] all.

XXII

Hawthornden MSS. Volume 15, ff. 8-9. The lines are here subscribed *J. H.* They are attributed to Mr Hoskins in *MS. Chetham 8012*, p. 78. See *Grosart Chetham 8012*, I, 86-7.

XXIII

MS. Harl. 3911, ff. 120. b-121. b. The lines are signed *J. H.*
Since their light, whimsical, satirical vein is not unlike Hoskyns' I
have included the verses among his writings.

XXIV

The text of 'Absence' is that printed by Sir Herbert Grierson in
The Poems of John Donne (Clarendon Press, Oxford, 1912, two
volumes, I, 428-29). There Sir Herbert prints it in an appendix as
probably by John Hoskyns. In 1921 in *Metaphysical Lyrics and Poems
of the Seventeenth Century* (pp. 23-4) he prints the poem as Hoskyns',
and in 1929 in *The Poems of John Donne* (pp. 387-88) as 'probably by
John Hoskins'. In the edition of 1912 (*op. cit.*, II, lvii) Sir Herbert
remarks: 'It has been the custom of late to assign to Donne the
authorship of one charming lyric in the *Rhapsody*, "Absence hear thou
my protestation." I hope to show . . . that this is the work, not of
Donne, but of another young wit of the day, John Hoskins, whose
few extant poems are a not uninteresting link between the manner of
Sidney and the Elizabethans and of Donne and the "Metaphysicals." '
After tracing the history of the poem (*ibid.*, cl-cli), Sir Herbert concludes that the '*onus probandi* lies with those who say the poem is
by Donne.' He finds the tone of the poem 'airier, the prosody more
tripping,' and the stressed syllables 'less weighted emotionally and
vocally' than are characteristic of Donne's work.

'Absence' appeared in print for the first time in Davison's *Poetical
Rhapsody* in 1602. There and in the editions of 1608, 1611, and 1621
it is anonymous. This anonymity suggests that Davison did not
attribute the poem to Donne, for Davison has recorded his desire to
search out the works of that poet. (See A. H. Bullen, *Davison's
Poetical Rhapsody*, London, 1890, two volumes, I, liii.) 'Absence' also
appeared anonymously in *Wit Restor'd* (London, 1658, pp. 108-109).
It was attributed to Donne in print for the first time in 1721 by
W. Walsh in *The Grove: or, a Collection of Original Poems, Trans-
lations, &c.* (London, pp. 37-9). Walsh's authority was 'an old
Manuscript of Sir John Cotton's of Stratton in Huntington-Shire.'
Sir John Simeon (*Miscellanies of the Philobiblon Society*, London,
1856-7, III, 27) printed the poem as Donne's upon the authority of a
small manuscript volume 'formerly in the collection of the late Mr.
Utterson.' Grosart (*The Complete Poems of John Donne*, London,
1873, two volumes, II, 238-39), following Walsh and Simeon, assigns
the poem to Donne; but this ascription to Donne by Simeon and,
indeed, all of his except one have been rejected by Sir Herbert
Grierson and by Mr. Geoffrey Landon Keynes (*Bibliography of the
Works of John Donne*, Cambridge, 1914). A. H. Bullen (*op. cit.*, II,
117-18 and lxxxiv) assigns the poem to Donne. Sir Edmund

Chambers (*Poems of John Donne*, London, 1896, two volumes, II, 249) relegates it to an appendix as doubtful. John Haywood omits the poem from his edition of Donne (*John Donne Dean of St. Pauls Complete Poetry and Selected Prose*, London, 1929). Hyder Edward Rollins (*A Poetical Rhapsody*, Harvard University Press, Cambridge, Massachusetts, 1931, two volumes, II, 51-2 and 185-86) notes Sir Herbert Grierson's ascription to Hoskyns but contributes no further evidence toward the solution of the problem of its authorship. Sir Arthur Quiller-Couch prints the poem as Donne's in *The Oxford Book of English Verse* (1931).

In manuscripts of the seventeenth century the poem is occasionally assigned to Donne, but it does not occur in the manuscripts that Sir Herbert Grierson considers most trustworthy. (See his edition of 1912, II, cli.) In *MS. Carnaby* (pp. 65-6) it is signed *J. D.* It occurs in *MS. Stowe 961* (f. 80), the whole collection there being described as 'Dr. J. Donne Poems.' It occurs anonymously in *MS. Stevens* (p. 236); *MS. O'Flahertie* (p. 309); *MS. Lansdowne 740* (ff. 99. b-100); and on page 425 of a seventeenth-century manuscript collection chiefly of Donne's poetry in the possession of Percy Dobell, Esq., who kindly permitted me to examine it in 1929. In the Dobell manuscript the poem is marked with a small cross in the margin as are also the poems beginning 'Send home my longe stray'd eyes to me' and 'Loue bred of glances 'twixt amorous eyes.' Sir Herbert Grierson names two manuscripts in which it occurs but which I have not seen: one in the Earl of Ellesmere's library at Bridgewater House and one in the possession of Captain C. Shirley Harris of Oxford. Besides the manuscripts mentioned, *MS. Hawthornden*, Volume 15 (ff. 65-6), contains the poem, here signed *J. H.*

It is upon the Hawthornden manuscript that Sir Herbert Grierson chiefly bases his claims for Hoskyns' authorship and upon which they must at present primarily rest. This manuscript is the authoritative collection of poems transcribed by William Drummond of Hawthornden and endorsed 'poems belonging to Jhon Don,' that is, in the possession of Donne, not necessarily by him. Certain lyrics are assigned, with apparent correctness, to the Earl of Pembroke, to Benjamin Rudyerd, and to Donne himself. A circumstance that strengthens the claim of Hoskyns is the fact that his poem beginning 'Loue is a foolish melancholie,' assigned to him in *MS. Chetham 8012*, appears on folio 8 of the Hawthornden manuscript, there signed *J. H.* (Unlike Sir Herbert Grierson, however, I have not found this poem in *MS. Additional 10,309*, although Hoskyns' poem 'You nimble dreams with cob-web wings' does occur in that manuscript as well as in *MS. Chetham 8012*.)

The only new evidence that I can bring forward in an attempt to establish Hoskyns' authorship of 'Absence' is of an entirely indirect and yet important kind. Those who have felt that Hoskyns' extant work

did not warrant the supposition that he could have composed a lyric
so charming as this one may be referred to his command of language
and imagery in his letter to his bride of three months, now printed
for the first time (Letter I, Chapter VII, above). That letter,
together with the best passages from his other hitherto unpublished
letters, now printed in this volume, and with the best passages from
his *Direccõns For Speech and Style*, will doubtless dispel the feeling
that he was incapable of composing upon occasion so pleasing a lyric
as 'Absence.' True enough, his greater power lay in prose composition, but it seems he may indeed have written 'Absence.'

XXV

*Oxoniensis Academiæ Funebre Officium in memoriam Elizabethæ,
nvper Angliæ, Franciæ, & Hiberniæ Reginæ*, printed by Barnes at
Oxford in 1603, pp. 140-41.

The poems in this volume were published in the name of the University, this one signed *Jo. Hoskins Nov. Coll. Socius.* Since John
Hoskyns the younger was by this time a fellow of New College, it is
possible that these lines were written by him. Since, however, John
Hoskyns the elder contributed to the Oxford volume celebrating the
accession of James, this is likely his also. See notes on No. XXVI,
below.

XXVI

*Academiæ Oxoniensis Pietas Erga Serenissimvm &t Potentissimvm
Iacobvm Angliæ Scotjæ Franciæ & Hiberniæ Regem, Fidei defensorem, Beatissimæ Elizabethæ nuper Reginæ legitimè & auspicatissimè
succedentem.* Oxford, 1603, p. 168.

Hoskyns is described as jurist and fellow of New College, and is
the 253rd contributor of congratulatory verse on James's accession.

XXVII

*Most Approved, and Long Experienced VVater-VVorkes. Contain-
ing, The manner of Winter and Summer-drowning of Medow and
Pasture, by the aduantage of the least, River, Brooke, Fount, or
Water-prill adiacent; by Rowland Vavghan, Esquire . . . London . . .
1610.*

These commendatory verses, signed *Iohn Hoskins*, appear on Sig.
D₂ *v.*, in this quaint volume on irrigation, dedicated to William
Herbert, Earl of Pembroke. Vaughan lived at Newcourt in the
Golden Valley, Herefordshire, and was a nephew of Blanche Parry, a
favoured attendant upon Queen Elizabeth, according to a manuscript
note in the British Museum copy of the *Most Approved VVater-
VVorkes.*

XXVIII

The text of the *Convivium philosophicum* is that printed by Andrew Clark in the notes of his edition of *Aubrey's 'Brief Lives,'* two volumes, Oxford, 1898, II, 50-3. Clark's version is from folio 185, *v.,* of an old commonplace book in the Library of Lincoln College, Oxford. The same Latin poem, he says, in an old copy owned by the late Falconer Madan is headed 'Mr. Hoskins, his Convivium Philosophicum' and at the end is marked '*per Johannem Hoskins,* London.' See Clark, *op. cit.,* I, 50, 53. On the same pages with the Latin verses, Clark prints an English version lent him by Falconer Madan and attributed to John Reynolds, which I quote in these notes, below.

The Latin version appears anonymously in *MS. Rawl. Poet. 117,* f. 192. a-191. b (reading in reverse order). It also is found among the *State Papers, Domestic, James I,* Vol. 66, no. 2. In the latter version the revellers are listed as Christoferus Brooke, Johannes Donne, Magister Cranefeild, Arthurus Ingram, Sr Robert Phillips; Sr Henry Nevile, Mr Connioke, Mr Hoskins, Ricardus Martin, Sr Henry Goodyear, John West, Hugo Holland, and Inigo Jones. On the outside of the latter manuscript is the endorsement 'Latin Rimes of Tom Coryate.' Since the lines in the manuscript owned by Madan are ascribed to Hoskyns and since the subject matter makes it plausible to construe the endorsement of the manuscript in the Public Record Office as indicating that the verses are '*of* Tom Corriat' in the sense of *about* or *belonging to* him, I have included them among Hoskyns' writings.

Clark fixes the date of the *convivium* as 2 September, from a phrase in the title, *in clauso Termini S^{tt}. Michaelis in crastino festi S^{tt}. Egridii in campis.* He also points out that the meeting must have taken place between 1608, the date of Coryate's departure on his trip to Venice, and 6 November 1612, the date of Prince Henry's death.

John Reynolds' English version follows:

[Mr. Hoskins, his Convivium Philosophicum]

Whosoever is contented
That a number be convented
    Enough but not too many;
The *Miter* is the place decreed,
For witty jests and cleanly feed,
    The betterest of any.

There will come, though scarcely current,
Christopherus surnamèd *Torrent,*
    And John ycleped *Made,*
And Arthur *Meadow-pigmies'-foe,*
To sup, his dinner will foregoe,
    Will come as soon as bade.

Sir Robert *Horse-lover* the while
Ne let Sir Henry count it *vile*
     Will come with gentle speed;
And *Rabbit-tree-where-acorn-grows*
And John surnamèd *Little-hose*
     Will come if there be need.

And Richard *Pewter-waster* best
And Henry *Twelve-month-good* at least
     And John *Hesperian* true.
If any be desiderated
He shal bee amerciated
     Forty-pence in issue.

Hugh the *Inferior Germayne*,
Nor yet unlearned nor prophane
     Inego *Ionicke-piller*
But yet the number is not ri<gh>ted;
If *Coriate* bee not invited,
     The jeast will want a tiller.

For wittily on him, they say,
As hammers on an anvil play,
     Each man his jeast may breake.
When Coriate is fudled well,
His tongue begins to talke pel-mel,
     He shameth nought to speake.

A boy he was devoid of skill
With white-pots and oaten-cakes at will
     Somersetizated.
And is a man with Scots and Angles
With silken scarfes and with spangles
     Fitly accommodated.

Are you in love with London citty?
Or else with Venice? he will fitt ye;
     You have his heart to prize it.
Or love you Greeke—of tongues <the> chiefe,
Or love you Latin? hee'le in briefe
     Sir Edward Ratcliffize itt.

This orator of Odcombe towne
Meaning to civilize the clowne,
     To parlé 'gan to call
The rusticks and the Coridons,
The naturalls and morions,
     And dis-coxcombde them all.

To pass the sea, to pass the shore,
And Fleet-street it all Europe o're,
    A thing periculous.
And yet one paire of shoes, they say,
And shirt did serve him all the way,
    A thing pediculous.

Whoso him exouthenizeth,
Garretating swaberizeth,
    And for this injurie
He shall walk as disrespected,
Of good fellows still neglected,
    In city and in curie.

To a fool thus elevated,
Mountebanke-like thus hee prated,
    Harringuizing rowndly.
Whosoe will be counted prudent,
Let him be no other student
    But to drinke profoundly.

Whatsoever you speak or doe
With your friends, in jocund row,
    It cannot be misdeemed.
For he that lives not ramp and scramp,
According to the swaggering stampe,
    Can never be esteemed.

The king religion doth out-bear,
The people doe allegiance sweare,
    Citizens usurize it.
The soldiers and the merchants feare,
The boyes and girles do love their paire,
    And women cuculize it.

Prince Henry cannot idly liven,
Desiring matter to be given
    To prove his valour good.
And Charles, the image of his father,
Doth imitate his eldest brother,
    And leades the noble blood.

The Chancellour relieveth many,
As well the wyse as fooles, or any
    In humble-wise complayninge.
The Treasurer doth help the rich,
And cannot satisfy the stitch
    Of mendicants disdayninge.

Northampton, seeking many wayes
Learning and learned men to rayse,
    Is still negotiated.
And Suffolke, seeking, in good sorte,
The king his household to supporte,
    Is still defatigated.

The noblemen do edifye,
The bishops they do sanctifie,
    The cleargie preach and pray:
And gentlemen their lands doe sell,
And, while the clownes strive for the shell,
    The fish is lawyers' prey.

Thus every man is busy still,
Each one practising his skill,
    None hath enough of gayne.
But Coriate liveth by his witts,
He looseth nothinge that he getts,
    Nor playes the fool in vayne.

XXIX

Coryats Crudities Hastily gobled vp in five Moneths trauells . . . .
London, 1611, Sig. e₅ to Sig. e₆, *v*. Two measures of music are added
on the latter page 'to be sung by those that are so disposed.'
    The lines also appeared in *The Odcombian Banqvet: Dished foorth
By Thomas the Coriat, and Serued in by a number of Noble Wits in
prayse of his Crvdities and Crambe too. London for Thomas Thorpe.
1611.* Here the verses are printed on Sig. H, *v*. to Sig. H₃. Coryate's
note on *Gymnosophist* in line 9 explains that Hoskyns calls him a
naked philosopher 'because one day he went without a shirt at Basil
while it was washing.'
    The stanza beginning 'Even as the waues of brainlesse butter'd fish'
is also found in *MS. Malone 19*, p. 157.
    In the introduction to the *Crudities* Coryate assures the reader that
he did not solicit 'halfe those worthy Wights' for their verses. At
last when he 'saw the multitude to increase to so great a number,'
he resolved to put a 'thousand of them into an Index expurgatorius,
and to detaine them from the presse.' However, Henry, Prince of
Wales, gave him 'strict and expresse commandement to print all
those verses' which he had read to 'his Highnesse.' Thereupon
Coryate 'communicated that copious rhapsodie of poems to the world,'
even though many of them were 'disposed to glance at' him 'with their
free and merry jests.'
    John Taylor the Water Poet 'paraphrased' these verses. See *All
the Workes of Iohn Taylor . . . newly Imprinted*, 1630. Sig. Gg₂, *v*.

XXX

MS. Add. 4130, f. 92. b. The poem is addressed to his fellow-prisoners in the Tower. See Chapter V, above.

XXXI

Carreglwyd Papers, A 830, endorsed 'Verses made by Sergeant Hoskins.' These papers, commonly known as the Conway-Griffith Manuscripts, are now on loan to the National Library of Wales at Aberystwyth, and were catalogued in the *Fifth Report of the Historical Manuscripts Commission*.

The English version of Hoskyns' poem to his son, written from the Tower, is found in eleven manuscripts: the **Carreglwyd Papers*; **MS. Add. 21,433*, f. 147; **MS. Add. 25,303*, f. 163; *MS. Add. 10,309*, f. 148; *MS. Ashmole 36-7*, f. 213; **MS. Rawlinson D. 727*, f. 94. b (*i.e.*, the manuscript of John Aubrey's Life of John Hoskyns); *MS. Rawl. Poet. 26*, f. 2. b; *MS. Rawl. Poet. 117*, f. 16. a; *MS. Add. 4130*, f. 93; **MS. Malone 19*, p. 149; **MS. Rawlinson B. 151*, f. 103.

The asterisks indicate manuscripts containing the Latin as well as the English version. Both were printed by Hannah (*op. cit.*, p. 121).

The verses appeared in the third edition of *Reliquiae Wottonianae*, 1672, p. 398, and were printed by William Harris, *An Historical and Critical Account of the Lives and Writings of James I and Charles I, etc.*, five volumes, London, 1814, I, 231. They were also printed by Hannah (*op. cit.*, p. 121).

XXXII

The Abbotsford Club Miscellany, edited by James Maidment, Edinburgh, 1837, I, 131-32. The poem is printed in that volume from the Balfour Manuscripts in what is now the National Library of Scotland, Edinburgh. Hoskyns' poem, it seems, was sent from the Tower to King James.

It is also found in *MS. Rawl. Poet. 26*, f. 41, where this contemporary note is attached: 'presented (it seemes) a New-yeares Gift, Petition to the King. These verses were made by Mr Hoskins Counsello^r of Law, when he was a Prisoner.'

In *MS. Harl. 1221*, f. 76, the poem is headed: 'John Hoskins New-yeares gift to the Kings Ma:^tie.' Other copies of the poem are found in *MS. Add. 4130*, f. 92, in Latin only, and in *MS. Harl. 6038*, ff. 20. b-21. b, in Latin and English.

XXXIII

MS. Harl. 1221, f. 77, signed *J. H.*

XXXIV

MS. Harl. 6947, ff. 252-53. In this manuscript a lengthy introduction precedes the poem: 'Mr John Hoskins of the Middle Temple, Counsell at Law, being committed to the Tower by the King for certaine speeches vttered in the Parliament house, not long after his comittm^t. (wch he caused his wife to p^resent to the Kings Matie) entituling the same A Dreame.'

The poem was frequently transcribed and may be found in these manuscripts: *MS. Ashmole 781*, pp. 129-31, printed by Wood (*op. cit.*, II, col. 627-28); *MS. Add. 25,303*, ff. 162-63; *MS. Ashmole 36-7*, f. 213; *MS. Add. 4130*, ff. 92. b.-94. b, entitled *Insomniũ*; *MS. Add. 21,433*, ff. 145. b.-147. a; *MS. Add. 4149*, ff. 211-13. a; and *MS. Malone 19*, pp. 71-3.

A shortened form of the poem frequently appears in the commonplace books of the time and in that form was printed from *MS. Malone 16*, p. 20, by Hannah (*op. cit.*, p. 121). *MS. Rawlinson D. 160*, f. 3. b; *MS. Egerton 923*, f. 11; and *MS. Ashmole 781*, p. 131 present this extract, which begins with the line, 'The worst is told; the best is hid,' and continues to: 'He err'd but once; once, king, forgive!' In *MS. Rawlinson 160* it is mistakenly recorded that the King graciously granted her suit.

In *MS. Egerton 923* this passage is headed: 'Mr. Hoskins to the king sent by his wife.'

Line 39 in *MS. Harl. 6947* reads: 'to speake to men & not to misse.' Most MSS. give the reading as I have printed it.

In line 58 I have supplied *me*, found in other MSS.

XXXV

MS. Malone 19, p. 148. I have expanded a contracted Greek form (χρε in MS.) to *Christe*, in the second line. The verses also appear in *Carreglwyd Papers, A 830.*

XXXVI

'Brief Lives' . . . *by John Aubrey*, edited by Andrew Clark, II, 48. The quatrain, Aubrey says, was written in Richard Martin's Bible, and signed *J. Hoskyns.*

The other verses attributed to Hoskyns by Aubrey may be seen in the Temple Church at the base of the 'faire monument' erected to the memory of Richard Martin, but, in 1930 at least, relegated to the balcony in the round gallery of that Church. Martin is represented life-size, wearing a red robe over black, kneeling, prayer-book in hand.

XXXVII

Epigrammatum Joannis Ovven Cambro-Britanni, Oxoniensis, etc.,
1620, Lipsiæ, Sig. A₂. These epigrams were written for Owen's third
edition, which came out in 1607. Though they might have been
inserted earlier in the text to preserve as far as possible the natural
order of composition, they are here placed just before the epitaph on
Owen.

XXXVIII

MS. Harley 3910, f. 57. The heading in the manuscript reads: 'In
eundem Audœnum Joh. Hoskins.' The lines follow an epitaph on
Owen by Sir John Roe.
John Owen died in 1622.

XXXIX

MS. Rawlinson B. 151, f. 102. b. The poem is dated 'April. 1621.'
At the end is written: 'Thought to be done by Mr Hoskins of
Hereford.'
The poem appears anonymously in *MS. Rawlinson Poet. 117*,
f. 22. b, and with variants in *MS. Harl. 6038*, ff. 27-8.

XL

MS. Malone 19, p. 148.

XLI

Reliquiae Wottonianae, London, 1651, p. 517. The poem appeared
again in the third edition in 1672, II, 378-79 and in the fourth in 1685.
I have not seen a second edition. Hannah, (*op. cit.*, pp. 88-9) printed
it in 1870.

XLII

'*Brief Lives,*' . . . *by John Aubrey*, edited by Andrew Clark, I, 424.
The tomb of Benedicta is at Vow Church, Herefordshire, not Bowe
Church, as stated by Aubrey.
The second epitaph was for Hoskyns' stepson John Bourne, who
died sometime between 1624 and 1627.

XLIII

'*Brief Lives,*' . . . *by John Aubrey*, edited by Andrew Clark, I, 419-21.
Aubrey says the first distich was at the gatehouse beside 'the picture
of the old fellowe that made the fires, with a block on his back, boytle
and wedges and hatchet.' The second distich was written on the wall
by the porch; the third, in the chapel; the fourth, in the gallery; the
fifth, on the garden wall.

XLIV

Faceticæ: *Musarum Deliciæ*: *or The Muses Recreation. Conteining Severall Pieces of Poetique Wit,* London, two volumes, 1817, II, 238. This poem appeared in the first edition of the *Faceticæ* in 1655 and in subsequent editions and in Camden's *Remaines.* In *MS. Sloane 1446* it is headed: 'On Mrs Anne Prideaux daughter of M^r D^r· Prideaux Regius professor she died aged 6 yeeres.' The child was thus the daughter of John Prideaux (1578-1650), Regius professor at Oxford and later Bishop of Worcester. The *D. N. B.* states that his wife died in 1627 and was buried with two of her children in St. Michael's Church, Oxford.

The lines also appear in *MS. Sloane 1827,* f. 32; *MS. Harl. 6917,* p. 115; *MS. Lansdowne 777,* f. 60; *MS. Egerton 2421,* f. 2; *MS. Harl. 3910,* f. 4; *MS. Egerton 923,* f. 16; *MS. Add. 25,303,* f. 163.

XLV

MS. Harl. 3910, f. 54. b. Compare John Owen's epigrams on Gifford in *Epigrammatum Joannis Ovven . . . etc.,* 1620, Lipsiæ, Sigg. E₆ and F₂.

See also Letter XV in Chapter VII, above.

XLVI

MS. Add., 23,229, f. 50, of the Conway Papers. Here the poem is anonymous, as it is in *MS. Tanner 465,* f. 62, and in *MS. Add. 25,303,* f. 151. It is ascribed to Hoskyns with no authority except its connection with an incident recorded by Aubrey, who relates (*op. cit.,* I, 422) that the Serjeant, upon hearing that Pye had died on Christmas, exclaimed, 'The devill haz a Christmas pye.' However, Aubrey was mistaken in supposing that the subject of Hoskyns' wit was Robert Pye. It was his brother, Sir Walter, who was Attorney of the Court of Wards, and who died on 26 December 1635.

XLVII

MS. Rawl. Poet. 26, f. 11. a. Hoskyns' verses in that manuscript are headed 'Vpon the birth of the Said Prince,' and follow others on the subject, one of them by Ben Jonson. In *MS. Rawl. Poet. 160,* f. 30, the same poem appears in the Latin and English versions, the former signed 'Ser: Hoskins; Med: Temp.,' and dated 30 May 1630. The English form appears anonymously in *MS. Add. 30,982,* f. 28. b, and in *MS. Harl. 6071,* f. 16. b. The Latin and English versions appear in *MS. Add. 15,227,* f. 37. b, where they are described as 'Certaine verses sent from Serjeant Hotchkins to one Mr Hyrne of Bramford who then preached at Pauls crosse, on that day the King came thither to offer up his oblation for the birth of his sonne.'

The lines celebrate the birth of Prince Charles on 29 May 1630.
A note in *MS. Rawl. Poet. 26* explains that there was an eclipse of
the sun on 31 May.

XLVIII

MS. Rawl. D. 727, f. 94. The lines are described by Aubrey
(*op. cit.*, I, 421) as having been written on the Serjeant's desk at
Morehampton under his picture. The poem occurs in slightly modified
form in *Carreglwyd Papers, A. 830*, where it is attributed to Hoskyns
and headed '*De Seipso*, 1634.'

The English version, probably by Hoskyns, as well as the Latin,
is found among the papers and letters of Hoskyns now in the possession of Henry Hornyold-Strickland, Esq. There the lines are headed
'Verse composed by Serjeant Hoskyns. 1632 or 1633.' They are in
a hand perhaps somewhat later than one of the first half of the
seventeenth century.

The Latin lines are cut in his table-tomb in the south choir of
Abbey Dore, Herefordshire.

APPENDIX B

DOUBTFUL VERSES

I

(From Camden's *Remaines*)

William Camden, before making a reluctant end of his *Remaines* ... *Concerning Britaine* (London, 1605) remarks (p. 56): 'But I feare now I haue ouer-charged the Readers mind, with dolefull, dumpish, and vncomfortable lines. I will therefore for his recomfort, end this part with a few conceited, merry, and laughing Epitaphes, the most of them composed by maister *Iohn Hostines* when he was young.' *Hostines* is changed to *Hoskines* in later editions. Some of the verses Camden prints are ascribed elsewhere to Hoskyns; others appear frequently in the commonplace books alongside his recognized work. Since Camden's ascriptions are vaguely expressed, those verses in his edition of 1605 not attributed elsewhere to Hoskyns and obviously not by other hands are printed in this appendix as probably Hoskyns'. Introductory matter of Camden's necessary to the point of the epitaph is printed in italics.

The first is an epitaph upon Elderton, the ballad maker beloved of the little page Michael Drayton before his mild tutor improved the boy's taste by reading to him from 'honest Mantuan.' (See *The Works of Michael Drayton, ed. cit.*, III, 227.) Camden is evidently in error in calling him Thomas Elderton, for William, the well-known if inebriate 'ballater,' must be meant.

> Hic situs est sitiens atque ebrius Eldertonus
> Quid dico hic situs est? hic potius sitis est.

* * *

Of him also was made this.

> Here is Elderton lyeing in dust,
> Or lyeing Elderton, chose [*sic*] which you lust.
> Here he lyes dead, I doe him no wrong,
> For who knew him standing, all his life long.

* * *

> Here lyeth Thom Nicks bodie
> Who liued a fool and dyed a nodye:
> As for his soule aske them that can tell,
> Whether fooles soules go to heauen or to hell.

* * *

> Hic est Durandus positus sub marmore duro,
> An sit saluandus ego nescio, nec ego curo.

Here lyeth father Sparges
That died to saue charges.

* * *

Here lyeth he
Which with himself could neuer agree.

* * *

Vpon merry Tarlton I haue heard this.

Hic situs est cuius vox, vultus, actio possit
    Ex Heraclito reddere Democritum.

* * *

Here lyeth Richard a Preene,
One thousand, fiue hundred, eighty nine,
Of March the 22. day,
And he that will die after him may.

* * *

Here lyes the man that madly slaine,
In earnest madnesse did complaine,
On nature, that she did not giue,
One life to loose, another to liue.

* * *

Here lyeth N. a man of fame
The first of his howse and last of his name.

* * *

For old Th. Churchyard the poore Court-Poet this is now commonly current.

Come Alecto and lend me thy torch
To find a Church-yard in the Church-porch.
Pouerty, and Poetry this tombe doth enclose,
Therefore Gentlemen be mery in Prose.

* * *

With these memoriales of the dead which giue a little liuing Breath to the dead: for as he saith, Mortuorum vita in memoria viuorum posita est, I conclude:

Et veniam pro laude peto: laudatus abundè
Non fastiditus si tibi Lector ero.

* * *

To the fifth edition of Camden's *Remaines* (1637) many more poems were added. How many of these are by Hoskyns it is impossible now to say. The final poem, 'Impossibilities,' is definitely suggestive of Donne's 'Go and catch a falling star.' But its lines 10, 11, and 12 are reminiscent of Hoskyns' reflections upon government as revealed

by his activities in Parliament. Therefore I include it in this appendix
as much for its general interest as for the possibility that it may be
Hoskyns'. Though there are similar poems on the pattern of Donne's
(see Grierson, II, 11-12), this particular version seems hitherto
unnoticed in relation to Donne's more famous lyric.

'Impossibilities' appears anonymously in *MS. Harl. 3511*, f. 71. b
and in *MS. Add. 33,998*, f. 30. b.

Impossibilities

Embrace a Sun-beame, and on it
The shadow of a man beget.
Tell me who raignes in the Moone,
Set the thunder in a tune,
Cut the Axel-tree that beares
Heaven and earth, or stop the spheares
With thy finger; or divide
Beggery from lust and pride,
Tell me what the Syrens sing,
Or the secrets of a King,
Or his power, and where it ends,
And how farre his will extends.
Goe and finde the bolt that last
Brake the clouds, or with like hast
Fly to the East, and tell me why
Aurora blushes: if to lie
By an old man trouble her minde,
Bid Cephalus be lesse unkinde.
Canst thou by thine art uncase
The mysteries of a Courtiers face?
Canst thou tell me why the night
Weeps out her eyes? If for the sight
Of the lost Sunne, she puts on blacke,
Post to his fall, and turn him backe,
If not for him, then goe and finde
A widdow, or all woman kinde,
Like to their outward shew, and be
More then a Delphian Deity.

II

Of one y^t had stolne much out of Seneca.

Put of thy buskins Sophocles ye greate,
and morter tread wth thy disarmed shankes.
for this mans heade hath had a happier sweat,
whereof ye worlde doth conn him little thankes.
Blush Seneca to see thy feathers loose,
pluckt from a Swann stuck vpon a goose.

The epigram quoted above from *MS. Chetham 8012, p. 76*, there signed *J. H.,* is printed as Henry Parrot's in his *Laquei ridiculosi: Or Springes for Woodcocks,* 1613, p. 163. Since the Chetham manuscript cannot be definitely dated, it is probable that the lines should be attributed to Parrot. Mr. Franklin B. Williams, Jr., has called my attention to the epigram in Parrot's volume. See his forthcoming work on Henry Parrot. I have seen the epigram in one other commonplace book, in the possession of Dr. A. S. W. Rosenbach (once owned by William Horatio Crawford); and there it is anonymous but follows 'An Epitaph Vpon a Bellowes-maker,' ascribed elsewhere to Hoskyns. In the Rosenbach MS. 'his Tragedies' is added in the title and *little* in the fourth line is replaced by *double.*

The epigram refers to Ben Jonson, whom Dekker (*Satiro-Mastix,* 1602, Sigg. C₄ v. and H₂) salutes as 'a poor lyme & hayre-rascall' and a 'foule-fisted Morter-treader.'

III

Aubrey (I, 418) attributes to Hoskyns the extraordinarily popular 'Censure' beginning 'Down came graue Sir John Crooke And read his message out of Booke.' These boisterous, jovial lines in questionable taste I have seen in some eighteen manuscripts as well as in *Facetiæ: Musarum Deliciæ* (compiled by Sir John Mennis, and printed in 1655, etc.) and in *Le Prince d'Amour,* 1660. Ben Jonson (in *The Alchemist,* 1612, Sig. D₂, v.) has Sir Epicure Mammon refer to the *authors* of these lines; and, indeed, it seems that the 'Censure' is the collaboration of several wits. In *MS. Sloane 2023,* f. 59, it is ascribed to Sir John Suckling, but in *MS. Add. 23,229,* ff. 16. a-17. b, to 'Ned Jones, Dick Martin, Hopkins [*sic*], and Cr Brooke.' Elsewhere it appears anonymously. Since, then, the lines are probably the result of collaboration, I have not printed them.

IV

I have found no proof of Hoskyns' authorship of 'Old Meg of Herefordshire,' lines on a Morris dance given in Herefordshire in 1609, referred to by Thomas Fuller (*Worthies of England,* 1662, II, 33). See also *The British Bibliographer,* IV, pp. 326-28 and *Miscellanea Antiqua Anglicana,* London, 1816, I.

Fuller says that Serjeant Hoskyns gave the entertainment for James I, but Nichols (*Progresses of James I,* pp. xix-xx) indicates that James was never in Herefordshire. In *MS. Add. 25,707,* is a letter from William Gibson Ward of Ross, Herefordshire, 1875, in which he declares that Hoskyns offered an old English welcome to the King and that the King accepted the invitation and that the

carved woodwork to serve as a canopy to a throne by day and as a
cover for the King's bed at night was to be seen in Herefordshire
until the eighteenth century. Apparently the King did not come and
proof is lacking that the verses for the occasion were by Hoskyns.

V

John Hoskins to the Lady Jacob

Oh loue whose powre & might non euer yet wthstood
thou teachest me to wrighte, come turne about Robin Hood.
Sole Mistresse of my rest, lett mee thus farre presume
to make this bolde request a black patch for ye Rume.
yor tresses finely wrought like to a golden snare
my louinge harte has cought, as Moss did catch his Mare:
yor eyes like starrs diuine make me renew this arrant
in my most silent speech a Buttock or a Warrant.
o women will yo^u nere beleiue but I doe flatter./
I vowe I lou'de yo^u euer but yet tis no great matter.
what is it I shoulde doe to purchase yor good smile./
bid me to Chyna goe & i'le stand still the while
I know that I shall dye loue so my harte bewitches
it makes mee howle and crye oh how my elbow itches.
teares over flow mine eyes wth floods of daily weepinge
that in the carefull night I take no rest for sleepinge.
Cupid is blinde mē say & yet mee thinkes he seeth
hee hitt my harte today a T——— in Cupids teeth.
my M^{rs} shee is fayre & yet her late disgraces
Haue made mee to despayre a pox of all good faces
but since my simple meritts her louinge lookes must lack
Ile stopp my vitall spiritts wth Claret & wth Sack.
regarde my strange mishaps Ioue father of ye Thunder
Send downe thy mighty clapps & rend her Smock asunder
but since that all relief & comfort doe forsake me
Ile hange my selfe for greif, nay then ye Diuell take me.

The preceding lines are from *MS. Add. 25,303*, f. 70. b, and are
followed by the lady's answer written in about the same vein. The
lines appear anonymously in *MS. Rawlinson Poet.* 172, f. 14. b, *MS.
Add. 22,601*, and *MS. Add. 24,665*, f. 81. b.

I have not included them in Chapter X, above, because in a manuscript belonging to Dr. A. S. W. Rosenbach, dated 1630, (No. 694
in catalogue of sale pasted in front) f. 14, the lines are headed 'Mr.
Poldens delight of New. Coll: Oxon:.' A Robert Polden matriculated
in New College, Oxford, 14 October 1597 (Clark, *Register*, II, ii,
p. 221).

VI

He that hath heard a princes Secrecy
hath his Deaths Wound, & let him looke to dye
ffor Princes Hearts cañot endure longe
to be obnoxious to a servants Tongue.
No Counsell but mans life will some way show it
then in some case as good doe ill as know it./

J : H :

The preceding lines are from *MS. Harl. 6038*, f. 12. a. The same manuscript contains the Latin and English versions of Hoskyns' recognised 'New Year's Gift' to the King, subscribed *J : H* : (ff. 20. b-21. b).

It seems likely that the six lines above are likewise by Hoskyns.

APPENDIX C

NOTES ON THE MINIATURE

The miniature reproduced as the frontispiece is probably the portrait of Serjeant John Hoskyns. It is the signed work of the miniaturist John Hoskins and has sometimes been described as possibly a self-portrait, although two authorities on miniatures, Charles Holme and H. A. Kennedy (*Early English Portrait Miniatures in the Collection of the Duke of Buccleuch*, 1917, 'The Studio,' London), reproduce it (Plate XXVI) as only probably a self-portrait of the artist, and in correspondence with me Dr. George C. Williamson has remarked that there is probability that it may represent Serjeant John Hoskyns.

Of the artist himself little is known except that his gift is attested by numerous examples of his work, notably those in the collection of the Duke of Buccleuch, those possessed by the Duke of Portland at Welbeck Abbey, others at Windsor, and others in the Victoria and Albert Museum and in various other collections. The artist was the uncle and teacher of Samuel Cooper, the great miniaturist. See Richard Graham (fl. 1680-1720), *The Art of Painting . . . . Ancient and Modern*, second edition, London, 1716, pp. 375-76. There may even have been two miniaturists, father and son, by the name of John Hoskins. Dr. George C. Williamson (*The Miniature Collector*, New York, 1921, p. 47) quotes the following comment from William Sanderson's *Graphice*, 1658: 'For Miniture or Limning in water Colours Hoskins and his Son the next modern since the Hilliards, Father and Son; those pieces of the Father (if my judgment faile not) incomparable.' Dr. Williamson also quotes (*ibid.*) a comment by George Vertue (1684-1756) found in *MS. Add. 23,072*, f. 74 (old pagination) to the effect that Flatman 'may well deserve the Title of a Master in the Art of Limning and indeed equal to Hoskins senior or junior and next in immitation of Samuel Cooper.' See also the late Richard W. Goulding's, *The Welbeck Abbey Miniatures Belonging To His Grace The Duke of Portland*, Oxford, at the University Press, 1916, and also Holme and Kennedy, *op. cit.*

That a John Hoskins was painting in the 1640's is evident from a reference to him in Aubrey (*op. cit.*, I, 409). Dated miniatures signed by the artist (or by the artists, if there were two) from 1638 to 1663 are catalogued in the works mentioned above. Many, of course, are undated and are doubtless earlier.

George Vertue, in his notes on painters edited by Horace Walpole (*Anecdotes of Painting in England*, second edition, 1765, II, 149) stated that Colonel Sothby had a portrait of Sir Benjamin Rudyerd by Hoskins and a profile which Vertue thought might be of the artist himself. At this point Vertue interestingly reveals his confusion of the artist and the subject of the present book by remarking that 'prefixed to Coryat's Crudities is a copy of verses with his name to them,' actually the work of John Hoskyns (1566-1638). Walpole (*ibid.*, p. 147) in a note declared that there was no extant portrait of the artist. In other notes on Vertue Walpole, however, observed that Lawrence Cross, an early eighteenth-century miniaturist owned 'a head almost in profile in crayons of Hoskins' and that he neither knew of 'any other portrait of that master nor where the picture itself now is.' See George C. Williamson, *The History of Portrait Miniatures*, London, 1904, I, 95-6.

An engraving of the portrait from which the frontispiece of the present book is reproduced was reproduced by S. and E. Harding in 1802 in *The Biographical Mirrour* (III, 64) and described as being 'in the collection of W. Sotheby, Esqr.' (*i.e.* William Sotheby, 1757-1833).

In 1864 the profile was again reproduced, this time by Amelia B. Edwards (*Historical Portrait Gallery*, 1864). Her book seems to have been prepared and issued privately for the dealers Colnaghi & Co. The firm still possesses a copy, I have been told by Dr. George C. Williamson.

A few years ago a plate from her book containing the miniature under discussion was found carefully preserved among family papers by the Reverend Sir Edwyn C. Hoskyns, Bart. He assumed that it was the portrait of Serjeant Hoskyns and that the original had perhaps been disposed of when Harewood, the Hoskyns estate in Herefordshire, was sold at auction in 1876.

Dr. Williamson has suggested to me that perhaps the firm distributed the plates to the persons who had lent the miniatures for reproduction. Many of them are known to have been in private hands when the book was prepared. From the firm of Colnaghi & Co., Dr. Williamson has been unable to learn details as to how the Edwards book was compiled or distributed.

I have been unable to learn when the miniature came into the collection of his Grace the Duke of Buccleuch. Thus at present obscurity surrounds the artist, and the history of the miniature itself is not known in full detail.

I summarise now the reasons for supposing the miniature may be a portrait of John Hoskyns (1566-1638): First there is Vertue's confusion of the artist and the author, noted above. Moreover, if the artist of this particular miniature died in 1664-5 (see *D. N. B.*), the only date at present known for the death of a John Hoskins, artist, the miniature can hardly be a self-portrait. Judging by the cut of the hair and beard, we may conclude that the portrait is of a man of about forty-five or fifty in, say, 1620. The sketch on the back of the miniature (reproduced facing page 305) is particularly interesting. It would

Sketch on the Back of the Miniature of John Hoskins
in the Collection of His Grace the
Duke of Buccleuch

have been characteristic of John Hoskyns to sketch himself and his family on the back of a portrait done for him by a distinguished artist. His Trusty Servant at Winchester and the figures on the walls at Morehampton indicate his flair for sketching. Of the quality of his work, it is true, we have scant evidence, but it seems unlikely that he should have decorated his walls at Morehampton with crude sketches. We do know that the Trusty Servant was so prized that it has become a famous tradition at Winchester. The sketch on the back of the miniature is admirable, but it may be that Hoskyns could draw with that degree of excellence. Furthermore, the family is interestingly congruous with his own. The older youth might represent John Bourne; the girl, Elizabeth Bourne; whereas the two younger children might easily be Benedict and Benedicta Hoskyns. From their apparent ages the sketch might then be dated about 1620. By 1620 Hoskyns' stepdaughter Frances Bourne had married Dr. John Hoskyns and would, therefore, hardly have been included in the sketch. Aubrey (*op. cit.*, I, 421) says that Hoskyns had black hair and eyes and that he had a picture of himself 'in the low gallery' near his desk. In the sketch on the back of the miniature the man has indeed a merry countenance, as one would expect in the Serjeant. His nose is prominent. That Hoskyns had a prominent nose is indicated by two lines in the so-called *censure* on Parliament referred to in Appendix A, III, above. In that piece of humourous verse, where every other reference to members of Parliament touches upon some salient trait, mannerism, or characteristic of the person, we find these lines:

> 'Well quoth Mr Hoskins, I dare pawn my nose
> The gentleman meant it noe further then's hose.'

Doubtless it is meant that Hoskyns was offering to pawn something quite considerable.

For these reasons I think it probable that the miniature may indeed be the likeness of John Hoskyns (1566-1638).

APPENDIX D

AN INDEX TO PRINCIPAL MANUSCRIPTS USED

MSS. Additional, British Museum:

4130	23,229
4149	24,491
5832	25,303
10,309	30,982
15,227	33,929
21,433	35,280
22,603	

MSS. Ashmole, Bodleian Library:

36-7	47
38	781

MS. Ash. Mus. d. 1, Bodleian Library.

MS. Aubrey 8, Bodleian Library.

MS. Carnaby, Harvard University.

Carreglwyd Papers, A 830. On loan in the National Library of Wales, Aberystwyth.

Chancery Bills and Answers, Charles I, Bundle H30/37, Public Record Office.

MSS. Chetham, 8011 and 8012, Library of the Chetham Society, Manchester.

MS. Dobell. A seventeenth-century MS. belonging to Percy Dobell, Esq., containing 'Absence, heare my protestation.'

MSS. Egerton, British Museum: 923, 2421.

MSS. Harley, British Museum:

280	4945
850	5353
1107	6038
1221	6071
3910	6395
3911	6726
4604	6947

MS. Hatfield 204, Library of the Marquis of Salisbury, Hatfield House.

MSS. Hawthornden, vol. 15, Library of the Society of Antiquaries, Edinburgh.

MSS. belonging to Henry Hornyold-Strickland, Esq., Sizergh, Kendal, Westmorland.

MSS. belonging to the Rev. Canon Sir Edwyn C. Hoskyns, Bart., Cambridge.

MS. King's 12 A. LXIV, British Museum.
MS. Lambeth 658, Lambeth Palace.
MSS. Lansdowne, British Museum:

104	777
740	984
741	

Lee, 127, Somerset House, London.
MSS. Malone, Bodleian: 16, 19, 36.
MS. O'Flahertie, Harvard University.
MS. Rawlinson B 151, Bodleian.
MS. Rawlinson D 160, Bodleian.
MS. Rawlinson D 727, Bodleian.
MS. Rawlinson D 1372, Bodleian.
MS. Rawlinson Poetry 26, Bodleian.
MS. Rawlinson Poetry 117, Bodleian.
MS. Rawlinson Poetry 160, Bodleian.
MS. Rawlinson Poetry 172, Bodleian.
MSS. belonging to Dr. A. S. W. Rosenbach:
    A seventeenth-century commonplace book with a bookplate of
    W. H. Crawford and a similar book inscribed 'Bishop 1630.'
MS. Stowe 961, British Museum.
MS. Western R. 7. 8, Library of Trinity College, Cambridge.
MS. Wood F 39, Bodleian.
MSS. Sloane, British Museum:

1446	1792
1489	1827
1757	

State Papers, Domestic, James I, Vol. 38, no. 80, Public Record Office.
State Papers, Domestic, James I, Vol. 40, no. 60.
State Papers, Domestic, James I, Vol. 66, no. 2.
State Papers, Domestic, James I, Vol. 77, no. 42.
State Papers, Domestic. James I, Vol. 90, no. 53.
State Papers, Domestic, Charles I, Vol. 122, no. 130.
MS. Tract Dd. 5.75, University Library, Cambridge.
Woodhall 30, Somerset House.

INDEX

In this index, spelling, except in titles of published works, has, in general, been modernised, with cross-references in the original spelling when it has seemed that confusion might arise. References to Hoskyns himself and his references to Sidney have not been indexed.

Hoskyns, Bennett, *see* Hoskyns, Sir Benedict, Bart.
Hoskyns, Charles (brother of John Hoskyns), 82, 250.
Hoskyns, Rev. Canon Sir Edwyn Clement, Bart., 216, 224, 235, 238, 304. 306.
Hoskyns, Elizabeth (grandmother of John Hoskyns), 16.
Hoskyns, Frances Bourne, 69, 72, 82, 83, 84, 85, 225, 229, 243, 248, 251, 305.
Hoskyns, Sir Hungerford, 229, 240.
Hoskyns, John, D. C. L. (1579-1631, brother of John Hoskyns), 16, 43, 50, 56, 66, 67, 72, 77, 78, 85, 86, 96, 222, 225, 227, 234, 235, 242, 243, 246, 248, 249, 251, 253, 254-55, 256, 287, 305.
Hoskyns, John (father of John Hoskyns), 16, 225.
Hoskyns, John (godson of John Hoskyns), 86.
Hoskyns, John (grandfather of John Hoskyns), 16.
Hoskyns, Sir John (grandson of John Hoskyns), 217, 219.
Hoskyns, John (not the author), 16.
Hoskyns, John (uncle of John Hoskyns), 16.
Hoskyns, John the younger (probably father or uncle of John Hoskyns), 227.
Hoskyns, Magdalen (niece of John Hoskyns), 97, 253, 254.
Hoskyns, Margery (mother of John Hoskyns), 16, 86, 225.
Hoskyns, Margaret (niece of John Hoskyns), 90, 253.
Hoskyns, Oswald (brother of John Hoskyns), 43, 49, 74, 82, 83, 86, 226, 227, 235, 242, 243, 250, 251, 254.
Hoskyns, Philip (brother of John Hoskyns), 86.
Hoskyns, Thomas (brother of John Hoskyns), 54, 75, 77, 78, 79. 84, 86, 248, 250.
Hoskyns, Thomas (uncle of John Hoskyns), 16.
Hoskyns, William (nephew of John Hoskyns), 90, 91, 93, 94, 242, 253, 254, 257.
Hoskyns, William (uncle of John Hoskyns), 16.
Hoskyns, spelling of, 216.
Howard, Frances, Countess of Essex, 246.

Howard, Henry, Earl of Northampton, 40, 246, 291.
Howard, Thomas, 1st Earl of Suffolk, 256.
Howarth, Mr., 91.
Howell, Thomas B., 221, 236.
Hudson, Hoyt H., 104, 107, 108, 217, 218, 219, 222, 223, 235, 258, 260, 262, 263, 264, 265, 266, 267, 268, 269, 270.
Hughs, John, 96.
Hughs, Robin, 96.
Humphreys, A. L., 229.
Hungerston, Herefordshire, 51.
Hunter, Joseph, 229.
Hynde, Thomas, 78.
hyperbole, 139, 143.
Hyrne, of Bramford, 295.

Ilchester, Somersetshire, 19, 20, 22, 227.
illustration, 131, 154-65.
Imagines, see Theophrastus.
impositions, 34-5.
'Impossibilities,' 298.
induction, 160.
Infanta of Spain, 49.
Ingpen, Arthur R., 228, 236.
Ingram, Arthur, 196, 288.
ink horn terms, 99.
Inns of Court, 7, 8, 98, 221, 222, 228.
Inns of Court and the English Drama, The, see Green, A. Wigfall.
Institutio Oratoria, see Quintilian.
interrogation, 146-47, 153.
intimation, 110, 131, 139-40.
invention, 118, 138, 142.
Ireland and the Irish, 34, 124, 134, 264.
ironia, 125, 139, 142, 144.
Isocrates, 4, 132, 152.

Jackson, J. E., 280.
Jacob, the Lady, 301.
James I, 2, 3, 9, 10, 11, 26, 27, 28, 32, 35, 36, 39, 43, 44, 46, 48, 52, 69, 87, 90, 195, 203-206, 222, 225, 233, 235, 237, 287, 290, 292, 300, 301.
'Jeffrey, Mris,' 51.
Jesuits, 58.
Jewers, Arthur J., 229.
John Donne Dean of St. Pauls, see Haywood, John.
John Florio, see Yates, Frances A.
Johnson, Richard, 236.